UNDERSTANDING GANDHI

Published Volumes in the Series

- Mahatma Gandhi on Ethics
- Revisiting Hind Swaraj

About the Author

Dr. Anil Dutta Mishra (*b.* 1965) started his career as an Assistant Professor in the Department of Non-violence and Peace Studies, Jain Vishva Bharati University, Ladnuṇ, Rajasthan. His area of specialization includes Public Administration, Grass Root Politics, Gender Issues, Ecology and Human Rights.

Besides a number of research papers in leading professional journals, he has to his credit 16 books including *Problems and Prospects of Working Women in Urban India* (1994); *Fundamentals of Gandhism* (1995); *Gandhian Approach to Contemporary Problems* (1996); *Decentralized Planning in India : A Study of Objectives and Operational Framework* (1999); *Gender Perspectives : Participation, Empowerment and Development* (1999); *Perspectives on Human Rights* (2002); *Rediscovering Gandhi* (2002); *Patterns of Gender Violence* (2002); *Challenges of Twenty First Century and Gandhian Alternative* (2003); *India and Canada; Past, Present and Future* (2003); *Public Governance and Decentralization : Essays in Honour of T.N. Chaturvedi* (2003); *Gandhian Alternative to Contemporary Problems* (2004); *Globalization Myth and Reality* (2004); *Gandhian Alternative,* Vol. III, *Socio-Political Thought* (2005); *Inspiring Thoughts of Mahatma Gandhi* (2008); and *Terrorism : A Global Challenge* (2009).

Email: anilduttamishra@gmail.com

Understanding Gandhi

Speeches and Writings

That Reveal His Mind, Methods and Mission

Dr. Anil Dutta Mishra

CONCEPT PUBLISHING COMPANY PVT. LTD.,
NEW DELHI-110 059

ISBN-13 : 978-81-8069-778-4

First Published 2012

Published and Printed by

Concept Since 1974

Concept Publishing Company Pvt. Ltd.
A/15-16, Commercial Block, Mohan Garden
New Delhi-110059 (India)
T: 25351460, 25351794, *F*: 091-11-25357109
E: publishing@conceptpub.com, W: www.conceptpub.com
Editorial Office: H-13, Bali Nagar, New Delhi-110 015, India.

Cataloging in Publication Data--*Courtesy:* D.K. Agencies (P) Ltd. <docinfo@dkagencies.com>

Gandhi, *Mahatma,* 1869-1948.
[Selections]
Understanding Gandhi : speeches and writings : that reveal his mind, methods and mission / Anil Dutta Mishra.
p. cm.
Includes bibliographical references and index.
ISBN 9788180697784

1. India—Politics and government—1919-1947. 2. Nationalism—India. I.Mishra, Anil Dutta, 1965- II. Title.

DDC 954.035 23

Dedicated to
My Guru Acharya Mahashraman—
An Apostel of Peace and
Non-Violence . . . . . .

Preface

Mahatma Gandhi popularly known as Bapu or Father of the Nation is tallest among the leaders of the world of the twentieth century ever produced. He is remembered all over the world for his love of peace, non-violence, truth, honesty, pristine purity, compassion and his success in using these instruments to bring together the entire population and helping the country to attain independence from the colonial power and show the new way to the world. Gandhi changed the course of history and created history. He was a man of principles and great convictions and always practiced what he preached. There was no dichotomy between theory and practice and between public and private life. He left an everlasting impact on the world at large because he always spoke and understood the language of the masses, socially deprived and downtrodden. Even after sixty-three years of his death, Gandhi continues to attract the attention of scholars, social activists, media, policy makers and dreamers not only in India but abroad too.

Gandhi was a multifaceted personality. He was a great man in every sense and many ways. It is difficult to understand a great person. Bhavbhuti, a great scholar of Sanskrit, rightly said, "who indeed can claim to know and understand the mind of the great?" This is true in case of Gandhi. Different persons see Gandhi with different perspective. Gandhi is the most misunderstood and misinterpreted person/philosopher. Because of preconceived notion of ideology or something else people have not understood him properly. A large number of books have been written on Gandhi but no one has yet understood objectively his complex and magnificent personality.

Anthony J. Parel rightly mentioned that a number of approaches---the Nationalist, the Marxist, the Orientalist, the

Post colonial and the Subaltern, etc.—to study Gandhi's thought are in practice today. To understand Gandhiji amidst his conflicting statements, one has perhaps to go into the meaning of meaning. To know their deeper significance, going by the literal meaning of the words would be futile and burdensome. As Vinoba says, "Gandhiji was a great man", nevertheless, he had laid bare his mind in its fullness before the world. For his part, he had permitted no secrecy. Even so, I must confess, the last chapter of his life, which I have called the "Swargarohan Parva", or the chapter of the "Ascent to Heaven", remains a mystery to me. Indeed, in my eyes, it stands equal to the last phase of Lord Krishna's Leela. To unravel its mystery, it may become necessary for Gandhiji himself to be born again.

In this background, an attempt has been made to put his writings and speeches at one place for proper understanding of Gandhi's life, thought and action. To make the book reader friendly it has been divided into two parts.

Part one comprises two Historical writings : (a) The green pamphlet in which Gandhi described in detail the condition of Indian people in South Africa; and (b) *Hind Swaraj* or Indians Home Rule in which Gandhi set goal for himself and for Indians. Through *Hind Swaraj* Gandhi wanted to establish self esteem of individual and moral regeneration of India. In other words, Gandhi through *Hind Swaraj* wanted to transform (a) India as a nation and polity; and (b) Indians. It is a source book for evaluation of India and Indians. It is a manual of action for people and a critique of excessiveness of materialistic western society. It is a pointer to down side of modern civilization, i.e., colonialism, neo-colonialism, violence, alienation, etc. It is also a pointer to Political democracy because political democracy without social democracy is not a democracy at all.

Second part comprises of seventeen historical speeches given by Gandhi at different places in different times. These speeches are touching almost all aspects and are of contemporary relevance.

After thirty years of my experience, I have come to the conclusion that immorality is often taught in the name of morality in the institutions known for spreading morality in the society. Ethics and honesty are dear to me and I stand firm on this conviction. The fact is that Gandhians' and Gandhian Institutions are becoming epic centre of all sorts of immoral activities and ethical and honest men are becoming casualty in these institutions. Gandhian Institutions till mid sixties were pride for the nation and now are in the shameless, pitiable condition due to undemocratic, anti-national, anti-people attitude of the persons who are at the helm of running these institutions. No one can think of transparency and accountability in these organizations. Government and the workers are blind spectators.

Where there is light, there is also shadow. It is our moral duty to set matters right. Evil has wings. It spreads fast like the wild fire. But good moves slowly at the pace of snail. Evil triumphs over the good because good people sit idle and do nothing. Gandhi's greatness lay in doing what everyone could do but does not.

Frankly speaking this work is an outcome of the darkest and brightest period of my life. I paid the price of honesty. I fought alone with the so called Gandhians. Ultimately the truth prevailed. In this period the people who got all sorts of benefit from me changed their colour and exhibited the real nature of selfishness. By God's grace in the same period I also came in contact with a number of people and they helped me and stood like rock. This strengthens my belief in God. In fact, this work is the result of inner strength. Great events in life always produce great results. Without God's grace, family support and reading *Gita*, this work would not have been completed. I have no words to thank God, *Gita*, family and friends for giving me inner strength to fight against un-Gandhian activities in Gandhian institutions. Whether I did right or wrong the time and the people will judge. Like Gandhi one step is enough for me.

This work would not have been possible in the present form without the support and help from friends and well-wishers. There are a number of persons behind the scene whose ideas, comments and suggestions have been included in the present book. I shall be failing in my duty if I do not record my appreciation to all of them.

First and foremost, I would like to express my sincere gratitude to Shree T.N. Chaturvedi, Former CAG and Governor of Karnataka and Kerala and Prof. R.P. Misra, former Vice-Chancellor, University of Allahabad, Allahabad, for their guidance and constant encouragement.

I am equally grateful to Prof. N. Radhakrishnan, former Director, GS&DS; Prof. D. Gopal of IGNOU; Prof. J.N. Sharma and Prof. M.L. Sharma of Punjab University, Chandigarh; Prof. K.S. Bharthi of Nagpur University, Nagpur; Prof. R.P. Dwivedi of Kashi Vidyapeeth, Varanasi; Prof. Amita Singh of JNU; Dr. A.K. Dubey, IAS; Mr. Atual Tiwari, IAS; Mr. Virendra Singh, IPS; Mr. Prabhat Ranjan, IRTS; Dr. Y.P. Anand, former Chairman, Railway Board; Dr. Pravin Kumar of Delhi University; Prof. M.P. Dubey of Allahabad University; Dr. Rajshekar Basu of Calcutta University; Dr. H.S. Rathore of Jodhpur University; Prof. Madhukar Shyam Chaturvedi and Dr. Sheela Rai of University of Rajasthan; Prof. S. Narayanasamy of Gandhi Gram Rural University; Prof. Suresh Misra of IIPA; Dr. Devendra Kakar of University of Delhi; Prof. Himanshu Bourai of H.B.N.Garhwal University and Prof. B.R. Dugar of JBVI, Ladnun, for their guidance and comments.

As always I received full support and patience of my dear family when I was busy with completion of this volume. My special thanks are due to my wife, Dr. Sweta Mishra, Gargi College , University of Delhi, Delhi and my daughters, Sanstuti and Sansriti for their patience and help.

My special thanks to my brother, Sunil Dutta Mishra, ADJ, and Purushottam Sharma Tripathi, Advocate, Supreme Court of India, for helping and relieving me from other works to complete this work in a stipulated time frame.

I would like to express my sincere gratitude to Sri Sudhir Nandrajog, Senior Advocate, whose human approach changed my attitude towards the legal profession. Words are inadequate to express my heartfelt regards to him.

Last but not the least, I am grateful to Shri Ashok Kumar Mittal of Concept Publishing Company Pvt. Ltd., for bringing out this book in present form and that too within record time.

15th November, 2011 **Anil Dutta Mishra**

Contents

Introduction

Understanding Gandhi the *third volume of the series* containing Gandhi's original writings and speeches. The purpose of this book is to revisit Gandhi. Gandhi was a simple person and whatever he has written can be understood by the illiterates and literates alike. Yet his was a complex personality. Behind the veneer of simplicity, there was a complex Gandhi—A Gandhi who can be understood only if we tune our life to that of Gandhi. His mind, methods and mission were old, nay ancient indeed, but they went against the main currents of his times. They made history, and set the agenda for generations to come. He could interact with kings and prime ministers with the same ease as he could with peasants and artisans. He was not an academic in the ordinary sense of the word but he has become one of the major subjects of academic discourse. He was a practical philosopher, an applied social scientist, a grass root social worker, a political mobilizer, a revered national leader, a scientist and a saint, all at the same time. His was a simple but complex personality. No matter how deep we penetrate his writings and life, we fail to understand him for we can neither relive his times nor can we disentangle ourselves from the myths, experiences, and prejudices of the past. To understand him, we have to read and re-read Gandhi, meditate over what he said and did and why and above all experiment with truth and non-violence to resolve the problems we face with similar, if not the same, resolve, dedication, and mission. Gandhi changed the world he lived in and gave new direction to what is now known as development. This series is being published to enable the reader to know Gandhi first hand, in his own words.

To understand Gandhi we have to be objective and analytical but at the same time synergic, interdisciplinary, and holistic. Unfortunately, we are trained to be specialists; we see the parts but not the whole. But if everything is related to everything else, and nothing stands apart, knowing the part alone would lead to knowing the whole. Universe is a system of which the solar system is a sub-system; in the solar system, the earth is sub-system; in the earth as a system, lithosphere, hydrosphere, ionosphere, atmosphere and biosphere are sub-systems; in the biosphere, human species form a sub-system; in the human species each family and individual forms a sub-system. This being the case, to understand even an individual in full, we have to treat him as a part of the whole universe. True he is more closely related to the systems nearer him but he is influenced and he influences by his thoughts and deeds not only his fellow human beings, but also all that surrounds him, nature included. All that we do has its implications far wider than we realize. This is how the problem of global warming and climate change has emerged. Real Gandhi is a systems man and unless we see him that way, we cannot understand him.

Further, Gandhi is so much an inseparable part of our modern history that we tend to be emotional about him and refuse to hear anything critical of him although those who see nothing great in him are not few. On the one hand, he is treated as the father of Indian Nationhood, on the other there are many who think that he wanted to take India to primitive days; who consider him an impractical man, and a man who mixed up religion, politics, and economics. We can understand Gandhi only if we distance ourselves, both physically and intellectually from dogmatism, fanaticism, and barren logic; if we see life in all its manifestation, and as a part and parcel of other life forms in general and human beings in particular.

Gandhi worked all through his life to liberate India from British colonialism; but this mission of his was only a part of a larger and more encompassing mission of liberating humanity from the mythos that grip its soul, mind, and body. He lived so simply not only because he wanted to identify himself with the poorest of the poor, but also because he followed the dictum of simple living and high thinking. Gandhi saw unity in diversity; unity of souls and diversity of bodies with oscillating minds in between. Gandhi had no enemies : he had no hatred for anyone. He accepted differences of opinions, perceptions, thoughts, and approaches natural for each individual saw the truth differently. These and other differences can be transcended and ironed out when the contenders are overflowing with love for each other and talk to each other as brothers and sisters.

He was at once saint and revolutionary, politicians and social reformer, economist and man of religion, educationist and satyagrahi; devotee alike of faith and reason, Hindu and inter-religious, nationalist and internationalist, man of action and dreamer of dreams. He was a great reconciler of opposites and he was that without strain or artificiality. Rabindranath Tagore called him Mahatma; Subash Chandra Bose, 'Father of the Nation'; Lord Mountbatten, 'One Man Boundary Force'; Hindu fundamentalists—'Pro-Muslim', Jinah 'Pro-Hindu'. And Winston Churchill called him 'half-naked, seditious fakir'. Whenever he went wrong, he stopped, looked around, retraced his steps and then moved again. What Gandhi did was the immediate concern of the people. He was a creative man and created history. Each of us has the potential to become something like him by experimenting with Truth as we move forward on the road to higher levels of consciousness.

Gandhi was not a theorist or model builder. He was a *Karma Yogi* seeking knowledge and wisdom through action. When people asked him to put his experiments in writing, he replied : "I am not built for academic writings. Action is my domain."[1] Yet he wrote copiously. As we scan through the 100 volumes of his Collected Works, we are struck by the depth and breadth of his reach. We wonder how this man of action wrote so much in so short a time. Even a four line letter he wrote contains pearls of wisdom. Yet, he was so humble as to say "There is no such thing as 'Gandhism' and I do not want to leave any sect after me, I do not claim to have originated any new principle or doctrine. I have simply tried in my own way to apply the eternal truths to our daily life and problems...Well, all my philosophy, if it may be called by that pretentious name, is contained in what I have said. You will not call it 'Gandhism' : there is no 'ism' about it".[2] He climbed step by step to transcend all isms and proclaimed Truth is God.

Gandhi tried to solve problems as they arose, following the law of Truth (morality), keeping in view the cultural background of the people, and good of the society at large. He was often accused of being inconsistent, which he indeed was because "At the time of writing I never think of what I have said before. My aim is not to be consistent with my previous statements on a given question, but to be consistent with truth as it may present itself to me at a given moment. The result has been that I have grown from truth to truth; I have saved my memory from an undue strain; and what is more, whenever I have been obliged to compare my writing even of fifty years ago with the latest, I have discovered no inconsistency between the two. But friends who observe inconsistency will do well to take the meaning that my latest writing may yield unless, of course, they prefer the old. But before making the choice they should try to see if there is not an underlying and abiding consistency between the two seeming inconsistencies"[3].

Not many have been able to fathom his depth. Gandhi believed in the unity of human life, which is a synthetic whole. It cannot be divided into separate, watertight compartments—religious, moral, political, economic, social, individual and collective. Gandhi said "Drops in separation could only fade away, drops in cooperation made the ocean which carried on its broad bosom ocean greyhounds.[4] A drop torn from the ocean perished without doing any good. If it remained a part of the ocean, it shared the glory of carrying on its bosom a fleet of mighty steps.[5]

Gandhi changed his approaches to conflict resolution depending on the nature of problem, people involved, and the circumstances surround it; certain timeless laws he followed and adhered to ever remained his guiding stars. *One*, he firmly believed that the process of evolution Darwin unravelled did not stop with the chimpanzees turning into Homo Sapiens.

Once the physical evolution was over, the evolution of the inner self began and it would continue until the humans evolve into superconscious beings. Anything that took man backward to his animal past was regressive, and that which took him to the next milestone of consciousness was progressive. *Two,* Truth and non-violence were the driving forces of this evolutionary journey to higher consciousness. *Three,* everything was related to everything else, and hence nothing stands independent and isolated. All that we feel, think, and act upon, has wider implications. Those nearer us are affected more than those at distant places. *Four,* since the journey of life adds new experiences, truth is not absolute; it is relative. As such all of us can be victims of truth or untruth depending on our perception of the reality. One should, therefore, change one's views as new truths come to light. One should not be dogmatic. *Five,* all life is a united whole; humans have to love not only their fellow human beings but also the nature—the plants, insects, and animals, and all that is created by the cosmic force otherwise known as God. And *six,* there is enough on this earth to satisfy everyone's need but not everyone's greed"[6] and hence follow the dictum of simple living and high thinking.

Gandhi lived in a world of wars, colonialism, survival of the fittest, and eye for eye, Gandhi's truth and non-violence appeared to many, as weapons of the weak. They gathered around him as co-workers and followers only when it appeared to work as a potent force against violence appearing in different garbs : injustice, exploitation, colonialism, and wars, to mention a few. Gandhi's weapons proved more powerful but least destructive *vis-a-vis* the conventional weapons of war. His *satyagraha* evoked worldwide attention and crossed the borders of India to reach many other countries, the USA, Russia, China, EU, and South Africa included. It proved beyond doubt that his means of fighting injustice ennobled both sides and left them in win-win situation. Globalization of Gandhian praxis did not go far enough to usher in a civilization of peace and harmony. It remained a movement which petered off when war mongering returned with a big bang in the form of modernization and globalization. Modernization means westernization and globalization means deprivation of the rights of the people to fully participate in production and consumption of the goods and services they need and use. It converts people from being prosumers to consumers.

Rejection of Gandhian ways began soon after India became independent. It proved too difficult for the leaders of the time, even though they followed Gandhi during the freedom struggle, to carry forward his legacy of truth and non-violence. Gandhi was soon enshrined in museums spread over different parts of the country, and Gandhi Bhawans of select universities. He became a research topic and a name to be prefixed with institutions, organizations and individuals to acquire prestige. Many development schemes sponsored by the Central and state governments are being named after Gandhi. But in all these cases it is name, not the spirit of Gandhi that pervades.

Gandhi advocated development from below. He wanted each village of India to function as an autonomous republic. The situation today is just the same as it was during the British days. It is development from above. Development is delivered by the Central and State governments to the people; it is not created by the local government—the village panchayats and city municipalities. It is clear from the fact that two-fifths (42 per cent) of the public expenditure on salaries is claimed by the Central Government employees; a little more than that (45 per cent) by the State Government employees; and only one-sixth (12-13 per cent) goes to local governments which are closest to the people; in China it is 43 per cent. It is not to suggest that more money will make local governments better. But it points to how far we have followed Gandhi.

Education and health are the most basic functions of the local government. But what is the situation on both of these fronts? We have failed to make people literate and those who claim to be literate (around 65 per cent) are literates on in name. Functional literacy rate would be less than 50 per cent. How tragic it is that the village panchayats have no say in schooling of the children, the future of our country. There is a plethora of officials who are supposed to inspect the schools, but rampant corruption has crippled them. Pay a monthly amount to the Basic Shiksha Adhikari (BSA), and you do not have to go to school or you can appoint a proxy to do the work you are supposed to do. Gandhi advocated Hindi and mother tongue as the medium of instruction. But in the land of Gandhi, English occupies the top choice of parents and children alike. Even those leaders who advocated Hindi as the medium of instruction, sent their children to UK and USA but asked the people to learn and love Hindi. Israel introduced Hebrew, a defunct language and made it national language. But we have failed to revive our living languages, Hindi included.

The same is the case with Primary Health Centres (PHCs). Most doctors go to the centres only once in a week or month. They pay the district CMO a fixed amount each month and run their private clinic in the city or nearby town fearlessly. British are gone but the British system of administration continues. The only major change is incursion of corruption in a big way. Worst is the situation with regard to law and order. Police Stations do not register FIR as they want their area to be crime free. The bureaucracy all the way from Central Secretariat to Panchayat Samitis has gone corrupt. It is not that we do not have honest and able civil servants. But the rot is spreading very fast. What has gone wrong is the nexus between corrupt politicians and corrupt bureaucrats. Had they been honest, India would have gone far ahead of China; there would have been no illiterate in the country; and abject poverty would have been a thing of the past. This is just a sample of how Gandhi has been sidelined, and the common people who constitute more than 75 per cent of the population of the country have been robbed of their livelihood. Unless we return to Gandhi at least in broad perspectives otherwise we would make India a land of perpetual violence.

A number of approaches to study of Gandhi's thought are in practice today—the Nationalist, the Marxist, the Oriental, the Post-colonial and the Subaltern, etc. To understand Gandhiji amidst his conflicting statements, one has perhaps to go into the meaning of meaning. To know their deeper significance, going by the literal meaning of the words would be futile and burdensome.[7] Even Vinoba Bhave, the spiritual heir of Gandhi failed to comprehend his Guru. "Gandhiji . . .laid bare his mind in its fullness before the world. For his part, he had permitted no secrecy. Even so, I must confess, the last chapter of his life, which I have called the 'Swargarohan Parva', or the chapter of the 'Ascent to Heaven', remains a mystery to me. Indeed, in my eyes, it stands equal to the last phase of Lord Krishna's Leela. To unravel its mystery, it may become necessary for Gandhiji himself to be born again".[8]

In this background, an attempt has been made in this and other volumes of the series to lift his writings and speeches from the maize of his other writings and to reproduce them theme-wise and put in book form to enable the reader to see what Gandhi had to say on different issues in a chronological order. This volume is a collection of his writings and speeches on subjects and issues that open up the rebel in Gandhi and continue to be debated to this day. To make the volume reader friendly the material has been presented in two parts. Part One comprises of two historical writings :

1. The Green Pamphlet published in; and
2. Hind Swaraj or Indian Home Rule published in 1909

Part Two contains sixteen speeches delivered by Gandhi on different topics, and at different places and different times.

REFERENCES

1. *Harijan*, 3-3-1946, p. 28.
2. *Ibid*, 28-3-1936, p. 49.
3. *Ibid*, 30-9-1939, p. 228.
4. CWMG : 89 : 97.
5. CWMG : 87 : 23.
6. Anil Dutta Mishra and Ravi Gupta, *Inspiring Thoughts of Mahatma Gandhi* (*Gandhi in Daily Life*), New Delhi, Concept, 2008, p. 63.
7. CWMG : 93 : 153.
8. CWMG : 86 : IX-X.

PART ONE

HISTORICAL WRITINGS OF MAHATMA GANDHI

1

The Green Pamphlet

THE GRIEVANCES OF THE BRITISH INDIANS IN SOUTH AFRICA

AN APPEAL TO THE INDIAN PUBLIC

On June 5, 1896, Gandhiji left South Africa on a visit to India for domestic reasons. The leading men of the Indian community in South Africa commissioned him to lay the grievances of the Indians residing there before the authorities and the public in India. The first step which Gandhiji took in this direction, during his stay of nearly five months in India, was to publish a pamphlet on the subject under the title The Grievances of the British Indians in South Africa. *The pamphlet later became known as the Green Pamphlet because of the colour of its cover. It received wide circulation and Gandhiji soon found it necessary to issue a second edition.*

Preface

The rush for copies of this pamphlet at the Madras Meeting in Pachaiyappa's Hall has necessitated the issue of the second edition. It was a scene never to be forgotten.

The demand proved two things—the importance of the question of the grievances of the British Indians in South Africa, and the interest shown by the Indian Public in the welfare of their countrymen beyond the waters.

It is to be hoped that the second edition will be disposed of as soon as the first, showing the continuance of the interest. Publicity is perhaps the chief remedy for the grievances and the pamphlet is one of the means to that end.

The appendix is an addition to the first edition and is a part of the address read before the Madras Meeting, being a reply to the Natal Agent-General's statement to Reuter.[1]

The Natal Immigration Law Amendment Act referred to in the pamphlet has, unfortunately for the poor Indians in South Africa, received the Royal assent. It is respectfully submitted that the question requires the closest study by our public men and there should be no rest till the Act is repealed or State-aided emigration to Natal suspended. The Madras Meeting has passed a Resolution requesting suspension of such emigration if the repeal of the Act cannot be brought about.

Calcutta, 1-11-1896 M.K. GANDHI

This is an appeal to the Indian public on behalf of the 100,000 Indians in South Africa. I have been commissioned by the leading members representing that community in South Africa to lay before the public in India the grievances that Her Majesty's Indian subjects are labouring under in that country.

South Africa is a continent by itself and is divided into many States of which the Colonies of Natal and the Cape of Good Hope, Zululand, a Crown Colony, the South African Republic of the Transvaal, Orange Free State and the Chartered Territories, are inhabited, more or less, by the Indians together with the Europeans and the natives of those countries. The Portuguese territories, viz., Delagoa Bay, Beira and Mozambique, have a large Indian population, but there the Indians have no grievances, apart from the general population.

Natal

From an Indian standpoint, Natal is the most important portion of South Africa. It has a native population of about 400,000, a European population of nearly 50,000 and an Indian population of about 51,000, of whom about 16,000 are those at present serving their indenture, about 30,000 are those who, having once been under indenture, are freed therefrom and have settled in the Colony on their own account, and about 5,000 belong to the trading community. These latter, of course, came to the Colony on their own means and some of them brought capital also into the country. The indentured Indians are drawn from the labouring population of Madras and Calcutta and are nearly equally divided. Those from Madras speak, as a rule, the Tamil language, and, those from Calcutta, the Hindi. They are most of them Hindus, a good few are Mahomedans. Strictly speaking, they do not observe caste restrictions. After becoming free, they either take to gardening or hawking vegetables and earn from 2 to 3 pounds sterling per month. A few become petty storekeepers. That business, however, is practically in the hands of the 5,000 Indians, who are drawn chiefly from the Mahomedan community in the Bombay Presidency. Some of these latter are doing well. Many are large landowners, two are now shipowners also. One of them has a small oil machine worked by steam. They come either from Surat, districts surrounding Bombay, or Porbandar. Many merchants from Surat have settled in Durban with their families. Most of them, including the assisted immigrants, can read and write their own language to a greater extent than one would think they do.

I venture to quote the following from my 'Open Letter' to the Members of the Legislative Assembly and the Legislative Council of Natal to show what treatment the Indian receives at the hands of the general run of Europeans in the Colony :

> The man in the street hates him, curses him, spits upon him, and often pushes him off the footpath. The Press cannot find a sufficiently strong word in the best English dictionary to damn him with. Here are a few examples.[2] 'The real canker that is eating into the very vitals of the community', 'these parasites', 'wily wretched semi-barbarous Asiatics', 'A thing black and lean and a long way from clean, which they call the accused Hindoo', 'He is chokeful[2] of vice and he lives upon rice. I heartily cuss the Hindoo', 'Squalid coolies with truthless tongues and artful ways'. The Press almost unanimously refuses to call the Indian by his proper name. He is 'Ramysamy'. He is Mr. 'Samy'.[3] He is Mr. 'Coolie'. He is the 'black man'. And these offensive epithets have become so common that they (at any rate, one of them, Coolies) are used even in the sacred precincts of the Courts, as if the Coolie were the legal and proper name to give to any and every Indian. The public men, too, seem to use the word freely. I have often heard the painful expression, 'coolie clerk', from the mouths of men who ought to

> know better.[4] The tramcars are not for the Indians. The railway officials may treat the Indians as beasts. No matter how clean, his very sight is such an offence to every White man in the Colony that he would object to sit, even for a short time, in the same compartment with the Indian. The hotels shut their doors against them.[5] Even the public baths are not for the Indians no matter who they are .... The vagrant law is needlessly oppressive and often puts respectable Indians in a very awkward position.

I have quoted this because the statement has been before the South African public for nearly one year and a half, has been commented upon freely by almost every newspaper in South Africa and remains practically uncontradicted (indeed, it has even been endorsed by one newspaper with approval) and because, during the interval that has elapsed, I have seen nothing to change that view. The Right Hon'ble Mr. Chamberlain, however, while in full sympathy with its object, in his reply to the deputation headed by the Hon'ble Mr. Dadabhai[6] is said to have stated that our grievances were more sentimental than material and real and that, if he could be shown any instances of real grievance, he should deal with them effectively. *The Times of India*, which has done us much service and has laid us under deep obligation to it by its persistent advocacy on our behalf, rebuked Mr. Chamberlain for calling our grievances sentimental. To give, however, proof of real grievances and to strengthen the position of the advocates of our cause in India, I shall beg leave to cite my own testimony and that of those who have undergone grievances personally. Every word of every statement to be made immediately can be established beyond the shadow of a doubt.

In Dundee last year, during the Christmas time, a gang of White men set fire to the Indian stores without the slightest provocation, in order to enjoy themselves. Mr. Abdulla Haji Adam, a shipowner and one of the leading members of the Indian community in South Africa, was travelling with me as far as Krantzkloof Station. He alighted there to go by postal cart to Natal. No one there would sell him even bread. The hotel-keeper would not allow him a room in his hotel and he had to sleep in the coach shivering the whole night with cold.

And the winter in that part of Africa is no joke. Mr. Haji Mohamed Haji Dada, another leading Indian gentleman, was travelling in a coach some time ago from Pretoria to Charlestown. He was forced out of the coach and had to walk a distance of three miles because he had not got a pass—whatever that may mean.[7]

A Parsee gentleman, Mr. Rustomjee, whose generosity goes much further than his purse would allow, has been unable to take a Turkish bath for the sake of his health in Durban, although the public baths are the property of the Durban Corporation, to which Mr. Rustomjee pays his rates just as well as the other ratepayers. In Field Street, Durban, last year during Christmas time, some youths threw burning crackers in the Indian stores doing some damage. Three months ago, in the same street, some youths shot lead bullets into an Indian store with a sling, hurting a customer who nearly lost his eye. Both these matters were brought to the notice of the Superintendent of Police who promised to do all he could. Nothing more has been heard of the matter. Yet, the Superintendent is an estimable gentleman, anxious to protect all the communities in Durban. But what could the poor man do against the tremendous odds? Will his subordinates take the trouble to find out the miscreants? When the aggrieved gentleman saw the constables at the police station, they first laughed and then asked him to get a warrant from the Magistrate for their arrest. No warrant is required in such cases when a constable wants to do his duty. Only the day before I left Natal, the son of an Indian gentleman, spotlessly dressed, was walking along the pavement in the principal street in Durban. Some Europeans pushed him off the pavement without any reason but to amuse themselves. Last year, the Magistrate at Estcourt, a village in Natal, had an Indian who was a prisoner in the dock forced out of it. His cap was forcibly removed and he was brought back bare-headed, in spite of the protest from the man that the removal of the cap was contrary to Indian custom and it offended his religious feeling also. A civil action was brought against the Magistrate. And the Judges held that the Magistrate was not civilly liable for acts done by him in his capacity as such. When we went to law, we knew that such would be the decision. Our object was to have the matter thoroughly thrashed out. This question at one time was a very great question in the Colony.

An Indian official, whenever he accompanies his superior during his periodical tours, is unable to secure accommodation in the hotels. He is obliged to sojourn in huts. The grievance had reached such a stage, when I left Natal, that he was seriously thinking of sending in his resignation.

A Eurasian gentleman, Mr. DeSilva by name, who was for some time employed in a responsible position in Fiji, happened to come to Natal to seek fortune. He is a certified chemist. He received an appointment as chemist by letter. When, however, his employer saw that he was not quite White, he dismissed him. I know other Eurasians who, being fair enough to pass as "White men", are not molested. This last instance I have quoted to show how unreasonable the prejudice is in Natal. I could go on relating such instances. But, I hope, I have adduced sufficient instances to show that our grievances are real and as one of our sympathizers in England says in a letter, "They have only to be known to be removed."

Now, what is our mode of action in such cases? Are we to go to Mr. Chamberlain in every case and turn the Colonial Office into one for hearing petty complaints from Indians in South Africa? I have used the word "petty" advisedly, for I admit that most of these cases are cases of petty assault and inconvenience. But when they occur pretty regularly, they assume a sufficiently big shape to be a source of constant irritation to us. Just picture a country where you never know you are safe from such assaults, no matter who you are, where you have a nervous fear as to what would happen to you whenever you undertake a journey, where you cannot be accommodated in a hotel even for a night and you have a picture of the state we are living in Natal. I am sure I am not exaggerating when I say that, if any of the Indian High Court Judges came to South Africa, I doubt very much whether any hotel would admit him, unless he took extraordinary precautions, and I am almost positive that he will have to travel from Charlestown to Pretoria in a Kaffir compartment, unless he is dressed in European clothing from top to toe.

I am aware that in some of the instances cited above Mr. Chamberlain could not very well afford relief, as for example the case of Mr. DeSilva, but the fact is clear that such instances occur because of the rooted prejudice against the Indians in South Africa, which is due to the indifference of the Home and the Indian Governments to the complaints of the Indians. In all the cases of assault, our mode of action, as a rule, is not to take any notice of them. We follow the principle, so far as we can, of going two miles when we are asked to go one. Sufferance is, really and sincerely, the badge of the Indians in South Africa, especially in Natal. I may state, however, that we follow this policy not from philanthropic but from purely selfish motives. We have found by painful experiences that to bring the offenders to justice is a tedious and expensive process. The result is often contrary to our expectations. The offender would either be discharged with a caution or fined "five shillings or one day". The very man, after getting out of the box, assumes a more threatening attitude and puts the complainant in an awkward position. And the publication of such acts incites others to similar ones. We, therefore, do not, as a rule, even mention them before the public in Natal.

Such a feeling of deep-seated hatred towards the Indians is reproduced all over South Africa, in special legislation for Indians, which has for its object the degradation of the Indian community in that country. The Attorney-General of Natal wants to keep the Indians forever "hewers of wood and drawers of water". We are classed with the natives of South Africa—Kaffir races. He defines the status of the Indians in the following words : "These Indians were brought here for the purpose of supplying labour for development of local industries and were not intended to form portion of the South African nation which was being built up in the various States." The policy of the Orange Free State, which, in the words of its leading organ, "has made the British Indian an impossibility by simply classifying him with the South African native", is cherished by the other States as a model policy. What that State has completely accomplished, the other States would accomplish within a very short time but for the vigilance of the Indian public. We are passing through a crisis now. We are hemmed in on all sides by restrictions and high-handed measures.

I shall now show how the feeling of hatred above described has been crystallized into legislation. An Indian cannot leave his house after 9 o'clock at night, unless he has a pass signed by someone showing that he is out under instructions or can give a good account of himself. This law applies to the natives and Indians only. The police use their discretion and do not, as a rule, trouble those who are dressed in the Memon costume, as that dress is supposed to be the Indian trader's dress. Mr. Aboobaker, now deceased, was the foremost Indian trader in Natal and much respected by the European community. He, with his friend, was once arrested by the police. When he was brought to the police station for being out after 9 p. m., the authorities knew at once that they had committed a mistake. They told Mr. Aboobaker that they did not want to arrest gentlemen like himself, and asked him if he could point out any distinguishing mark between a trader and a labourer. Mr. Aboobaker pointed to his robe, and, ever since, it has been a tacit understanding between the police and the public that those wearing the flowing robe should not be arrested, even though they may be out after 9 p.m. But there are Tamil and Bengali traders, equally respectable, who do not wear the robes. There are, again, the Christian Indian educated youths—a most sensitive class—who do not wear robes. They are constantly molested. A young Indian, well-educated, and a Sunday school teacher, another a schoolmaster, were arrested only four months ago and locked up in a dungeon the whole night, in spite of their protestations that they were on their way home. They were discharged by the Magistrate but that was a poor consolation. An Indian lady, a teacher, the wife of the Indian Interpreter at Ladysmith, was a short time ago, on her return from the church on a Sunday evening, arrested by two Kaffir policemen and roughly handled, so much so that her dress was soiled, not to speak of all sorts of bad names she was called. She was locked up in a cell. She was promptly released when the Superintendent of Police came to know who she was. She was carried home senseless. The bold lady sued the Corporation for damages for wrongful arrest and got £20 and costs from the Supreme Court. The Chief Justice remarked that her treatment was "unjust, harsh, arbitrary and tyrannical". The result, however, of these three cases is, that the Corporations are now clamouring for more powers and an alteration of the law, in order that they may, to put it bluntly, subject all Indians, irrespective of their position, to restrictions so that, as a member of the Legislative Assembly said on the occasion of the passing of the Immigration Bill of 1894, "the intention of the Colony to make the Indian's life more comfortable in his native land than in the Colony of Natal" may be fulfilled. In any other country, such instances would have excited the sympathy of all right-minded people and the decision quoted above would have been hailed with joy.

Some eight months ago, about 20 Indians, pure labourers on their way to the Durban market with vegetable baskets on their heads, a sufficient indication that they were not vagrants, were arrested at 4 o'clock in the morning under the same law. The police prosecuted the case vigorously. After a two days' trial, the Magistrate discharged them, but at what cost to the poor people ! They were carrying their day's earnings in prospect on their shoulders. These were gone. They were, I believe, detained for two days in gaol and had to pay their attorney's fees in the bargain, for having ventured to be up and doing in the early morning, a fitting reward for industry ! And Mr. Chamberlain wants instances of real grievances !

There is a system of passes in Natal. Any Indian who, whether in the day-time or the night-time, does not show a pass as to who he is, is liable to arrest. This is meant to prevent desertion by the indentured Indians and to facilitate identification, and is thus far, I believe, necessary, but the working of the law is extremely irritating and a crying grievance. But for the cruel feeling, no injustice need occur under that law. Let the papers speak for themselves as to the working of the law. *The Natal Advertiser* of the 19th June, 1895, has the following on the subject :

> I wish to bring before your notice a few facts regarding the manner in which the Cato Manor[8] tenants are arrested under Section 31,

> Law 25 of 1891. When they are walking on their grounds, the policemen come and arrest them and ask for their free passes. When they call out for their wives or relatives to produce the passes, before they can be produced the policemen begin to drag the Indians to the police station. When the passes are produced on the road to the station, the policemen simply look at them and throw them to the ground. The Indians are taken to the police station, detained for a night and made to wash the cell out in the morning and are then brought before the Magistrate. The Magistrate, without taking their pleas, fines them. When they reported this to the Protector,[9] he told them to go to the Magistrate, yet (adds the correspondent) he is appointed to protect the Indian immigrants. If such things exist in the Colony (continues the writer), to whom are they to appeal?

The statement that the Magistrate does not take pleas must, I think, be a mistake.

The Natal Mercury, the Government organ in Natal, of 13th April, 1895, has the following from the Editor :

> A point of considerable importance to respectable Indians and which causes much heart-burning, is their liability to arrest. Let me give a case in point. A well-known Durban Indian who has property in various parts of the town, a well-educated and exceedingly intelligent man, was the other night, with his mother, visiting Sydenham, where also he has property. Met by two native constables, the young man and his mother were taken into custody and marched off to the police station, though it is only fair to say the native police conducted themselves admirably. The young Indian referred to explained who he was and gave references and the trooper at length bade him begone, warning him, however, that if he did not have a pass next time he would be detained and prosecuted. Being a British subject in a British Colony, he objects to being treated in this way, though, of course, he recognizes the necessity of watchfulness in general. He makes a very strong point, however, and one which the authorities should certainly consider.

It will be only fair to state what the authorities have to say. They admit the grievance but ask how they are to distinguish between an indentured Indian and a free Indian. We, on the other hand, submit that nothing can be easier. The indentured Indian never is dressed in a fashionable dress. The presumption should be in favour of, not against, the Indian, especially an Indian of the type I am referring to. There is no more reason to presume a man to be a thief than to presume an Indian to be a deserter. Even if an Indian did desert and made preparations to look decent, it will be difficult for him to remain undetected for a long time. But, then, the Indian in South Africa is not credited with any feelings. He is a beast, "a thing black and lean", "the Asian dirt to be heartily cursed".

There is, again, a law which says that natives and Indians, when driving cattle, must be provided with certain passes; also a bye-law in Durban which provides for the registration of native servants and "others belonging to the uncivilized races of Asia". This presupposes that the Indian is a barbarian. There is a very good reason for requiring registration of a native in that he is yet being taught the dignity and necessity of labour. The Indian knows it and he is imported because he knows it. Yet, to have the pleasure of classifying him with the natives, he too is required to be registered. The Superintendent of the Borough Police has never, so far as I know, put the law in motion. Once I raised an objection, in defending an Indian servant, that he was not registered. The Superintendent resented the objection and said he never applied the law to Indians and asked me if I wanted to see them degraded. The law, however, being there, may at any time be used as an engine of oppression.

But we have not attempted to have any of these disabilities removed. We are doing what we can to have their rigour mitigated locally. For the present, our efforts are concentrated towards preventing and getting repealed fresh legislation. Before referring to that, I may further illustrate the proposition that the Indian is put on the same level with the native in many other ways also. Lavatories are marked "natives and Asiatics" at the railway stations. In the Durban Post and Telegraph Offices, there were separate entrances for natives and Asiatics and Europeans. We felt the indignity too much and many respectable Indians were insulted and called all sorts of names by the clerks at the counter. We petitioned the authorities to do away with the invidious distinction and they have now provided three separate entrances for natives, Asiatics and Europeans.

The Indians have, up to now, enjoyed the franchise rights under the general franchise law of the colony, which requires ownership of immovable property worth £50 or payment of an annual rental of £10 to qualify an adult male to be placed on the Voters' Roll. There is a special franchise law for the natives. Under the former, in 1894, there were 9,309 European voters and 251 Indians, of whom only 203 were living at the time, the populations being equal. Thus the European vote in 1894 was 38 times as strong as the Indian vote. Yet, the Government thought or pretended to think that there was a real danger of the Asiatic vote swamping the Europeans. They, therefore, introduced into the Legislative Assembly of Natal a Bill disfranchising all Asiatics save those who were then rightly contained in any Voters' List, the preamble of the Bill stating that the Asiatics were not acquainted with elective representative institutions. Against this Bill we memorialized both the Legislative Assembly[10] and the Legislative Council[11] of Natal but to no purpose. We then memorialized Lord Ripon[12] and forwarded copies of the memorial to the Press and the public in India and England, with a view to enlist their sympathy and to secure their active support which, we are thankful to say, we received to some extent.

As a result, that Act has now been repealed and replaced by an Act which says "no persons shall be qualified to have their names inserted in any list of electors who (not being of European origin) are natives or descendants in the male line of natives of countries which have not hitherto possessed elective representative institutions founded on the parliamentary franchise unless they shall first obtain an order from the Governor-in-Council, exempting them from the operation of the Act." It also exempts from its operation those persons that are rightly contained in any Voters' List. This Bill was first submitted to Mr. Chamberlain who has practically approved of it. We, yet, thought it advisable to oppose it and, with a view to secure its disallowance, have sent a memorial[13] to Mr. Chamberlain and hope to secure the same measure of support that has been extended to us hitherto. We believe that the real reason for all such legislation is to accord a different treatment to the Indian in South Africa, such that, under it, a respectable Indian in that country may become an impossibility. There is no real danger of the Asiatic vote swamping the European or the Asiatic ruling South Africa. Yet this was the main point urged in support of the Bill. The whole question has been well thrashed out in the Colony and Mr. Chamberlain has got all the materials before him to judge. Here are the Government giving their own view in their organ, *The Natal Mercury*, of the 5th March, 1896, dealing with the present Bill and supporting it. After quoting the figures from the Voters' List it says :

> The fact of the matter is that apart from numbers altogether the superior race will always hold the reins of Government. We are inclined to the belief therefore that the danger of the Indian vote swamping the European is a chimerical one. We do not consider that the danger of being swamped is at all a likely one, as past experience has proved that the class of Indians coming here, as a rule, do not concern themselves about the franchise and further that the majority of them do not even possess the small property qualification required.

This admission has been reluctantly made. The *Mercury* supposes, and we believe, that the Bill will fail in its purpose if it is to debar the Asiatic from the franchise and says that it would not matter if it does. What, then, is the object if it be not to harass the Indian community? The real reason why the Bill has been introduced is thus guardedly but frankly stated by the *Mercury* of the 23rd April, 1896 :

> Rightly or wrongly, justly or unjustly, a strong feeling exists among the Europeans in South Africa, and especially in the two Republics, against Indians or any other Asiatics being allowed unrestricted right to the franchise. The Indian argument, or course, is that there is only one Indian to every 38 European voters on the Roll at present with the open franchise and that the danger anticipated is imaginary. Perhaps it is, but we have to deal with it as if it were a real danger, not altogether, as we have explained, because of our views, but because of the views we know to be strongly held by the rest of the Europeans in the country. We do not want isolation again under the far greater and more fatal ban of being a semi-

> Asiatic country out of touch and out of harmony with the other European Governments of the country.

This, then, is the naked truth. In obedience to the popular outcry, justly or unjustly, the Asiatic must be put down. This Bill has been passed after a secret meeting was held by the Government at which they explained the real reasons for passing the Bill. It has been condemned by the Colonists' and the other newspapers as inadequate from their point of view and by the very members who voted for it. They hold that the Bill will not apply to the Indians because they possess in India "elective representative institutions founded on the Parliamentary franchise and that it will involve the Colony in endless litigation and agitation". We, too, have taken up the same ground. We have urged that the Legislative Councils in India are "elective representative institutions founded on the Parliamentary franchise". Of course, in the popular sense of the term, we have no such institutions, but in the opinion of the *London Times* and an able jurist in Durban our institutions can well be legally classified under those described in the Bill. *The Times* says "the argument that he (the Indian) has no franchise whatever in India is inconsistent with facts." Mr. Laughton, an eminent lawyer in Natal, writing to a newspaper on the subject, says :

> Is there, then, a Parliamentary (or legislative) franchise in India, and what is it? There is, and it was created by the Acts 24 and 25 Victoria, Chapter 67, and 55 and 56 Victoria, Chapter 140, by the regulations made under Section 4 of the latter Act. It may not be founded on what we call a liberal basis, it may indeed be founded on a very crude basis, but it is the Parliamentary franchise nevertheless and, under the Bill it is on it that elective representative institutions of India have to be founded.

This is also the opinion of other eminent men in Natal. Mr. Chamberlain, however, in his dispatch[14] in connection with the matter says :

> I also recognize the fact that the natives of India do not possess representative institutions in their own country and that they themselves, in those periods of their history when they were

> exempt from European influence, have never set up any such system themselves.

The opinion, as will be noticed, is opposed to the view expressed by *The Times* partly quoted above and has naturally frightened us. We are anxious to know what the best legal opinion here is. We cannot, however, too often urge that it is not political power that we want but it is the degradation which these Franchise Bills involve that we resist. If a Colony is allowed to treat the Indians on a different footing from the Europeans in one respect, there would be no difficulty in going further. Their goal is not merely disfranchisement. Their goal is total extinction of the Indian. He may be allowed to exist there as a pariah, as an indentured labourer, at the most a free labourer, but he must not aspire higher. At the time the first Franchise Bill was introduced, in response to the clamour for Municipal disfranchisement of the Indians, the Attorney-General said that [that] would be dealt with in the near future. The Natal Government, about a year ago, wished to convene what was called a "Coolie Conference", so that there might be uniformity in Indian legislation throughout South Africa. At that time also, the Deputy Mayor of Durban moved a resolution that the Asiatics should be induced to live in separate locations. The Government are vexing themselves to find out how they can directly and effectively check the influx of the Indian traders, whom Mr. Chamberlain describes to be "peaceable, law-abiding, meritorious body of persons whose undoubted industry and intelligence and indomitable perseverance", he hopes, "will suffice to overcome any obstacles which may now face them in pursuit of their avocations". The present Bill, therefore, we humbly think, has to be taken in connection with these facts and treated accordingly. The *London Times* has put the franchise question in this form :

> The question now before Mr. Chamberlain is not an academic one. It is not a question of argument but of race-feeling. We cannot afford a war of races among our own subjects. It would be as wrong for the Government of India to suddenly arrest the development of Natal by shutting off the supply of immigrants as it would be for Natal to deny the rights of citizenship to British Indian subjects

who, by years of thrift and good work in the Colony, have raised themselves to the actual status of citizens.

The Second Bill that has been passed by the Natal Legislature proposes to keep the indentured Indians always under indenture, or if they do not relish it, to send them back to India at the end of the first indenture of five years, or if they would not go back, then to compel them to pay an annual tax of £ 3.[15] How, in a British Colony, such a measure could even be thought of passes our comprehension. Almost all the public men in Natal are agreed that the prosperity of the Colony depends upon the Indian labour. In the words of a present member of the Legislative Assembly, "at the time the Indian immigration was decided upon the progress and almost the existence of the Colony hung in the balance !" But in the words of another eminent Natalian :

> Indian immigration brought prosperity, prices rose, people were no longer content to grow or sell produce for a long, they could do better. If we look to 1859, we shall find that the assured promise of Indian labour resulted in an immediate rise of revenue which increased four-fold within a few years. Mechanics who could not get a wage and were earning 5 shillings a day and less found their wages more than doubled and progress gave encouragement to everyone from the Burgh to the Sea.

Yet they want to tax these industrious and indispensable people who, in the words of the present Chief Justice of Natal, have turned out to be "trustworthy and useful domestic servants", after having taken the very life-blood out of them. The following opinion was held by the present Attorney-General ten years ago. He is now the framer of this Bill which a Radical newspaper in London says "is a monstrous wrong, an insult to British subjects, a disgrace to its authors and a slight upon ourselves".

> With reference to the time-expired Indians, I do not think that it ought to be compulsory on any man to go to any part of the world save for a crime for which he is transported. I hear a great deal of this question. I have been asked again and again to take a different view but I have not been able to do it. A man is brought here in

> theory with his own consent, in practice very often, without, he gives the best five years of his life, he forms new ties, forgets the old ones perhaps, establishes a home here and he cannot, according to my view of right and wrong, be sent back. Better by far to stop the further introduction of Indians altogether than to take what work you can out of them and order them away.

But now that which was meritorious 10 years ago in the Indian, namely, his service to the Colony for 5 years for a paltry wage, has become a crime for which he would deserve transportation to India, if the Natal Attorney-General be allowed to do so by the Indian and the Home Governments. I may mention that the Indian Government, on the representation of an *ex parte* Commission[16] that visited India from Natal in 1893, have accepted the principle of compulsory indenture. We, however, are hoping confidently that the facts brought out in the memorials to the Home and the Indian Governments[17] are sufficient to induce the latter to alter their views.

Although we have not moved in the matters specially affecting the Indians now serving their indenture, one may well presume that their lot will not be practically comfortable on the estates. We think that the alteration in the Colony's tone with regard to the general population will affect the masters also of the indentured Indians. One or two matters, however, I have been asked to especially bring to the notice of the public. A representation was made, even as far back as 1891, by an Indian Committee headed by Mr. Haji Mohamed Haji Dada, one of the prayers whereof being that the Protector of Immigrants should be a man knowing the Tamil and the Hindustani languages and should, if possible, be an Indian. We have not receded from that position, but the interval has merely confirmed that opinion.

The present Protector is an estimable gentleman. His ignorance of the languages, however, cannot but be a serious drawback. We humbly consider also that the Protector should be instructed to act as an advocate for the Indians more than as Judge between the employers and the immigrants. I shall illustrate what I say. An Indian named Balasundaram was, in 1894, so ill-treated by his master that two of his teeth were nearly knocked out; they came out through his upper lip causing an issue of blood sufficient to soak his long turban in it. His master admitted the fact but pleaded grave provocation, denied by the man. On receiving the punishment, he seems to have gone to the Protector's house which was closed by his master's. The Protector sent word that he must go to his office the next day.

The man went, then, to the Magistrate who was much moved at the sight. The turban was kept in court and he was at once sent to the hospital for treatment. The man after having been kept in the hospital for a few days was discharged. He had heard about me and came to my office. He had not recovered sufficiently to be able to speak. I asked him, therefore, to write out his complaint in Tamil which he knew. He wanted to prosecute the master so that his contract of indenture might be cancelled. I asked him if he would be satisfied if his indenture was transferred. On his nodding consent to what I said, I wrote to his master asking if he would consent to transfer the services of the man. He was at first unwilling but subsequently consented. I sent the man also to the Protector's office with a Tamil clerk of mine who gave the man's version to the Protector. The Protector desired the man to be left in his office and sent word that he would do his best. The master, in the meanwhile, went to the Protector's office and changed his mind, saying his wife would not agree to the transfer because his services were invaluable. The man was then said to have compromised and to have given the Protector a written document to the effect that he had no complaint to make. He sent me a note to the effect that as the man had no complaint to make and his master did not consent to transfer the services he would not interfere in the matter. I ask if this was right. Was it right for the Protector to have taken such a document from the man? Did he want to protect himself against the man? To proceed, however, with the painful story, naturally the note sent a shock through my body. I had hardly recovered when the man came to my office crying and saying the Protector would not transfer him. I literally ran to the Protector's Office and inquired what the matter was. He placed the written document before me and asked me how he could help the man. He said the man should not have signed the document. And this document was an affidavit attested by the Protector himself. I told the Protector that I should advise the man to go to the Magistrate and lodge a complaint. He said the document would be produced before the Magistrate and it would be useless. He advised me, therefore, to drop the matter. I returned to my office and wrote a letter to his master imploring him to consent to the transfer. The master would do nothing of the kind. The Magistrate treated us quite differently. He had seen the man while the blood was yet dropping from his lips. The deposition was duly made. On the day of hearing, I explained the whole circumstances and again appealed to the master in open court and offered to withdraw the complaint if he consented to the transfer. The Magistrate then gave the master to understand that, unless he considered my offer more favourably than he seemed to do at the time, consequences might be serious for him. He went on to say that he thought the man was brutally treated. The master said he gave provocation. The Magistrate retorted : "You had no business to take the law in your own hands, and beat the man as if he were a beast." He adjourned the case for one day in order to enable the master to consider the offer made by me. The master, of course, came down and consented. The Protector then wrote to me that he would not agree to transfer unless I submitted a European name he could approve of. Happily, the Colony is not quite devoid of benevolent men. A Wesleyan local preacher and solicitor, out of charity, undertook to take over the man's services, and thus ended the last act of this painful drama. Comment is superfluous as to the procedure adopted by the Protector. This is only a typical instance showing how hard it is for the indentured men to get justice.

We submit that no matter who he is, his duties should be clearly defined as are those of Judges, Advocates, Solicitors and others. Certain things, for the sake of avoiding temptations, he should not be able to do in spite of himself. Just fancy a Judge being the guest of a criminal who is being tried before him. Yet, the Protector, when he goes to the estates to enquire about the condition of the men and to hear complaints, can and does often become the guest of the employers. We submit that this practice is wrong in principle, no matter how high-minded the Protector may be. As a Surgeon-Superintendent of Immigrants remarked the other day, the Protector should be easily approachable to the meanest coolie, but he should be unapproachable to the lordliest employer. He may not be a Natal man. It also looks a strange procedure to appoint as Protector a member of a Commission whose object is to induce the Indian Government to consent to pass harsher laws for the indentured Indians. When the Protector has to perform such a conflicting duty, who is to protect the indentured men?

It should be easy for the immigrant to have his services transferred. There are in the gaol some Indians who have been there for years because they refuse to go to their employers. They say they have complaints which, owing to the peculiar circumstances in which they are placed, they cannot substantiate. A Magistrate was so much disgusted with the business that he wished he had not to try such cases. *The Natal Mercury* of 13th June, 1895, thus comments on such a case :

> When a man, even a coolie immigrant, prefers to go to prison rather than work for the master to whom he has been indentured, the natural inference is that something is wrong somewhere, and we are not surprised at Mr. Dillon's remarks on Saturday, when he had three coolies before him, all charged with the same offence of refusing to work, all giving the same excuse, viz., that they were ill-treated by their masters. Of course, it is just possible that these particular coolies prefer gaol work to plantation work. On the other hand, it is just possible that the coolies have some ground for their complaint as to their treatment and the matter is one that ought to be investigated, and at least these men who complain in this way should be transferred to another master and, if they again refuse to work, it can be readily seen that they do not want to work. If a coolie is ill-treated it may be said that he can complain to the Magistrate, but it is not an easy matter for any coolie to prove such cases. It is a matter altogether for the Protector of Immigrants to inquire into and remedy, if possible.

There is an Immigration Trust Board that consists of employers of Indians. They have now received very wide powers. And seeing the position they occupy, their acts will have to be very jealously watched by the Indian Government. The punishment for desertion is heavy enough, and yet, they are now seriously considering whether some stiffer mode of dealing with such cases could not be devised. It should be remembered, however, that, in at least 9 cases out of 10, the so-called deserters complain of ill-treatment, and such deserters are protected under the law from punishment, but, as the poor fellows cannot establish their complaints, they are treated as real deserters and sent by the Protector to the Magistrate for punishment accordingly. Under such circumstances, any alteration for the worse in the law about desertion should, we submit, require careful consideration.

There is a sad mortality among these people from suicides. They are not satisfactorily accounted for. I cannot do better than quote the *Advertiser* of the 15th May, 1896 :

> A feature of the annual report of the Protector of Immigrants, to which more public attention should be given than is the case, is that referring to the number of suicides which take place every year among the indentured coolies on the estates. This year the number recorded is six out of a total of 8,828. A large number occurred in 1894. It is, however, a very high percentage and raises the suspicion that on some estates a system of treatment exists towards the coolie labourers much akin to slave-driving. It is extremely significant that so many suicides should occur on certain estates. This is a point which calls for investigation. Apparently, no inquiry of any kind is held into the cases with a view to ascertain whether the treatment meted out to unfortunate wretches, who prefer death to life, is such as to render existence an intolerable misery. The matter is one which is apt to pass unnoticed. It, however, ought not to do so. In a recent case of desertion on the part of several coolies from an estate down South, the prisoners openly declared in Court that they would rather kill themselves than return to their employer. The Magistrate said he had no option but to order them back to serve out their indentures. It is time the Colony took steps to afford such complainants an opportunity of bringing the facts in connection with their complaints before some Court of Inquiry and the public. It is also desirable that a Secretary of Indian Affairs should be added to the Ministry. As matters stand at present, the indentured Indian has no effectual mode of appeal against whatever brutality may be inflicted on him on the plantations.

We, however, wish to guard ourselves against being understood to say that the life of the indentured Indians in Natal is harder than in any other country, or that this is a part of the general grievances of the Indians in the Colony. On the other hand, we know that there are estates in Natal where the Indians are very well treated. At the same time, we do humbly submit that the lot of the indentured Indians is not all that it might be and that there are points which require attention.

When an indentured Indian loses his free pass, he is charged £3 for the duplicate. The reason for this is the alleged fraudulent sale by the Indians of their passes. But, surely, such fraudulent sale can be criminally punished. A man who has sold his pass should never be able to get a duplicate even on a payment of £30. On the other hand, it should be as easy for an ordinary Indian to get a duplicate as the original. They are supposed to carry their passes about their persons. No wonder if they are frequently lost. I know a man who could not get a duplicate because he had not £3 with him. He wanted to go to Johannesburg and he could not go. The practice in the Protector's department in such cases is to issue temporary passes so that the men may be able to make a present of their first £3 earned to the Protector's office. In the case I am referring to, the man had a temporary pass issued for six months. He could not earn £3 during that time. There are dozens of such cases. I have no hesitation in saying that this is nothing but a system of blackmail.

Zululand

In the Crown Colony of Zululand there are certain townships. There are regulations published with reference to the sale of land in these townships, and the regulations for the townships of Eshowe and Nondweni prevent the Indians from owning or acquiring land,[18] although the Indians own land worth nearly £2,000 in the township of Melmoth in the same country. We have sent a memorial to Mr. Chamberlain[19] and it is now engaging his attention. The Colonists in Natal say that, if such disabilities can be placed on Indians in a Crown Colony, a responsibly governed Colony such as Natal should be allowed to do what it liked with regard to the Indians. Our position in Zululand is no better than in the Free State. It is so dangerous to go to Zululand that the one or two who ventured to go there had to return back. There is a good opening for the Indians there, but the ill-treatment comes in the way. This is a matter that we are earnestly hoping will be set right without much delay.

The Cape Colony

In the Cape Colony, the Mayoral Congress has passed a resolution signifying its desire for legislation prohibiting the influx of Asiatics in that Colony and hoping that prompt action will be taken. The Cape Legislature has, lately, passed a measure which gives the East London Municipality in that Colony the power to make bye-laws compelling natives and Indians to remove to and reside in certain locations and prohibiting them from walking on foot-paths. It is difficult to conceive a better instance of cruel persecution. The following is the position of the Indians in East Griqualand under the Cape Government, according to the *Mercury* of 23rd March, 1896 :

> An Arab, named Ismail Suliman, erected a store in East Griqualand, paid customs duty upon goods and applied for a license, which the Magistrate refused. Mr. Attorney Francis, on the Arab's behalf, appealed to the Cape Government who upheld the Magistrate and have issued instructions that no coolies or Arabs are to have trading licenses in East Griqualand and the one or two that have licenses are to be closed up.

Thus, in some parts of Her Majesty's Dominions in South Africa, even the vested rights of Her Indian subjects are not to be protected. What happened to the Indian in the end, I was unable to ascertain. There are many cases where Indians have been unceremoniously refused licenses to trade. There is a Bluebook on Native Affairs published in Natal. One of the Magistrates therein says, he simply refuses to issue trading licenses to Indians and thus prevents Indian encroachments.

Chartered Territories

In the Chartered Territories, the Indians are receiving the same kind of treatment. Only lately, an Indian was refused a license to trade. He went to the Supreme Court who decided that the license could not be refused to him. Now the Rhodesians have sent a petition to the Government requesting them to alter the law so as to prevent the Indians from getting licenses under the request of the petitioners. This is what the correspondent of the South African *Daily Telegraph* has to say about the meeting that sent the petition :

> It affords me pleasure to be able to say, and say truthfully, that the meeting was in no way a representative one. Had it been so, little credit would thereby have been reflected on the inhabitants of the town. Some half a dozen leading store-keepers, the editor of a paper, a sprinkling of minor Government officials and a fairly large collection of prospectors, mechanics and artisans made up the assembly, which, those under whose direction it was held would, have us believe represented the voice of the police of Salisbury. The resolutions, which I have already wired you with the [names of] proposers and seconders, were nicely cut and dried before the meeting commenced and the figures were set in order and worked in their places when the time arrived. There were no Indians present and no one ventured a word on their behalf, why, it is hard to say, for it is certain that the feeling of by far the majority in this town is altogether adverse to the one-sided, selfish and narrow-minded opinion expressed by those who essayed to speak on the question. . . . I cannot help thinking that little, if any, harm need be feared from the advent of a race who are industrious and steady and who, in higher sphere, have on occasion given evidences of their capabilities in upholding positions which they maintain ably and honourably side by side with their lighter-skinned brother.

The Transvaal

Coming now to the non-British States, i.e., the Transvaal and the Free State, there were in the Transvaal nearly two hundred traders in 1894 whose liquidated assets would amount to £100,000. Of these, about three firms imported goods directly from England, Durban, Port Elizabeth, India and other places, and had thus branches in the other parts of the world whose existence mainly depended upon their Transvaal business. The rest were small vendors having stores in different places. There were, then, nearly two thousand hawkers in the Republic who buy goods and hawk them about. Of the labouring Indian population, who are employed as general servants in European houses or hotels, there were about 1,500 men, of whom about 1,000 lived in Johannesburg. Such, roughly, was the position at the end of 1894 A.D. The numbers have now considerably increased. In the Transvaal, the Indians cannot own landed property; they can be ordered to reside in locations. No new licenses to trade are issued to them. They are made to pay a special registration fee of £3. All these restrictions are unlawful, being in contravention of the London Convention which secures the rights of all Her Majesty's subjects. But the previous Secretary of State for the Colonies having consented to a departure from the Convention, the Transvaal has been able to impose the above restrictions. They were the subject of an arbitration in 1894-95 which has decided against the Indians, that is to say, which has declared that the Republic was entitled to pass those laws. A memorial[20] against the award of the arbitrator was sent to the Home Government. Mr. Chamberlain has now given his decision on the memorial and, while sympathising with the prayer thereof, has accepted the award of the Arbitrator. He has, however, promised and retained the right to make friendly representations to the Transvaal Government from time to time. And, if the representations are emphatic enough, we have no doubt that we shall get justice in the end. We, therefore, implore the public bodies to exert their influence so that these representations may be such as to have their desired effect. I shall venture to quote an instance in point. When, during the Malaboch war, the British subjects were being commandeered, many protested against it and asked for the interference of the Home Government. The reply first sent was to the effect that they could not interfere with the affairs of the Republic. The papers, however, were enraged and memorials strongly worded were repeated. At last came the request to the Transvaal Government not to commandeer British subjects. It was not an interference, yet the request had to be granted and the commandeering of British subjects was stopped. May we hope for such a request which carries with it its fulfilment? If we are not as important a community as that concerned with the commando movement, our grievances, we submit, are much more so.

Whether such or any representations are made or not, there will arise questions out of the award that will engage Mr. Chamberlain's attention. What shall be done with the hundreds of Indian stores in the Transvaal? Will they all be closed up? Will they all be made to live in locations, and if so, what locations? The British Agent has thus described the Transvaal locations with reference to the removal of the Malays in Pretoria, the Metropolis of the South African Republic :

> To be forced into a small location on a spot used as a place to deposit the refuse of the town, without any water except the polluted soakage in the gully between the location and the town, must inevitably result in malignant fevers and other diseases breaking out amongst them whereby their lives and the health of the community in town will be endangered. (Green Book No. 2, 1893, page 72)

Will they, or will they not, receive any compensation if they are made to sell off? Again, the very law is ambiguous. The Arbitrator was called upon to decide upon the interpretation which he has now left to the High Court of the Transvaal. We contend that by the law the State can only compel us to reside in locations. The State contends that residence includes trading stores also and that, therefore, we may not, under that law, even trade except in specified locations. The High Court is said to favour the State interpretation.

Nor are these the only grievances in the Transvaal. These were the subject of the arbitration. But there is a law which prevents the railway authorities in the Transvaal from issuing first or second-class tickets on the railways. There is a tin compartment reserved for natives and other coloured people in which we are literally packed like sheep, without regard to our dress, our behaviour, or our position. In Natal, there is no such law but the petty officials give trouble. The hardship is not insignificant. In Delagoa Bay, the authorities so respect the Indian that they would not allow him to travel third class, so much so that, if a poor Indian could not afford the second class fare, he is allowed to travel second class under a third class ticket. The same Indian, as soon as he reaches the Transvaal border, is compelled to put his dignity into his pocket, asked to produce a pass and then unceremoniously thrust into the third class compartment, no matter whether he has a first class or a second class ticket. The journey is long enough to be felt like a month's journey in those uncomfortable quarters. The same thing happens on the Natal side. Four months ago, an Indian gentleman got a second class ticket for Pretoria at Durban. He was assured that he would be all right, yet, he was not only forcibly put out at Volksrust, a station on the Transvaal border, but could not proceed by that train because it did not carry any third class compartment. These regulations seriously interfere with our carrying on our trade also. There are many who, owing to such inconveniences, would not move from place to place unless they could not possibly avoid it.

Then, in the Transvaal, an Indian, like the native of South Africa, has to carry a travelling pass which costs a shilling. This is the Indian's permit to travel about. It is, I believe, available only for a single journey. Thus, Mr. Haji Mahomed Haji Dada was put out of his post-cart and had to walk a distance of three miles, at the point of the policeman's *sjambok*, which serves the purpose of the bayonet, in order to get the pass. The pass master, however, knew him and so would not issue any pass to him. All the same, he had to miss his coach and walk from Volksrust to Charlestown.

The Indians cannot, as of right, walk on the foot-path in Pretoria and Johannesburg. I use the word "as of right" advisedly, because the traders are, as a rule, not interfered with. In Johannesburg, there is a bye-law to that effect passed by the Sanitary Board. A gentleman, named Mr. Pillay, a graduate of the Madras University, was violently pushed off the foot-paths in Pretoria. He wrote about it to the papers. The attention of the British Agent also was drawn to the matter. But, sympathetic as he was towards the Indians, he declined to interfere.

The gold mining laws of Johannesburg prevent Indians from taking out mining licenses and render it criminal for them to sell or possess native gold.

The treaty, exempting the British subjects from commando service, has been accepted by the Transvaal with the reservation that British subjects therein shall mean only "Whites". That is now the subject of a memorial to Mr. Chamberlain.[21] Under it, apart from the serious disability it places upon the Indian subjects of Her Majesty, we might, as the London *Times* puts it, "now see a levy of British Indian subjects driven at the point of the Transvaal bayonets against the bayonets of British Troops".

The Orange Free State

The Orange Free State, as I have already quoted from a newspaper, has made the British Indian an impossibility. We are driven away from that State, causing to us a loss of £9,000. Our stores were closed up and no compensation was given to us. Will Mr. Chamberlain consider this a real grievance and get us our £9,000 from the Orange Free State, not to speak of the future blighting of the prospects of the traders particularly concerned? I know them all, and most of them have not been able to regain their former position, although at the time they were thus driven out they were supposed to be the wealthiest firms. The law, which is entitled "the law to prevent the inrush of Asiatic coloured persons", prevents any Indian from remaining in the Orange Free State for more than 2 months, unless he gets the permission from the President of the Republic, who cannot consider the application to reside before thirty days have elapsed after the presentation of the petition and other ceremonies have been performed. He can, however, on no account, hold fixed property in the State or carry on any mercantile or farming business.

The President may or may not, "according to the state of things", grant such mutilated permission to reside. Any Indian resident, moreover, is subject to an annual poll-tax of £10. The first contravention of the section relating to mercantile and farming business renders the delinquent liable to a fine of £25 or three months' imprisonment, with or without hard labour. For all subsequent contraventions, the punishment is to be doubled.

But, gentlemen, you have been told lately by the Natal Agent-General[22] that the Indians are nowhere better treated than in Natal; that the fact that a majority of the indentured labourers do not avail themselves of the return passage is the best answer to my pamphlet, and that the railway and tram-car officials do not treat the Indians as beasts nor do law courts deny them justice.

With the greatest deference to the Agent-General, all I can say as to the first statement is that he must have very queer notions of good treatment, if to be locked up for being out after 9 p.m. without a pass, to be denied the most elementary right of citizenship in a free country, to be denied a higher status than that of bondman and, at best, a free labourer, and to be subjected to other restrictions referred to above are instances of good treatment. And if such treatment is the best the Indians receive throughout the world, then the lot of the Indians in other parts of the world and here must be very miserable indeed, according to the commonsense view. The thing is that Mr. Walter Peace, the Agent-General, is made to look through the official spectacles and to him everything official is bound to appear rosy. The legal disabilities are condemnatory of the action of the Natal Government, and how can the Agent-General be expected to condemn himself? If he, or the Government which he represents, only admitted that the legal disabilities mentioned above were against the fundamental principles of the British Constitution, I should not stand before you this evening. I respectfully submit that statements of opinion made by the Agent-General cannot be allowed to have greater weight than those of an accused person about his own guilt.

The fact that the indentured Indians, as a rule, do not avail themselves of the return passage we do not dispute, but we certainly dispute that it is the best answer to our complaints.

How can that fact disprove the existence of the legal disabilities? It may prove that the Indians, who do not take advantage of the return passage, either do not mind the disabilities, or remain in the Colony in spite of such disabilities. If the former be the case, it is the duty of those who know better to make the Indians realize their situation and to enable them to see that submission to them means degradation. If the latter be the case, it is one more instance of the patience and the forbearing spirit of the Indian nation, which was acknowledged by Mr. Chamberlain in his despatch in connection with the Transvaal Arbitration. Because they bear them is no reason why the disabilities should not be removed or why they should be interpreted into meaning the best treatment possible.

Moreover, who are these people who, instead of returning to India, settle in the Colony? They are the Indians drawn from the poorest classes and from the most thickly populated districts, possibly living in a state of semi-starvation in India. They migrated to Natal with their families, if any, with the intention of settling there, if possible. Is it any wonder if these people, after the expiry of their indenture, instead of returning to face semi-starvation, as Mr. Saunders has put it, settle in a country where the climate is magnificent and where they may earn a decent living? A starving man, generally, would stand any amount of rough treatment to get a crumb of bread.

Do not the Uitlanders make out a terribly long list of grievances in the Transvaal? And yet, do they not flock to the Transvaal in thousands, in spite of the ill-treatment they receive there, because they can earn their bread in the Transvaal more easily than in the old country?

This, too, should be borne in mind that, in making his statement, Mr. Peace has not taken into account the free Indian trader who goes to the Colony on his own account and who feels most the indignities and disabilities. If it does not do to tell the Uitlander that he may not go to the Transvaal if he cannot bear the ill-treatment, much less will it do to tell so to the enterprising Indian. We belong to the Imperial family and are children, adopted, it may be, of the same august mother, having the same rights and privileges guaranteed to us as to the European children. It was in that belief that we went to the Colony of Natal, and we trust that our belief was well-founded.

The Agent-General has contradicted the statement made in the pamphlet that the railway and tram-car officials treat the Indians as beasts. Even if the statements I have made were incorrect, that would not disprove the legal disabilities which, and which alone, have been made the subject of memorials and to remove which we invoke the direct intervention of the Home and the Indian Governments. But, I venture to say that the Agent-General has been misinformed, and beg to repeat that the Indians are treated as beasts by the railway and the tram-car officials. The statement was made now nearly two years ago in quarters where it could have been contradicted at once. I had the honour to address as 'Open Letter' to the members of the local Parliament in Natal. It was widely circulated in the Colony and noticed by almost every leading newspaper in South Africa. No one contradicted it then. It was even admitted by some newspapers. Under such circumstances, I ventured to quote it in my pamphlet published here.[23] I am not given to exaggerate matters, and it is very unpleasant to me to have to cite testimony in my own favour, but since an attempt has been made to discredit my statements and, thereby, the cause I am advocating, I feel it to be my duty for the sake of the cause to tell you what the papers in South Africa thought about the 'Open Letter' in which the statement was made.

The Star, the leading newspaper in Johannesburg, says :

> Mr. Gandhi writes forcibly, moderately and well. He has himself suffered some slight measure of injustice since he came into the Colony, but that fact does not seem to have coloured his sentiment, and it must be confessed that to the tone of the 'Open Letter' no objection can reasonably be taken. Mr. Gandhi discusses the questions he has raised with conspicuous moderation.

The Natal Mercury, the Government organ in Natal, says :

> Mr. Gandhi write with calmness and moderation. He is as impartial as any one could expect him to be, and probably a little more so than might have been expected, considering that he did not receive

very just treatment at the hands of the Law Society[24] when he first came to the Colony.

Had I made unfounded statements the newspapers would not have given such a certificate to the 'Open Letter'.

An Indian, about two years ago, took out a second class ticket on the Natal railway. In a single night journey he was thrice disturbed and was twice made to change compartments to please European passengers. The case came before the Court and the Indian got £10 damages. The following is the plaintiff's evidence in the case :

> Deponent got into a second class carriage in the train leaving Charlestown at 1.30 p.m. Three other Indians were in the same compartment but they got out at Newcastle. A White man opened the door of the compartment and beckoned to witness saying : "Come out, Sammy". Plaintiff, asked : "Why", and the White man replied : "Never mind, come out, I want to place someone here." Witness said : "Why should I come out from here when I have paid my fare"?... The White man then left and brought an Indian who, witness believed, was in the employ of the railway. The Indian was told to tell plaintiff to get out of the carriage. Thereupon the Indian said, "The White man orders you to come out and you must come out." The Indian then left. Witness said to the White man : "What do you want to shift me about for? I have paid my fare and have a right to remain here". The White man became angry at this and said : "Well, if you don't come out, I will knock hell out of you." The White man got into the carriage and laid hold of the witness by the arm and tried to pull him out. Plaintiff said : "Let me alone and I will come out." The witness left the carriage and the White man pointed out another second class compartment and told him to go there. Plaintiff did as he was directed. The compartment he was shown into was empty. He believed some people who were playing a band were put into the carriage from which he was expelled. This White man was the District Superintendent of Railways at Newcastle. To proceed, witness travelled undisturbed to Maritzburg. He fell asleep, and when he awoke at Maritzburg, he found a White man, a White woman and a child in the compartment with him. A White man came up to the carriage and said : "Is that your boy,[25] speaking to the White man in the compartment?" Witness's fellow-traveller replied : "Yes", pointing to his little boy. The other White man then said, "No, I don't mean him. I mean the damned coolie in the corner!" This

> gentleman with the choice language was a railway official, being a shunter. The White man in the compartment replied : "Oh never mind him, leave him alone". Then the White man outside (the official) said : "I am not going to allow a coolie to be in the same compartment with White people." This man addressed plaintiff, saying : "Sammy, come out." Plaintiff said : "Why, I was removed at Newcastle to this compartment." The White man said : "Well, you must come out", and was about to enter the carriage. Witness, thinking he would be handled as at Newcastle, said he would go out and left the compartment. The White man pointed out another second class compartment which witness entered. This was empty for a time but, before leaving, a White man entered. Another White man, (the official), afterwards came up and said : "If you don't like to travel with that stinking coolie I will find you another carriage." (*The Natal Advertiser*, 22nd November, 1893, Wednesday.)

You will have noticed that the official at Maritzburg maltreated the Indian passenger although his White fellow-passenger did not mind him. If this is not bestial treatment, I should very much like to know what is, and such occurrences take place often enough to be irritating.

It was found during the case that one of the witnesses for the defendant was coached. In answer to a question from the Bench whether the Indian passengers were treated with consideration, the witness, who was one of the officials referred to, replied in the affirmative. Thereupon, the presiding Magistrate who tried the case is reported to have said to the witness : "Then, you have a different opinion to what I have, and it is a curious thing that people who are not connected with the railway observe more than you."

The Natal Advertiser, a European daily in Durban, made the following remarks on the case :

> It was indisputable from the evidence that the Arab had been badly treated and seeing that second class tickets are issued to Indians of this description, the plaintiff ought not to have been subjected to unnecessary annoyance and indignity.... Some definite measures should be taken to minimise the danger of trouble arising between European and coloured passengers, without rendering the carrying out of such measures annoying to any person, whether black or white.

In the course of its remarks on the same case, *The Natal Mercury* observed:

> There is, throughout South Africa, a tendency to treat all Indians as coolies pure and simple, no matter whether they be educated and cleanly in their habits or not.... On our railways we have noticed, on more than one occasion, that coloured passengers are not, by any means, treated with civility, and although it would be unreasonable to expect that the White employees of the N.G.R.[26] should treat them with the same deference as is accorded to European passengers, still we think it would not be in any way derogatory to their dignity if the officials were a little more *suaviter in modo* when dealing with coloured travellers. (24-11-1893).

The *Cape Times,* a leading newspaper in South Africa, says :

> Natal presents the curious spectacle of a country entertaining a supreme contempt for the very class of people she can least do without. Imagination can only picture the commercial paralysis which would inevitably attend the withdrawal of the Indian population from that Colony. And yet the Indian is the most despised of creatures, he may not ride in the tram-cars nor sit in the same compartment of a railway carriage with the Europeans. Hotel-keepers refuse him food or shelter and he is denied the privilege of the public bath ! (5-7-1891).

Here is the opinion of an Anglo-Indian, Mr. Drummond, who is intimately connected with the Indians in Natal. He says, writing to *The Natal Mercury* :

> The majority of the people here seem to forget that they are British subjects, that their *Maharanee* is our Queen and, for that reason alone, one would think that they might be spared the opprobrious term of 'coolie' as it is here applied. In India, it is only the lower class of White man who calls a native a 'nigger' and treats him as if he were unworthy of any consideration or respect. In their eyes, as in the eyes of many in this Colony, he is treated either as a heavy burden or a mechanical machine.... It is a common thing, and a lamentable thing, to hear the ignorant and the unenlightened speak of the Indian generally as the scum of the earth, etc. It is depreciation from the White man and not appreciation that they get.

I think I have adduced sufficient outside testimony to substantiate my statement that the railway officials treat the Indians as beasts. On the tram-cars, the Indians are often not allowed to sit inside, but are sent 'upstairs', as the phrase goes. They are often made to remove from one seat to another or prevented from occupying front benches. I know an Indian officer, a Tamil gentleman, dressed in the latest European style, who was made to stand on the tram-car board, although there was accommodation available for him.

As to the statement that the Indians get justice in the law courts, I beg to say that I have never said they do not, nor am I prepared to admit that they get it at all times and in all courts.[27]

Quoting statistics to prove the prosperity of the Indian community is quite unnecessary. It is not denied that the Indians who go to Natal do earn a living and that in spite of the persecution.

Such then is the position of the Indians in South Africa, except Delagoa Bay where the Indians are very much respected, labour under no special disability and are owners of nearly half the fixed property in the principal streets of that city. They are all of them mostly traders. Some of them are in Government employment also. There are two Parsee gentlemen who are Engineers. And there is another Parsee gentleman whom, perhaps, even a child in Delagoa Bay knows by the name of "Senhor Edul". The trading class, however, chiefly consists of Mahomedans and Banias, mostly from Portuguese India.

It yet remains for me to examine the cause of this deplorable state of things, as also the remedy. The Europeans say that the habits of the Indians are insanitary, they spend nothing and that they are untruthful and immoral. These are the objections according to the most moderate journals. Others, of course, simply abuse us. The charge as to insanitary habits and untruthfulness is partially true, that is to say, the sanitary habits of the Indian community as a whole, in South Africa, are not as good as they might be from the highest point of view. The charge as laid against us by the European community and used in the way it has been, we totally deny, and we have quoted the opinions of Doctors in South Africa to show that "class considered, the lowest-class Indian lives better and in better habitation and with more regard to sanitary measures than the lowest-class White". Dr. Veale, B.A., M.B.B.S. (Cantab.), finds the Indians "to be cleanly in their persons and free from the personal diseases due to dirt or careless habits" and finds also that "their dwellings are generally clean and sanitation is willingly attended to by them."[28] But we do not say we are beyond improvement in this matter. We may not live quite satisfactorily if there were no sanitary laws. Both the communities err equally in this respect, as the newspaper records would show. That, however, cannot be a reason for all the serious disabilities that are imposed upon us. The cause lies elsewhere, as I shall presently show. Let them enforce the sanitary law very strictly, and we shall be all the better for that. Those of us who are lazy will be properly aroused from our lethargy. As to untruthfulness, the charge, to a certain extent, is true, with regard to the indentured Indians, utterly exaggerated with regard to the traders. But the indentured Indians, placed in the position they are, I venture to say, have done much better than any other community would do in a similar position. The very fact that they are liked as servants by the Colonists and called "useful and trusty", shows that they are not the incorrigible liars they are made out to be. However, the moment they leave India, they are free from the healthy checks that keep them on the narrow path. In South Africa, they are without any religious instruction, though they need it badly. They are called upon to give evidence against their masters for the sake of a fellow brother. This duty they often shirk. Gradually, therefore, their faculty for adhering to the truth, under all circumstances, becomes perverted and they become helpless afterwards.

I submit that they are more the objects of pity than of contempt. And this view I ventured to place before the public in South Africa two years ago, and they have not excepted to it. The facts that the European firms in South Africa give hundreds of Indians large credit, practically on their word of honour, and have no cause to regret having done so, and that the banks give Indians almost unlimited credit, while the merchants and bankers would not trust Europeans to that extent, conclusively prove that the Indian traders cannot be so dishonest as they are made out to be. I do not, of course, mean to convey that the European firms believe the Indians to be more truthful than the Europeans. But I do humbly think that, while they would perhaps trust both equally, they rely upon the Indian's thrift, his determination not to ruin his creditor and his temperate habits. A bank has been giving credit to an Indian to a very large extent. A European gentleman, known to the bank and a friend of this Indian, wanted £300 credit for speculation. The bank refused to give him credit without guarantee. The Indian friend pledged his honour, and that was all he had to pledge, and the bank accepted that security, although at the time, too, he was heavily in debt to the bank. The result is, the European friend has failed to refund the £300 to the bank, and the Indian friend, for the present, has lost the money. The European, of course, lives in a better style and requires some drink for his dinners, and our Indian friend drinks only water. The charges that we spend nothing and are immoral, i.e., more than those who bring the charges against us, we repudiate entirely. But the real cause is the trade jealousy, in the first instance, and want of knowledge about India and the Indians, in the second.

The hue and cry against the Indians was first raised by the traders and then taken up by the populace till, at last, the prejudice permeated the high and the low. This can be seen from the South African legislation affecting Indians. The Orange Free Staters have frankly stated that they hate the Asiatic because he is a successful trader. The Chambers of Commerce in the different States were the first movers. And they, of course, came out with the statements that we believed the Christians a natural prey, and that we believed our women to be soulless and were propagators of leprosy and syphilis and other diseases. The matters have now reached such a stage that for a good Christian gentleman it is as natural to see nothing unjust in the persecution of the Asiatics as it was in the olden days for the *bona fide* Christians to see nothing wrong or unchristian in slavery. Mr. Henry Bale is a legislator in the Natal Assembly, a typical English gentleman, and is dubbed Bale the conscientious because he is a converted Christian and takes a prominent part in religious movements and brings his conscience often into play on the floor of the Assembly House. Yet, this gentleman is one of the most powerful and uncompromising opponents of Indians, and gives his certificate that an annual poll-tax of £3 on a body of men who have been the mainstay of the Colony, and compulsory return of such men, are just and humane measures.

Our method in South Africa is to conquer this hatred by love. At any rate, that is our goal. We would often fall short of that ideal but we can adduce innumerable instances to show that we have acted in that spirit. We do not attempt to have individuals punished but, as a rule, patiently suffer wrongs at their hands. Generally, our prayers are not to demand compensation for past injuries, but to render a repetition of those injuries impossible and to remove the causes. Our grievances have been laid before the Indian public in the same spirit. If we have quoted instances of personal injuries, that we have done, not for the purpose of seeking compensation, but for that of laying our position vividly before the public in India. We are trying to remove any causes that may be in us for such treatment. But we cannot succeed without the sympathy and support of the public men in India, and without strong representations from the Home and Indian Governments. The want of knowledge about India is so great in South Africa that the people would not even believe us if we said that India is not dotted by huts only. The work done on our behalf by the *London Times*, the British Committee[29] of the Congress and by Mr. Bhownaggree and in India by *The Times of India*, has borne fruit already. Of course, the question of the position of the Indians has been treated as an Imperial question, and almost every statesman whom we have approached has expressed his full sympathy to us. We have letters of sympathy from both the Conservative and Liberal members of the House of Commons. The *Daily Telegraph* has also extended its support to us. When the Franchise Bill was first passed[30] and there was some talk of its disallowance, the public men and the newspapers in Natal said the Bill will be passed over and over again till Her Majesty's Government were tired. They rejected the British subject "humbug", and one paper went so far as to say that they would throw over their allegiance to the Queen if the Bill was disallowed. The Ministers openly declared that they would decline to govern the Colony if the Bill was disallowed. This was the time when the writer of the "Colonial Affairs" in the London *Times* favoured the Natal Bill. But the *Thunderer,* when it dealt with the matter, specially changed its tone. The Colonial Secretary seemed to be decisive and the despatch with reference to the Transvaal Arbitration arrived in time. This changed the whole tone of the Press in Natal. They protested but they were a part and parcel of the British Empire. *The Natal Advertiser,* which at one time proposed the formation of an anti-Asiatic League, thus dealt with the Indian question in a leading article, dated the 28th February, 1895. After alluding to the then reported disallowance of the Franchise Bill and the resolution of the Mayoral Congress in the Cape Colony before referred to, the article goes on :

> The problem, therefore, when looked at as a whole from the imperial to the purely local standpoint, is a very large and complex one. But however prone localities may be to regard the subject simply from the local standpoint, it should be apparent to all who wish to study the matter in all its bearings (the only way in which a sound and healthy judgment can be arrived at), that the wider or Imperial considerations must also be taken into account. And further, as regards the purely local aspect of the case, it is quite as necessary, and perhaps as difficult, to discover whether a comprehensive view of the position is being taken or whether imperfect opinions are being formed on one side or the other through the acceptance of only such data as prejudice or self-interest may find acceptable. The general opinion existing throughout South Africa, as regards Indian emigration, may be summed up in the words, "We don't want them". The first point to be weighed is this that, in belonging to the British Empire, we have to take whatever may be evil as well as whatever may be good as arising from that connection, provided, of course, it is inseparable therefrom. Now, as regards the destinies of India's population, it may be taken for granted that the Imperial Government will not readily permit of legislation in any British dependency which has for its avowed object the repulsion of India's surplus population from any part of the British dominions; or, to put it the other way, which embodies the principle, so far as the

particular legislating State is concerned, that India's teeming and fast increasing millions must be confined, and ultimately smothered, within India itself. On the contrary, the desire of the British Government is to remove from India the possibilities of such congestion, and to thereby render it a prosperous and happy, instead of a dangerous and discontented, portion of the British Empire. If India is to be retained as an advantageous part of the Empire, then it is absolutely necessary that means shall be found for relieving it of much of its present population, and it may be taken to be a part of the Imperial policy that India's surplus population is to be encouraged, rather than discouraged, to find fresh outlets in those other portions of the Empire which are in need of a labouring population. It will thus be seen that the question of coolie immigration into the British Colonies is one which reaches down to the deepest amelioration and salvation of India; it may even mean the inclusion or exclusion of that great possession in or from the British Empire. That is the Imperial aspect of the question, and is one which points directly to a desire on the part of the Imperial Government to do all in its power to prevent the raising, in other portions of the Empire, of barriers for the prevention of Indian immigration.

As regards the local aspect of Indian immigration, what has to be considered is whether and if so, how far, does this Imperial policy conflict with what is desirable for this particular locality? There are those who absolutely condemn Indian immigration into this Colony, but it is doubtful whether these have given full consideration on all the bearings of the case. In the first place, those who so oppose Indian immigration have to answer the question : What would this Colony have done without them in those departments of industry in which they have undoubtedly proved useful? There is unquestionably much that is undesirable about the coolie, but before his presence here is condemned as an unmixed evil, it has to be shown that the Colony would have been better without him. This, we think, would be somewhat difficult to prove. There can be no question that the coolie is the best fitted, under existing local conditions, for the field labour required in connection with the agriculture of the Colony. Such work can never be undertaken in this climate by White men; our natives show little disposition or aptitude for it. This being so, who is ousted by the presence of the coolie as an agricultural labourer? No one. The work had either to be done by him or left undone altogether. Again, the coolie is largely employed by Government, especially on the railway. What is the objection to him there? It may be said he is taking the place of the White man there; but is he? There may be a few isolated cases in which this contention holds good, but it cannot for a moment be supposed that the Colony could afford to replace all the Indians employed in the Government service by White men. Further, the towns in Natal are almost entirely dependent for their supply of vegetables upon the coolies, who farm plots of ground in the vicinity. With whom does the coolie interfere in this direction? Certainly not with the White man. Our farmers, as a body, have not yet acquired a taste for kitchen gardening sufficient to keep the market fully supplied. Neither does he interfere with the native, who, being the incarnation of indolence, does not, as a rule, trouble about the cultivation of anything except mealies[31] for himself. Our own natives ought to have been our labouring class, but the fact has to be faced that, in this respect, they are almost a dead failure. Consequently, coloured labour of a more active and reliable kind had to be procured from some other source, and India has offered the necessary supply. The debt which the White man owes to these coloured labourers is this that they, by occupying the lowest stratum of society in those mixed communities of which they form a part, raise the White man one stratum higher right through the social scale than he otherwise would have occupied, had the menial offices been discharged by a European class. For instance, the White man, who is 'boss' over a gang of coolies, would have had himself to form one of the gang of labourers, had there been no black labourer. Again, the man who, in Europe, would have been that man's foreman, in this country develops into a master tradesman. And as in every other direction, by the presence of a black labouring class, the Whites are set free to throw their efforts into higher planes than they could have done, had the majority of them had to devote their lives to the arduous labours of toilers of the lowest order. It will, therefore, probably yet be found that the removal of the drawbacks, at present incidental to the immigration of Indians into British Colonies, is not to be effected so much by the adoption of an obsolete policy of exclusion as by an enlightened and progressive application of ameliorating laws to those Indians who settle in them. One of the chief objections to Indians is that they do not live in accordance with European rules. The remedy for this is to gradually raise their mode of life by compelling them to live in better dwellings and by creating among them new wants. It will probably be found easier, because more in accord with the great onward movement of mankind, to demand of such settlers that they shall rise to their new conditions, than to endeavour to maintain the *status quo ante* by their entire exclusion.

Such articles (and they can be quoted by the dozen from the various newspapers) show that application of sufficient pressure from the Home Government can bring about a healthy change in the Indian policy of the Colonies, and that, even in the worst places, British love of justice and fair play can be roused. These two are the sheet-anchor of our hope. No amount of spreading information about India on our part can do any good without the much-needed application of the pressure.

The following article, from the pen of a veteran journalist in South Africa, shows also that there are men in South Africa who would rise above their surroundings and disclose the true British character :

> It sometimes happens in life that men are called upon to decide decisively between the claims of justice and the claims of self. With men of honourable inclination, the task is, of course, a far heavier one than with men whose natures have long ago cast overboard any conscientious scruples with which they may have been endowed at the outset of their unlovely existence. From men who will puff rotten companies at the very moment they are selling out and individuals of a like character, it is, of course, perfectly absurd to expect any other result than that self will predominate, but with the average commercial man, justice is more often the victor in the ethical conflict. Amongst the causes of these conflicts, as they affect South Africans generally and British Transvaalers in particular, is the question of the 'coolie traders', as our Indian and Arab fellow citizens are designated. It is the position of these merchants, for so they really are, which has aroused so much attention and which is still productive of no little interest and hostility to this day. And, it is in considering their position that their rivals in trade have sought to inflict upon them, through the medium of the State, what looks, on the face of it, something very like an injustice for the benefit of self.
>
> The outcry, which was raised in the capital of the Transvaal against the coolie trader some little time ago, is brought to the mind by occasional paragraphs in the morning papers regarding the doings of the Indian and Arab dealers.
>
> In the face of such reminders as these, one may reasonably expect to be pardoned for referring, for a few moments, to a body of respectable, hard-working men, whose position is so misunderstood that their very nationality is overlooked, and a name labelled to them which tends to place them on an exceedingly low level in the estimation of their fellow-creatures. In the face, too, of financial operations, the success of which many of their detractors would envy, one fails to understand the agitation which would place the operators in the same category as the half-heathen

native and confine them to locations and subject them to the harsher laws by which the Transvaal Kaffir is governed. The impression, which is but too prevalent both in the Transvaal and this Colony, that the quiet and altogether inoffensive 'Arab' shopkeeper, and the equally harmless Indian, who carries his pack of dainty wares from house to house, is a 'coolie', is due largely to an indolent ignorance as to the race whence they sprung. When one reflects that the conception of Brahminism, with its poetic and mysterious mythology, took its rise in the land of the 'coolie trader', that in that land, twenty-four centuries ago, the almost divine Buddha taught and practised the glorious doctrine of self-sacrifice, and that it was from the plains and mountains of that weird old country that are derived the fundamental truths of the very language we speak, one cannot but help regretting that the children of such a race should be treated as the equals of the children of black heathendom and outer darkness. Those who, for a few moments, have stayed to converse with the Indian trader, have been, perhaps, surprised to find they are speaking to a scholar and a gentleman. In the schools of Bombay, Madras, and even from under the very shadows of the Himalayas and from the plains of the Punjab, these unassuming individuals have drunk deep the springs of knowledge, it may be, unsuited to our requirements, foreign to our taste, and savouring too much of the mythical to be of use in our practical lives, but, nevertheless, a knowledge the acquisition of which requires as much application, as much literary application, and a far more sensitive and poetic nature than is required in the highest schools of Oxford or Cambridge. The philosophy of India, obscured by the dust of ages and the traditions of generations, was taught with delight, when the ancestors of the Superior Boer and the Superior Englishman were content to find their highest pleasures in the pursuit of the bear and the wolf over the marshes and through the forests of their native lands. When these same ancestors has had no thought of a higher life, when self-preservation was their first law, and the destruction of their neighbour's village and the capture of his wife and infant their keenest enjoyment, the philosophers of India had grown weary with a thousand years' conflict with the problems of existence. And it is the sons of this land of light who are despised as coolies and treated as Kaffirs.

It is about time that those, who cry out against the Indian merchant should have pointed out to them who and what he is. Many of his worst detractors are British subjects enjoying all the privileges and rights of membership in a glorious community. To them the hatred of injustice and the love of fair-play is inherent, and when it affects themselves, they have a method of insisting upon their rights and

> liberties, whether under a foreign government or under their own. Possibly, it has never struck them that the Indian merchant is also a British subject and claims the same liberties and rights with equal justice. To say the very least of it, if we may be permitted to employ a phrase of Palmerston's days, it is very un-English to claim rights one would not allow to others. The right of trade as an equal privilege has, since the abolition of the Elizabethan monopolies, become almost a part of the English Constitution, and were anyone to interfere with that right, the privilege of British citizenship would very suddenly come to the front. Because the Indian is more successful in competition and lives on less than the English merchant, is the unfairest and weakest of arguments. The very foundation of English commerce lies in the fact of our being able to compete more successfully with other nations. Surely, it is Protection running to madness when English traders wish the State to intervene to protect them against the more successful operations of their rivals. The injustice to the Indians is so glaring that one is almost ashamed of one's countrymen in wishing to have these men treated as natives, simply because of their success in trade. The very reason, that they have been so successful against the dominant race, is sufficient to raise them above that degrading level. (*Cape Times*, 13-4-1889)

The question resolves itself into this : "May the British Indians when they leave India," in the words of the London *Times*, "have the same status before the law as other British subjects enjoy? May they or may they not go freely from one British possession to another and claim the rights of British subjects in allied States?" Says the same journal again :

> The Indian Government and the Indians themselves believe that it is in Southern Africa that this question of their status must be determined. If they secure the position of British subjects in South Africa, it will be almost impossible to deny it to them elsewhere. If they fail to secure that position in South Africa, it will be extremely difficult for them to attain it elsewhere.

Thus, then, the decision of the question will affect not only the Indians at present settled in South Africa but the whole future emigration of Indians and, also, the position of Indian immigrants in other parts of Her Majesty's Dominions and allied States. In Australia they are endeavouring to pass laws to restrict the influx of Indians in those parts. Temporary and local relief, while absolutely necessary for the cases now before the two Governments for consideration, will be of no avail, unless the whole question is decided once for all, for "the whole body is rotten and not parts only". Mr. Bhownaggree has questioned Mr. Chamberlain "whether he will take immediate steps to arrest legislation of this description by the Government of Natal and other parts of Her Majesty's Dominions in Africa". There may yet be laws and regulations besides what have been alluded to herein and which may not be known to us. Unless, therefore, all such past legislation is declared illegal and further legislation stopped, we have a very dismal outlook before us, for the struggle is unequal, and how long are we to go on troubling the Colonial Office and the Indian Government? *The Times of India* has been our advocate when we were almost without any. The British Committee of the Congress has always worked on our behalf. The powerful aid of the London *Times* has, by itself, raised us a step higher in the estimation of the South Africans. Mr. Bhownaggree has been incessant in his efforts on our behalf ever since he entered Parliament. We know we have the sympathy of the public bodies in India, but our object in laying our grievances specially before the Indian public is to enlist the very active sympathy of all the public bodies in India. That is my commission, and our cause is so great and just that I have no doubt I shall return to Natal with satisfactory result.

Rajkot, Kathiawar **M.K. Gandhi**
14 August, 1896

PS. If any gentleman is anxious to study further the Indian question in South Africa and requires the various memorials referred to herein, an effort will be made to supply him with copies of the same.

M.K. Gandhi

From a copy printed at the Price Current Press, Madras, 1896, second edition, the first edition not being available.

GANDHIJI'S CREDENTIALS[32]

We, the undersigned, representing the Indian Community in South Africa, hereby appoint M.K. Gandhi, Esq., of Durban, Advocate, to represent the grievances the Indians are labouring under in South Africa before the authorities and public men and public bodies in India.

Dated at Durban, Natal, this 26th day of May 1896.

ABDOOL CARIM HAJI ADAM
(DADA ABDOOLLA & CO.)
ABDUL CADER
(MAHOMED CASSIM CAMROODEEN)
P. DAWAJEE MAHOMED
HOOSEN CASSIM
A.C. PILLAY
PARSEE RUSTOMJI
A.M. TILLY
HAJEE MAHOMED H. DADA
AMOD MAHOMED PARUK
ADAMJI MIANKHAN
PEERUN MAHOMED
A.M. SALOOJEE
DOWD MAHOMED
AMOD JEEWA HOOSEN MEERUM
K.S. PILLAY & CO.
મુનશી અહમદજી દાઉજી
i.e., AHMEDJI DOWJI MOGRARIA
MOOSA HAJEE CASSIM
G.A. BASSA

MANILAL CHATURBHAI
M.E. KATHRADA
D.M. TIMOL
દાવજી મહમદ શીદાત
DAVAJEE M. SEEDAT
ISMAIL TIMOL
SHAIK FAREED & CO.
SHAIKHJEE AMOD
મહમદ કાસમ આફીજી
MAHOMED CASSIM HAFFIJI
AMOD HOOSEN
MAHOMED AMOD BASSA
V.A. ESSOP
મહમદ સુલેમાન
MAHOMED SULEMAN
DAWJEE MAMAD MUTALA
SULEMAN VORAJI
EBRAHIM NOOR MAHOMED
મહમદ સુલેમાન ખોટા સહી
CHOOHURMAL LUCHERAM
NARAYAN PATHER
VIJAYA RAGAVALOO
SULIMAN DAWJEE

NOTES ON THE GRIEVANCES OF THE BRITISH INDIANS IN SOUTH AFRICA

These Notes *were published by Gandhiji to provide a brief consitutional background of Natal, the Cape Colony, the Transvaal, the Chartered Territories and the Orange Free State, and to give a succinct idea of Indian grievances against discriminatory legislation and legal disabilities. Gandhiji considered the* Notes *as necessary "for a proper study of the whole question" and an "aid to the study of the memorials and pamphlets which contain valuable information collected from various sources."* (Vide p. 69, infra). *These were enclosed with the* Notes, *but have not been reproduced here as the text of all those available has been published in Vol. I in their chronological sequence. Hence, the bare text of the* Notes *is being given.*

RAJKOT,
September 22, 1896

South Africa, for our purposes, consists of the two British Colonies of the Cape of Good Hope and Natal, the two Republics, viz., the South African Republic or the Transvaal and the Orange Free State, the Crown Colony of Zululand, the Chartered Territories and the Portuguese territories comprising Delagoa Bay or Lorenzo Marques and Beira.

Natal

Natal is a British self-governing Colony enjoying Responsible Government since 1893 A.D. Before September of 1893, Natal was a Crown Colony having a Legislative Council of 12 elective and 4 executive members, with a Governor representing the Queen, a Constitution not very unlike the Indian Legislative Councils. In 1893, Responsible Government was granted, whereby an upper and a lower chamber were created. The upper chamber, called the Legislative Council, consists of 11 members nominated by His Excellency the Governor of the Colony, and the lower chamber, styled the Legislative Assembly, consists of 37 members elected by the Colonists possessing the legal qualifications to be hereafter described. There is a movable Ministry of five members based on the model of the British Cabinet. Sir John Robinson is the present Prime Minister and the Hon'ble Mr. Harry Escombe, Q.C., the present Attorney-General.

The Constitution Act provides that no Acts, which have for their object class legislation and which curtail the rights of non-European British subjects, shall have the force of law unless they are sanctioned by Her Majesty. The Royal instructions to the Governor also include such prohibitory clauses.

Natal has an area of 20,851 square miles and a European population of about 50,000, a native population of about 400,000, and an Indian population of about 51,000, according to the latest census. The 51,000 Indians include 30,000 free Indians, i.e., those that have finished their indentured service and are engaged in the Colony in various pursuits of life as household servants, petty farmers, vegetable hawkers, fruiterers, goldsmiths, artisans, petty store-keepers, school-masters, photographers, attorneys' clerks, etc., 16,000 who are at present serving their indenture, and 5,000 traders who came to the Colony on their own means and are either traders or shop-keepers' assistants, the trade consisting in soft goods suitable to the natives of South Africa, called Zulus or Kaffirs, hardware, soft goods and groceries suitable to the Indian population. The soft goods and groceries for the Indians are imported from Bombay, Calcutta and Madras. The free and indentured Indians come from Madras and Calcutta and are pretty equally divided. Indian emigration was resorted to when, as a member of the Legislative Assembly of Natal, Mr. Garland, says, "the existence of the Colony hung in the balance". The terms of the contract briefly are that the indentured man has to serve his employer for a period of 5 years, the monthly wages for the first year being £10, to be increased by £1 every succeeding year, with food, clothing and lodging during the period and the passage to Natal also paid by the employer. If, after the first five years, he serves in the Colony as a free labourer for another five years, he becomes entitled to a free passage back to India for himself, his wife and children, if any. The immigrants are imported to work on the sugar fields and tea estates and replace the Kaffirs who were found by the Colonists to be indifferent and unsteady. They are also largely employed by the Government on the railways and for the sanitation of the Colony. The Colonists at first assisted the sugar and tea industries of the Colony by granting Rs. [£?] 10,000 towards the cost of the importation of the Indian immigrants. Almost the first act of the Responsible Government was to abolish this grant under the plea that the industries no longer required such support.

First Grievance in Natal—Franchise

The Royal Charter, dated the 15th July, 1850, provides that any adult male, not being a native of South Africa, possessing property to the value of £50 or who rents any such property of the yearly value of £10, shall be entitled to be placed on the Voters' Roll. There is a separate law governing the Native Franchise which requires, among other things, 12 years' residence on the part of the Native in a particular electoral district and exemption from the native law of the Colony.

Under the general franchise law of the Colony, i.e., the Royal Charter referred to above, the Indians as British subjects enjoyed full electoral rights till after 1893. In 1894, in the Second Parliament under the Responsible Government, an Act was passed, No. 25 of 1894, disqualifying persons of Asiatic extraction from having their names inserted in any Voters' List, exempting those whose names were then already rightly contained in any Voters' List. The preamble of the Act stated that such persons were not accustomed to the Franchise rights.

The real reason for passing such an Act was to lower the status of the Indian and gradually to bring him down to the level of the South African Natives so that, in time to come, the respectable Indian may become an impossibility. A petition was presented to the Legislative Assembly combating the view that the Indians were not accustomed to representative institutions and asking for the withdrawal of the Bill, or an enquiry as to whether or not the Indians were fit to exercise the franchise. (Enclosure I, Appendix A)[33]

The petition was rejected. Another was sent to the Legislative Council when the Bill came before it. That too was rejected and the Bill was passed. (Enclosure I, Appendix B)[34]

It, however, required Her Majesty's sanction before it could come into force. The Indian community sent a memorial to Her Majesty's Principal Secretary of State for the Colonies, protesting against the measure and requesting him either to disallow the measure or to institute an inquiry of the nature above indicated. The memorial was signed by nearly 9,000 Indians. (Enclosure I)[35]

A good deal of correspondence went on between Her Majesty's Government and the Natal Ministry. The result was that in the April of this year, the Franchise Act was withdrawn by the Natal Ministry and replaced by the following :

> No persons shall be qualified to have their names inserted in any list of electors who (not being of European origin) are natives or descendants in the male line of natives of countries which have not hitherto possessed elective representative institutions founded on the parliamentary franchise, unless they shall first obtain an order from the Governor-in-Council exempting them from the operation of this Act.

The measure also excepts those whose names are already rightly contained in any Voters' Lists.

A memorial was presented to the Legislative Assembly, showing that India contained, in its Legislative Councils, "elective representative institutions founded on the parliamentary franchise" and that, therefore, the Bill was a harassing measure. (Enclosure II, Appendix A).[36] Though our institutions cannot popularly be termed such as to satisfy the requirement of the above measure, it is respectfully submitted that legally they are so, and this is the opinion of the London *Times,* as also of an able jurist in Natal (Enclosure III, p. 11).[37] Mr. Chamberlain himself, in his despatch dated 12th September, 1895,[38] signifying his inability to approve of the first Franchise Bill above referred to, in answer to the Natal Ministers' arguments, says, among other things :

> I also recognize the fact that the Natives of India do not possess representative institutions in their own country and that they themselves, in those periods of their history when they were exempt from European influence, have never set up any such system among them. (Enclosure IV)

A memorial has been sent to Mr. Chamberlain (Enclosure II),[39] and private advice from London states that the matter is engaging his attention. Mr. Chamberlain has already approved of the principle of this Bill which was submitted to him by the Ministers, before it was introduced into the Natal Parliament. (Enclosure IV). The Indians in South Africa, however, believe that the facts brought out in the memorial should induce Mr. Chamberlain to alter his views.

Too much stress cannot be laid on the fact that there can be no comparison between the condition of the Indians in India and that of those in South Africa. Here it is political persecution and very little class legislation. There it is class legislation pure and simple and degradation of the Indian to the level of a pariah.

The London *Times* has put the franchise question in this form, in dealing with the first Bill above referred to :

> The question now put before Mr. Chamberlain is not an academic one. It is not a question of argument but of race feeling. We cannot afford a war of races among our own subjects. It would be as wrong for the Government of India to suddenly arrest the development of Natal by shutting all the supply of immigrants as it would be for Natal to deny the right of citizenship to British Indian subjects who, by years of thrift and good work in the Colony, have raised themselves to the actual status of citizens. (London *Times*, 27th June, 1896).

This article deals with the various arguments brought forward by the Colonists in support of disfranchisement of the Indians and shows that there is no question of swamping the European electors, because, out of nearly 10,000 electors, according to latest lists published, there are only 251 Indian electors and that there are very few Indians in the Colony who can command the necessary property qualifications (*see* Enclosure V).[40] The present Bill is meant merely to harass the Indian community and to involve them in endless litigation. (Enclosure II.)

Second Grievance—Indian Immigration

In the year 1893, a Commission consisting of Mr. Binns, a member of the Legislative Assembly of Natal, and Mr. Mason, the present Protector of Indian Immigrants in Natal, was sent by the Government of Natal to India in order to induce the Indian Government to consent to the following alterations in the terms of indenture entered into by the Indians at present and referred to above, that is to say :

(1) To raise the period of indenture from five years to an indefinite period, with a corresponding increase in wages up to twenty shillings per month.
(2) In the event of the Indian refusing to enter into such further indentures after the first five years' indenture, to compel him to return to India at the Colony's expense.

The present Viceroy, in his despatch to the Governor of Natal, says that, although personally he regrets that such a course should be desired by the Colonists, subject to the approval of the Home Government he would be prepared to consent to the alterations on the understanding that the breach of the clause about compulsory return should never become a criminal offence. (Enclosure V.)[41]

On the lines of the report of the Commission that visited India, the Natal Government, in the year 1895, introduced the Indian Immigration Law Amendment Bill, which provides, amongst other things, for the indefinite period of indenture or the compulsory return of the immigrants, and further provides that any such immigrant failing to enter into the further terms of indenture or to return to India shall be liable to take out an annual licence costing £3 yearly. Thus it would appear that this Bill goes further than the terms laid down in the Viceroy's despatch above alluded to. Memorials were presented to both the Houses in Natal taking exception to this Bill but to no purpose. (Enclosure V, Appendix A[42] and B[43].) A memorial has also been addressed to Mr. Chamberlain as well as to the Indian

Government praying either that the Bill should be disallowed or that further Indian immigration to Natal should be stopped. (Enclosure VI.)[44] These prayers have been strongly supported by the London *Times* in a leading article dated 3-5-95 [96?].[45]

Over ten years ago, a Commission was appointed by the then Governor of Natal to report upon various matters connected with Indian immigration. Evidence has been cited from this report to show that, at that time, the Commissioners as well as the best men of the day, including the present Attorney-General, thought that any such measure would be a cruel wrong to the Indians and a disgrace to the British name. The memorial is still engaging Mr. Chamberlain's and the Indian Government's attention. (Enclosure VI.)[46]

Third Grievance—The Curfew

There is a Law in Natal (No. 15 of 1869), which provides that, in the boroughs, no 'coloured person', unless he can give a good account of himself or unless he can produce a pass from his employer, shall be out at night after 9 o'clock. This Law is, perhaps, not absolutely unnecessary, but its working is often oppressive. Respectable Indians, such as schoolmasters and others, have often been locked up in horrible dungeons for having ventured out after 9 p.m., no matter on what business.

Fourth Grievance—The Pass Law

The Law provides that every Indian can be asked to produce a pass. It is really meant to detect indentured Indians who have deserted their masters, but is also used as an engine of oppression towards the Indians generally. The Indian community in Natal have not yet moved with regard to the last two matters, but they may be brought under the general grievances and can be used to show the tendency of the Colonists to make it as uncomfortable as possible for the Indians in Natal. As for the working of these two Laws, see Enclosure III, pp. 6 and 7.[47]

Zululand

This country is a Crown Colony governed by the Governor of Natal in the Queen's name. The Natal Ministry or the Governor of Natal as such has nothing to do with Zululand. There is a small European and a large native (Kaffir) population in it. There are townships established in Zululand. The township of Melmoth was the first to be established. In that township, in the year 1888, the Indians bought *erven*, i.e., specified pieces of land, worth about £2,000. The township of Eshowe was proclaimed in 1891 and that of Nondweni in 1896. The regulations for the purchase of *erven* in both these township are the same and they provide that only persons of European birth and descent shall be approved of as occupiers of *erven* or sites, (Enclosure VII.)[48]

A memorial[49] protesting against these regulations was presented to the Governor of Zululand last February, who declined to interfere.

Thereupon a memorial[50] was sent to Mr. Chamberlain, and the question is now engaging his attention. These regulations, it will be noticed, go much further than what the Colonists in the self-governing Colonies have been allowed to do, and follow the policy of total exclusion adopted by the Orange Free State.

Zululand gold mining laws make it criminal for an Indian to buy or possess native gold.

Cape Colony

The Colony of the Cape of Good Hope is, like the Colony of Natal, a responsibly governed Colony with a Constitution similar to Natal's. Only, the Legislative Assembly and the Legislative Council contain a greater number of members, and the franchise qualifications are different, viz., the property qualification is occupation for 12 months of a building worth £75, the salary qualification is £50 per annum. The person claiming to be registered must be able to sign his name and write his address and occupation. This Act was passed in 1892 and was really passed to check the Indian and the Malay vote. There would be no objection on the part of the Indian community to such educational qualifications being imposed or property qualifications being increased in Natal. This Colony contains an area of 276,320 square miles and a total population of about 1,800,000 persons, of whom not more than 400,000 are Europeans. The Indian population of the Colony would be roughly 10,000, consisting of traders, hawkers and labourers. They are to be found chiefly in the ports, viz., Port Elizabeth, East London and Cape Town and also in the mines in Kimberley.

All the informations relating to the disabilities placed on the Indians is not available. In 1894, the Parliament passed a Bill authorizing the East London Municipality to frame bye-laws prohibiting the Indians from walking on the foot-paths and compelling them to live in specified locations. No special representation on this head has been made to Mr. Chamberlain from South Africa. But the matter was touched upon by the Indian deputation that waited upon Mr. Chamberlain last year.

In the various parts or districts of the Cape Colony, it is extremely difficult for an Indian to get trading licences. In many cases the magistrates simply refuse the licences, declining to give reasons for so doing. The Magistrates are within their rights in declining to give reasons, but it has been found almost invariably that the licences have been granted to Europeans when they have been withheld from the Indian. The following is the position of the Indians in East Griqualand, a district in the Cape Colony, according to *The Natal Mercury* dated 3rd March, 1896 :

> An Arab named Ismail Suliman erected a store in East Griqualand, paid customs duty upon goods and applied for a licence which the Magistrate refused. Mr. Attorney Francis on the Arab's behalf (as the Indians are sometimes called in South Africa) appealed to the Cape Government, who upheld the Magistrate and have issued instructions that no coolies or Arabs are to have trading licences in East Griqualand and one or two that have licences are to be closed up.

This is outdoing the Transvaal.

Chartered Territories

These territories include Mashonaland and Matabeleland. About 100 Indian waiters and labourers have settled there. A few traders have also gone, but they are refused licences to trade, in the first instance. The law being in favour of the Indians, one enterprising Indian last year succeeded in securing a trading licence through the Superior Court at Cape Town.

The Europeans in the Chartered Territories have now applied for an alteration of the law so that the Indians may, henceforth, be prevented from getting trading licences in those territories. The newspapers in South Africa say that the Cape Government favour such an alteration.

The Transvaal or the South African Republic

This is an independent republic governed by the Dutch or the Boers. There are two chambers called the Volksraad, with an executive Government with the President at the head. It contains an area of about 113,642 square miles and a white population of 119,228. Its black population is said to be 653,662. The chief industry of the Republic is gold mining in Johannesburg, the largest town in the Transvaal. The total Indian population may be roughly put down at 5,000. They are traders, shopkeepers' assistants, hawkers, cooks, waiters or labourers, mostly settled in Johannesburg and Pretoria, the capital of the Republic. Of the traders, there are nearly 200, whose liquidated assets would amount to nearly £100,000. Some of these traders have branches in other parts of the world whose existence mainly depends upon their Transvaal businesses. There are nearly 2,000 hawkers in the Republic who buy goods and hawk them about. About 1,500 are employed as general servants in European hotels or houses. This estimate was formed in 1894. The numbers have since considerably increased in every department.

The Transvaal is subject to the Queen's suzerainty. There are two Conventions between the Governments of England and the Transvaal. Article 14 of the London Convention of 1884 and Article 26 of the Pretoria Convention of 1881 provide as follows :

> All persons, other than natives of South Africa, conforming themselves to the laws of the Transvaal State will have full liberty with their families to enter, travel or reside in any part of the Transvaal State. They will be entitled to hire or possess houses, manufactories, warehouses, shops, premises. They may carry on their commerce either in person or by any agents they may think fit to employ. They will not be subject, in respect of their persons and property, in respect of their commerce and industry, to any taxes, whether general, or local, other than those which are or may be imposed upon the Transvaal citizens.

This Convention, thus, completely secures the trading and property rights of British Indians. In January 1885, the Transvaal Government wanted so to interpret the word "natives", occurring in the Art. 14 of the Convention, as to include Asiatics. Sir Hercules Robinson, the then High Commissioner for South Africa, after consultation with Sir Henry de Villiers, the Chief Justice of the Colony, considered that the interpretation put upon the word "native" by the Transvaal Government could not be sustained and "that Asiatics were persons other than natives".

Negotiations then went on between the Transvaal Government and the Home Government with a view to an alteration in the Convention so as to except the Indians from the privileges secured to "all persons other than natives". Sir Hercules Robinson was favourably disposed towards the Transvaal Government and, in response to his suggestion, received the following reply from Lord Derby under dated 19th March, 1885 :

> I have carefully considered your suggestion as to the amendment of the Convention, and if you are of opinion that it would be preferable and more satisfactory to the Government of the South African Republic to proceed as you propose, Her Majesty's Government will be willing to amend the Convention as suggested. It seems to deserve consideration, however, whether it would be more correct for the Volksraad to legislate in the proposed sense, having received an assurance that Her Majesty's Government will

> not desire to insist upon any such construction of the terms of the Convention as would interfere with reasonable legislation in the desired direction.

In accordance with Lord Derby's suggestion, the Transvaal Volksraad passed bye-law No. 3 of 1885, which applies to all Indians and other coloured people, and provides that none of them could obtain the franchise, that they could not be owners of fixed property, that such coloured people, who settle in the Republic for the purpose of trading, must be separately registered within 8 days after the day of their arrival and that they should pay a registration fee of £25. Any contravention of this law subjects the defaulter to a fine of from £30 to £100 or, in default, from 1 to 6 months' imprisonment. It also provides that the Government shall have the right to point out to such coloured people streets, wards and locations for habitation. In 1886, this law was amended so as to reduce the £25 fee to £3 and the other sections were kept as they were. That now is the law with regard to the Indians in the Transvaal. After the law was passed, the Indians sent representations, telegraphic and otherwise, to the Indian and the Home Governments protesting against the Law 3 of 1885 and its amendment and pointing out that they were in direct violation of the London Convention. This brought out some representations from Lord Knutsford on behalf of the Indians. There has been voluminous correspondence between the two Governments with regard to the interpretation of the word 'habitation'. The Home Government insisted that the word 'habitation' meant residence only. The Transvaal Government insisted that it included not only residence but trading stores also. The ultimate result was that the whole became "confusion worse confounded", and it was agreed between the two Governments that the question of the validity of the Law 3 of 1885 and its amendment, as also interpretation, should be submitted to arbitration. The Chief Justice of the Orange Free State was selected as the sole arbitrator who gave his award last year and decided that the Transvaal Government was justified in passing Law 3 of 1885 and its amendments, but he left undecided the question of interpretation and held that, if the parties could not agree to interpretation, the Courts of the Transvaal were the proper tribunals to decide that question. (Enclosure VIII.)[51]

The Indians in the Transvaal sent memorials[52] to the Home and Indian Governments. Mr. Chamberlain has given his decision and has reluctantly accepted the award of the arbitrator, but sympathizes with the Indians and terms them "a peaceable, law-abiding, meritorious body of persons" whose undoubted industry, intelligence and indomitable perseverance perhaps will suffice to overcome any obstacles which may now face them in the pursuit of their avocations, and reserves to himself the liberty, later on, to make friendly representations to the Transvaal Government.

The question rests there at present. Although the award has been accepted, it will have been seen from what has preceded that there are many questions still undecided. Where will the Indians be now in the Transvaal? Will their stores be closed up? If so, what will 200 or 300 traders do to earn a living? Will they have to trade also in locations? This, however, does not complete the list of disabilities in the Transvaal.

Act 25 (10th January 1893), section 38, says :

> That it is not permitted to natives and other coloured people to travel in the carriage intended for the Whites, viz., the first and second class.

The most respectable Indian, spotlessly dressed, cannot, as of right, travel first or second class on the Transvaal Railways. He is huddled together with the natives of all sorts and conditions in a third-class compartment. This is a cause of very great inconvenience to the Indian community in the Transvaal.

There is a system of passes in the Transvaal which requires that any Indian, like the native, should take a shilling travelling pass when he moves about from one place to another.

In 1895, the Commandos Treaty was entered into between Her Majesty's Government and the Transvaal Government, exempting the British subjects from compulsory military service. This treaty came up before the Transvaal Volksraad for ratification in the same year.

The Volksraad ratified the treaty with the modification or reservation that the words "British subjects" shall mean "Whites" only. The Indians promptly telegraphed to Mr. Chamberlain and a memorial was also sent. (Enclosure IX.)[53] The question is now engaging his attention.

The London *Times* gave a very sympathetic and strong leading article on the subject. (Weekly Edn. 10-1-'96.)

The Gold Mining laws of Johannesburg make it criminal for the Indians to possess native gold. The curfew prevails also in the Transvaal, absolutely unnecessarily, so far as the Indians are concerned.

It may be as well to state here that those who wear the Memon costume are not, as a rule, molested under this Law, for certain reasons. (Enclosure III, p. 6.)[54]

There is a footpath bye-law in Johannesburg and there are instructions issued to the police in Pretoria to the effect that the Indians should not be allowed to walk on the footpaths. A graduate of the Madras University was violently kicked off a footpath in 1894.

Orange Free State

This is an independent Dutch Republic without any suzerain power to the Queen.

The Commission is very similar to that of the Transvaal. Mr. Steyn is the President of the Republic and Bloemfontein is the capital. Its area is 72,000 square miles and the total population is 207,503. Of these the Europeans number 77,716, and the coloured population 129,787. There are a few Indians employed there as general servants. In 1890, there were about 3 Indians stores in that Republic having liquidated assets over £9,000. These were driven out and their stores were closed up without any compensation. They were given a year's notice to clear. Representations were made to the British Government without any avail.

The Law of 1890, Chapter XXXIII, which is entitled the Law to prevent the inrush of the Asiatic coloured persons, prevents any Indian from remaining in that country for more than 2 months, unless he gets the permission from the President of Republic, who cannot consider the application to reside before 30 days have elapsed after the presentation of the application and other ceremonies have been performed. The applicant can, however, on no account hold fixed property in the State or carry on any mercantile or farming business. The President may or may not, according to the state of things, grant such mutilated permission to reside. Any Indian resident moreover is subject to an annual poll-tax of £10. The first contravention of the section relating to mercantile or farming business renders the delinquent liable to a fine of £25 or 3 months' imprisonment with or without hard labour. For all subsequent contraventions, the penalty is to be each time doubled. (Enclosure X.)[55]

This practically finishes the list of grievances.

These notes are not intended to replace the various enclosures. It is respectfully submitted they are necessary for a proper study of the memorials and pamphlets which contain valuable information collected from various sources.

The whole question has been thus put by the London *Times* :

> May the British Indians, when they leave India, have the same status before the law as other British subjects enjoy? May they or may they not go freely from one British possession to another and claim the rights of British subjects in allied States?

Again :

> The Indian Government and the Indians themselves believe that it is in Southern Africa that this question of their status must be determined. If they secure the position of British subjects in South Africa, it would be almost impossible to deny it to them elsewhere. If they fail to secure that position in South Africa, it will be extremely difficult for them to attain it elsewhere.

The question has been treated as an Imperial question and all parties without distinction have supported the British Indians in South Africa.

The following are the dates of the articles dealing with the question in the London *Times* :

28th June 1895 *Weekly Edition*
3rd August 1895 *Weekly Edition*
13th September 1895 *Weekly Edition*
6th September 1895 *Weekly Edition*
10th January 1896 *Weekly Edition*
7th April 1896 *The Times*
20th March 1896 *Weekly Edition*
27th January 1896 *The Times*

In the Portuguese territories of Delagoa Bay there are no grievances. They serve as a favourable contrast (Enclosure III).

M.K. Gandhi

REFERENCES

1. No 'appendix', as such, was included in the pamphlet. The reference is to matter on pp. 32-9, *infra* beginning with the paragraph: "But, gentlemen, you have been told . . . ." and ending with the paragraph: "Quoting statistics to prove. . . ." *Vide* footnote on p. 32 and also the Madras Address, pp. 105-112, *infra.*
2. *Vide* pp. 51-2, *infra.*
3. *Vide* Vol. I, pp. 142-163, for original text.
4. The original has "samples".
5. The original spells this as "chock-full".
6. The original has "Ramsamy" and "Sammy".
7. Two sentences following this, in the original, have been omitted in the Green Pamphlet. *Vide* Vol. I, p. 160.
8. A sentence from the original has been omitted here also; ibid, p. 160.
9. Dadabhai Naoroji.
10. *Vide* Vol. I, p. 207.
11. A suburb of Durban.
12. Protector of Indian Immigrants.
13. *Vide* Vol. I, pp. 92-96.
14. Ibid, pp. 107-111.
15. Ibid, pp. 116-128.
16. Ibid, pp. 324-345.
17. Dated September 12, 1895.

18. Vide Vol. I, pp. 212-214 and pp. 215-227.
19. The Binns-Mason Commission.
20. *Vide* Vol. I, pp. 215-230.
21. *Vide* Vol. I, pp. 292-294 and pp. 299-301.
22. *Ibid*, pp. 303-307.
23. *Vide* Vol. I, pp. 187-208.
24. *Vide* Vol. I, pp. 254-256.
25. On the publication of the first edition of the Green Pamphlet, Reuter issued a misleading report of its contents. The Natal Agent-General sought to refute charges of ill-treatment made by Gandhiji. The paragraphs from "But, gentlemen, . . ." to "Quoting statistics to prove. . . ." (p. 39, *infra*) constituted Gandhiji's reply to the Agent-General made at the Madras meeting. They were incorporated in the second edition of the Green Pamphlet and referred to, in the preface, as an "appendix". *Vide* pp. 105-112, *infra*, and for Gandhiji's letter on the subject to the Press, pp. 85-89, *infra*.
26. The reference is to the first edition of the Green Pamphlet.
27. The Law Society of Natal had opposed Gandhiji's admission as an Advocate to the Supreme Court.
28. A term used by Europeans, in Asia and Africa, for a native male servant.
29. Natal Government Railway.
30. This paragraph, which also formed part of the Madras Address, was found inadvertently omitted in the second edition of the Green Pamphlet.
31. *Vide* Vol. I, p. 203.
32. Set up in London by the Indian National Congress; Sir Mancherji Bhownaggree was one of its principal members.
33. On July 7, 1894; *vide* Vol. I, p. 115.
34. Maize or Indian Corn.
35. This document formed the last page of the Green Pamphlet and was probably drafted by Gandhiji. He refers to it in the opening paragraph of the Pamphlet (*vide*, p. 1, *supra*) and in his speeches at the Bombay and Madras meetings (*vide* p. 70 and p. 94, *infra*).
36. *Vide* Vol. I, pp. 92-96.
37. Ibid, pp. 103-105.
38. Ibid, pp. 116-128.
39. *Vide* Vol. I, pp. 312-320.
40. The reference is to the Green Pamphlet; *vide* p. 16, *supra*.
41. The photostat has 1885, obviously a typographical mistake.
42. *Vide* Vol. I, pp. 324-345.
43. This enclosure contained the Viceroy's despatch referred to in the following pages.
44. *Vide* footnote 1 at p. 58.

45. *Vide* Vol. I, pp. 176-179.
46. Ibid, pp. 212-214.
47. *Vide* Vol. I, pp. 215-27, and pp. 228-230.
48. *Vide* pp. 9-12, *supra*.
49. The enclosure is not available.
50. *Vide* Vol. I, pp. 292-294.
51. Ibid, pp. 303-307.
52. This was, probably, the Arbitrator's award.
53. *Vide* Vol. I, pp. 187-208 and pp. 209-212.
54. *Vide* Vol. I, pp. 254-256.
55. This probably was the text of the Law of 1890.

2

Hind Swaraj or Indian Home Rule

HIND SWARAJ

Preface

I have written some chapters on the subject of Indian Home Rule which I venture to place before the readers of *Indian Opinion*. I have written because I could not restrain myself. I have read much, I have pondered much, during the stay, for four months in London, of the Transvaal Indian deputation. I discussed things with as many of my countrymen as I could. I met, too, as many Englishmen as it was possible for me to meet. I consider it my duty now to place before the readers of *Indian Opinion* the conclusions, which appear to me to be final. The Gujarati subscribers of *Indian Opinion* number about 800. I am aware that, for every subscriber, there are at least ten persons who read the paper with zest. Those who cannot read Gujarati have the paper read out to them. Such persons have often questioned me about the condition of India. Similar questions were addressed to me in London. I felt, therefore, that it might not be improper for me to ventilate publicly the views expressed by me in private. These views are mine, and yet not mine. They are mine because I hope to act according to them. They are almost a part of my being. But, yet, they are not mine, because I lay no claim to originality. They have been formed after reading several books. That which I dimly felt received support from these books.

The views I venture to place before the reader are, needless to say, held by many Indians not touched by what is known as civilization, but I ask the reader to believe me when I tell him that they are also held by thousands of Europeans. Those who wish to dive deep, and have time, may read certain books themselves. If time permits me, I hope to translate portions of such books for the benefit of the readers of *Indian Opinion*. If the readers of *Indian Opinion* and others who may see the following chapters will pass their criticism on to me, I shall feel obliged to them.

The only motive is to serve my country, to find out the Truth, and to follow it. If, therefore, my views are proved to be wrong, I shall have no hesitation in rejecting them. If they are proved to be right, I would naturally wish, for the sake of the motherland, that others should adopt them. To make it easy reading, the chapters are written in the form of a dialogue between the reader and the editor.

MOHANDAS KARAMCHAND GANDHI

Kildonan Castle
22-11-1909 [From Gujarati]

2.1

The Congress and its Officials

READER : Just at present there is a Home Rule wave passing over India. All our countrymen appear to be pinning for National Independence. A similar spirit pervades them even in South Africa. Indians seem to be eager to acquire rights. Will you explain your views in this matter?

EDITOR : You have put the question well, but the answer is not easy. One of the objects of a newspaper is to understand popular feeling and to give expression to it; another is to arouse among the people certain desirable sentiments; and the third is fearlessly to expose popular defects. The exercise of all these three functions is involved in answering your question. To a certain extent the people's will has to be expressed, certain sentiments will need to be fostered, and defects will have to be brought to light. But, as you have asked the question, it is my duty to answer it.

READER : Do you then consider that a desire for Home Rule has been created among us ?

EDITOR : That desire gave rise to the National Congress. The choice of the word "National" implies it.

READER : That, surely, is not the case. *Young India* seems to ignore the Congress. It is considered to be an instrument for perpetuating British Rule.

EDITOR : That opinion is not justified. Had not the Grand Old Man of India prepared the soil, our young men could not have even spoken about Home Rule. How can we what Mr. Hume has written, how he has lashed us into action, and with what effort he has awakened us, in order to achieve the objects of the Congress? Sir William Wedderburn has given his body, mind and money to the same cause. His writings are worthy of perusal to this day. Professor Gokhale in order to prepare the nation, embraced poverty and gave twenty years of his life. Even now, he is living in poverty. The late Justice Budruddin Tyebji was also one of those who, through the Congress, sowed the seed of Home Rule. Similarly, in Bengal, Madras, the Punjab and other places, there have been lovers of India and members of the Congress, both Indian and English.

READER : Stay, stay; you are going too far, you are straying away from my question. I have asked you about Home or Self-Rule; you are discussing foreign rule. I do not desire to hear English names, and you are giving me such names. In these circumstances, I do not think we can ever meet. I shall be pleased if you will confine yourself to Home Rule. All other talks will not satisfy me.

EDITOR : You are impatient. I cannot afford to be likewise. If you will bear with me for a while, I think you will find that you will obtain what you want. Remember the old proverb that the tree does not grow in one day. The fact that you have checked me and that you do not want to hear about the well-wishers of India shows that, for you at any rate, Home Rule is yet far away. If we had many like you, we would never make any advance. This thought is worthy of your attention.

READER : It seems to me that you simply want to put me off by talking round and round. Those whom you consider to be well-wishers of India are not such in my estimation. Why, then, should I listen to your discourse on such people? What has he whom you consider to be the Father of the Nation done for it? He says that the English Governors will do justice and that we should co-operate with them.

EDITOR : I must tell you, with all gentleness, that it must be a matter of shame for us that you should speak about that great man in terms of disrespect. Just look at his work. He has dedicated his life to the service of India. We have learned what we know from him. It was the respected Dadabhai who taught us that the English had sucked our life-blood. What does it matter that, today, his trust is still in the English nation? Is Dadabhai less to be honoured because, in the exuberance of youth, we are prepared to go a step further? Are we, on that account, wiser than he? It is a mark of wisdom not to kick away the very step from which we have risen higher. The removal of a step from a staircase brings down the whole of it. When, out of infancy, we grow into youth, we do not despise infancy, but on the contrary, we recall with affection the days of our childhood. If, after many years of study, a teacher were to teach me something, and if I were to build a little more on the foundation laid by that teacher, I would not, on that account, be considered wiser than the teacher. He would always command my respect. Such is the case with the Grand Old Man of India. We must admit that he is the author of nationalism.

READER : You have spoken well. I can now understand that we must look upon Mr. Dadabhai with respect. Without him and men like him, we should probably not have the spirit that fires us. How can the same be said of Professor Gokhale? He has constituted himself a great friend of the English; he says that we have to learn a great deal from them, that we have to learn their political wisdom, before we can talk of Home Rule. I am tired of reading his speeches.

EDITOR : If you are tired, it only betrays your impatience. We believe that those, who are discontented with the slowness of their parents and are angry because the parents would not run with their children, are considered disrespectful to their parents. Professor Gokhale occupies the place of a parent. What does it matter if he cannot run with us? A nation that is desirous of securing Home Rule cannot afford to despise its ancestors. We shall become useless, if we lack respect for our elders. Only men with mature thoughts are capable of ruling themselves and not the hasty-tempercd. Moreover, how many Indians were there like Professor Gokhale, when he gave himself to Indian education? I verily believe that whatever Professor Gokhale does, he does with pure motives and with a view to serving India. His devotion to the Motherland is so great that he would give his life for it, if necessary. Whatever he says is said not to flatter anyone but because he believes it to be true. We are bound, therefore, to entertain the highest regard for him.

READER : Are we, then, to follow him in every respect?

EDITOR : I never said any such thing. If we conscientiously differed from him, the learned Professor himself would advise us to follow the dictates of our conscience rather than him. Our chief purpose is not to decry his work, but to believe that he is infinitely greater than we are, and to feel assured that compared with his work for India, ours is infinitesimal. Several newspapers write disrespectfully of him. It is our duty to protest against such writings. We should consider men like Professor Gokhale to be the pillars of Home Rule. It is a bad habit to say that another man's thoughts are bad and ours only are good and that those holding different views from ours are the enemies of the country.

READER : I now begin to understand somewhat your meaning. I shall have to think the matter over. But what you say about Mr. Hume and Sir William Wedderburn is beyond my comprehension.

EDITOR : The same rule holds good for the English as for the Indians. I can never subscribe to the statement that all Englishmen are bad. Many Englishmen desire Home Rule for India. That the English people are somewhat more selfish than others is true, but that does not prove that every Englishman is bad. We who seek justice will have to do justice to others. Sir William does not wish ill to India—that should be enough for us. As we proceed, you will see that, if we act justly, India will be sooner free. You will see, too, that if we shun every Englishman as an enemy, Home Rule will be delayed. But if we are just to them, we shall receive their support in our progress towards the goal.

READER : All this seems to me at present to be simply nonsensical. English support and the obtaining of Home Rule are two contradictory things. How can the English people tolerate Home Rule for us? But I do not want you to decide this question for me just yet. To spend time over it is useless. When you have shown how we can have Home Rule, perhaps I shall understand your views. You have prejudiced me against you by discoursing on English help. I would, therefore, beseech you not to continue this subject.

EDITOR : I have no desire to do so. That you are prejudiced against me is not a matter for much anxiety. It is well that I should say unpleasant things at the commencement. It is my duty patiently to try to remove your prejudice.

READER : I like that last statement. It emboldens me to say what I like. One thing still puzzles me. I do not understand how the Congress laid the foundation of Home Rule.

EDITOR : Let us see. The Congress brought together Indians from 251 different parts of India, and enthused us with the idea of nationality. The Government used to look upon it with disfavour. The Congress has always insisted that the Nation should control revenue and expenditure. It has always desired self-government after the Canadian model. Whether we can get it or not, whether we desire it or not, and whether there is not something more desirable, are different questions. All I have to show is that the Congress gave us a foretaste of Home Rule. To deprive it of the honour is not proper, and for us to do so would not only be ungrateful, but retard the fulfilment of our object. To treat the Congress as an institution inimical to our growth as a nation would disable us from using that body.

2.2
The Partition of Bengal

READER : Considering the matter as you put it, it seems proper to say that the foundation of Home Rule was laid by the Congress. But you will admit that this cannot be considered a real awakening. When and how did the real awakening take place?

EDITOR : The seed is never seen. It works underneath the ground, is itself destroyed, and the tree which rises above the ground is alone seen. Such is the case with the Congress. Yet, what you call the real awakening took place after the Partition of Bengal. For this we have to be thankful to Lord Curzon. At the time of the Partition, the people of Bengal reasoned with Lord Curzon, but in the pride of power he disregarded all their prayers. He took it for granted that Indians could only prattle, that they could never take any effective steps. He used insulting language, and in the teeth of all opposition partitioned Bengal. That day may be considered to be the day of the partition of the British Empire. The shock the British power received through the Partition has never been equalled by any other act. This does not mean that the other injustices done to India are less glaring than that done by the Partition. The salt-tax is not a small injustice. We shall see many such things later on. But the people were ready to resist the Partition. At that time feeling ran high. Many leading Bengalis were ready to lose their all. They knew their power; hence the conflagration. It is now well-nigh unquenchable; it is not necessary to quench it either. The Partition will go, Bengal will be reunited, but the rift in the English barque will remain; it must daily widen. India awakened is not likely to fall asleep.

The demand for the abrogation of the Partition is tantamount to a demand for Home Rule. Leaders in Bengal know this. British officials realize it. That is why the Partition still remains. As time passes, the Nation is being forged. Nations are not formed in a day; the formation requires years.

READER : What, in your opinion, are the results of the Partition?

EDITOR : Hitherto we have considered that for redress of grievances we must approach the throne, and if we get no redress we must sit still, except that we may still petition. After the Partition, people saw that petitions must be backed up by force, and that they must be capable of suffering. This new spirit must be considered to be the chief result of the Partition. That spirit was seen in the outspoken writings in the Press. That which the people said tremblingly and in secret began to be said and to be written publicly. The Swadeshi movement was inaugurated. People, young and old, used to run away at the sight of an English face; it now no longer awes them. They do not fear even a row, or being imprisoned. Some of the best sons of India are at present in banishment. This is something different from mere petitioning. Thus are the people moved. The spirit generated in Bengal has spread in the north to the Punjab, and in the south to Cape Comorin.

READER : Do you suggest any other striking result?

EDITOR : The Partition has not only made a rift in the Englishship but has made it in ours also. Great events always produce great results. Our leaders are divided into two parties : the Moderates and the Extremists. These may be considered as the slow party and the impatient party. Some call the Moderates the timid party, and the Extremists the bold party. All interpret the two words according to their preconceptions. This much is certain—that there has arisen an enmity between the two. The one distrusts the other and imputes motives. At the time of the Surat Congress there was almost a fight. I think that this division is not a good thing for the country, but I think also that such divisions will not last long. It all depends upon the leaders how long they will last.

2.3

Discontent and Unrest

READER : Then you consider the Partition to be a cause of the awakening? Do you welcome the unrest which has resulted from it?

EDITOR : When a man rises from sleep, he twists his limbs and is restless. It takes some time before he is entirely awakened. Similarly, although the Partition has caused an awakening, the comatose condition has not yet disappeared. We are still twisting our limbs and are still restless, and just as the state between sleep and awakening must be considered to be necessary, so may the present unrest in India be considered a necessary and, therefore, a proper state. The knowledge that there is unrest will, it is highly probable, enable us to outgrow it. Rising from sleep, we do not continue in a comatose state, but according to our ability, sooner or later, we are completely restored to our senses. So shall we be free from the present unrest which no one likes.

READER : What is the other form of Unrest?

EDITOR : Unrest is, in reality, discontent. The latter is only now described as unrest. During the Congress period, it was labelled discontent. Mr. Hume always said that the spread of discontent in India was necessary. This discontent is a very useful thing. As long as a man is contented with his present lot, so long it is difficult to persuade him to come out of it. Therefore, it is that every reform must be preceded by discontent. We throw away things we have, only when we cease to like them. Such discontent has been produced among us after reading the great works of Indians and Englishmen. Discontent has led to unrest, and the latter has brought about many deaths, many imprisonments, many banishments. Such a state of things will still continue. It must be so. All these may be considered good signs but they may also lead to bad results.

2.4

What is Swaraj ?

READER : I have now learnt what the Congress has done to make India one nation, how the Partition has caused an awakening, and how discontent and unrest have spread through the land. I would now like to know your views on Swaraj. I fear that our interpretation is not the same as yours.

EDITOR : It is quite possible that we do not attach the same meaning to the term. You and I and all Indians are impatient to obtain *swaraj*, but we are certainly not decided as to what it is. To drive the English out of India is a thought heard from many mouths, but it does not seem that many have properly considered why it should be so. I must ask you a question. Do you think that it is necessary to drive away the English, if we get all we want?

READER : I should ask of them only one thing, that is : "Please leave our country." If, after they have complied with this request, their withdrawal from India means that they are still in India, I should have no objection. Then we would understand that, in their language, the word "gone" is equivalent to "remained".

EDITOR : Well then, let us suppose that the English have retired. What will you do then ?

READER : That question cannot be answered at this stage. The state after withdrawal will depend largely upon the manner of it. If, as you assume, they retire, it seems to me we shall still keep their constitution and shall carry on the Government. If they simply retire for the asking, we should have an army, etc., ready at hand. We should, therefore, have no difficulty in carrying on the Government.

EDITOR : You may think so; I do not. But I will not discuss the matter just now. I have to answer your question, and that I can do well by asking you several questions. Why do you want to drive away the English?

READER : Because India has become impoverished by their Government. They take away our money from year to year. The most important posts are reserved for themselves. We are kept in a state of slavery. They behave insolently towards us and disregard our feelings.

EDITOR : If they do not take our money away, become gentle, and give us responsible posts, would you still consider their presence to be harmful?

READER : That question is useless. It is similar to the question whether there is any harm in associating with a tiger if he changes his nature. Such a question is sheer waste of time. When a tiger changes his nature, Englishmen will change theirs. This is not possible, and to believe it to be possible is contrary to human experience.

EDITOR : Supposing we get Self-Government similar to what the Canadians and the South Africans have, will it be good enough?

READER : That question also is useless. We may get it when we have the same powers; we shall then hoist our own flag. As is Japan, so must India be. We must have own our navy, our army, and we must have our own splendour, and then will India's voice ring through the world.

EDITOR : You have drawn the picture well. In effect it means this : that we want English rule without the Englishman. You want the tiger's nature, but not the tiger; that is to say, you would make India English. And when it becomes English, it will be called not Hindustan but *Englistan*. This is not the *Swaraj* that I want.

READER : I have placed before you my idea of *Swaraj* as I think it should be. If the education we have received be of any use, if the works of Spencer, Mill and others be of any importance, and if the English Parliament be the Mother of Parliaments, I certainly think that we should copy the English people, and this to such an extent that, just as they do not allow others to obtain a footing in their country, so we should not allow them or others to obtain it in ours. What they have done in their own country has not been done in any other country. It is, therefore, proper for us to import their institutions. But now I want to know your views.

EDITOR : There is need for patience. My views will develop of themselves in the course of this discourse. It is as difficult for me to understand the true nature of *Swaraj* as it seems to you to be easy. I shall, therefore, for the time being, content myself with endeavouring to show that what you call *Swaraj* is not truly *Swaraj*.

2.5

The Condition of England

READER : Then from your statement I deduce that the Government of England is not desirable and not worth copying by us.

EDITOR : Your deduction is justified. The condition of England at present is pitiable. I pray to God that India may never be in that plight. That which you consider to be the Mother of Parliaments is like a sterile woman and a prostitute. Both these are harsh terms, but exactly fit the case. That Parliament has not yet, of its own accord, done a single good thing. Hence I have compared it to a sterile woman. The natural condition of that Parliament is such that, without outside pressure, it can do nothing. It is like a prostitute because it is under the control of Ministers who change from time to time. Today it is under Mr. Asquith, tomorrow it may be under Mr. Balfour.

READER : You have said this sarcastically. The term "sterile woman" is not applicable. The Parliament, being elected by the people, must work under public pressure. This is its quality.

EDITOR : You are mistaken. Let us examine it a little more closely. The best men are supposed to be elected by the people. The members serve without pay and, therefore, it must be assumed, only for the public weal. The electors are considered to be educated and, therefore, we should assume that they would not generally make mistakes in their choice. Such a Parliament should not need the spur of petitions or any other pressure. Its work should be so smooth that its effects would be more apparent day-by-day. But, as a matter of fact, it is generally acknowledged that the members are hypocritical and selfish. Each thinks of his own little interest. It is fear that is the guiding motive. What is done today may be undone tomorrow. *It is not possible to recall a single instance in which finality can be predicted for its work.* When the greatest questions are debated, its members have been seen to stretch themselves and to doze. Sometimes the members talk away until the listeners are disgusted. Carlyle has called it the "talking shop of the World". Members vote for their party without a thought. Their so-called discipline binds them to it. If any member, by way of exception, gives an independent vote, he is considered a renegade. If the money and the time wasted by Parliament were entrusted to a few good men, the English nation would be occupying today a much higher platform. Parliament is simply a costly toy of the nation. These views are by no means peculiar to me. Some great English thinkers have expressed them. One of the members of that Parliament recently said that a true Christian could not become a member of it. Another said that it was a baby. And if it has remained a baby after an existence of seven hundred years, when will it outgrow its babyhood ?

READER : You have set me thinking; you do not expect me to accept at once all you say. You give me entirely novel views. I shall have to digest them. Will you now explain the epithet "prostitute" ?

EDITOR : That you cannot accept my views at once is only right. If you will read the literature on this subject, you will have some idea of it. Parliament is without a real master. Under the Prime Minister, its movement is not steady but it is buffeted about like a prostitute. The Prime Minister is more concerned about his power than about the welfare of Parliament. His energy is concentrated upon securing the success of his party. His care is not always that Parliament shall do right. Prime Ministers are known to have made Parliament do things merely for party advantage. All this is worth thinking over.

READER : Then you are really attacking the very men whom we have hitherto considered to be patriotic and honest?

EDITOR : Yes, that is true; I can have nothing against Prime Ministers, but what I have seen leads me to think that they cannot be considered really patriotic. If they are to be considered honest because they do not take what are generally known as bribes, let them be so considered, but they are open to subtler influences. In order to gain their ends, they certainly bribe people with honours. I do not hesitate to say that they have neither real honesty nor a living conscience.

READER : As you express these views about Parliament, I would like to hear you on the English people, so that I may have your view of their Government.

EDITOR : To the English voters their newspaper is their Bible. They take their cue from their newspapers which are often dishonest. The same fact is differently interpreted by different newspapers, according to the party in whose interests they are edited. One newspaper would consider a great Englishman to be a paragon of honesty, another would consider him dishonest. What must be the condition of the people whose newspapers are of this type?

READER : You shall describe it.

EDITOR : These people change their views frequently. It is said that they change them every seven years. These views swing like the pendulum of a clock and are never steadfast. The people would follow a powerful orator or a man who gives them parties, receptions, etc. As are the people, so is their Parliament. They have certainly one quality very strongly developed. They will never allow their country to be lost. If any person were to cast an evil eye on it, they would pluck out his eyes. But that does not mean that the nation possesses every other virtue or that it should be imitated. If India copies England, it is my firm conviction that she will be ruined.

READER : To what do you ascribe this state of England?

EDITOR : It is not due to any peculiar fault of the English people, but the condition is due to modern civilization. It is a civilization only in name. Under it the nations of Europe are becoming degraded and ruined day-by-day.

2.6

Civilization

READER : Now you will have to explain what you mean by civilization.

EDITOR : It is not a question of what I mean. Several English writers refuse to call that civilization which passes under that name. Many books have been written upon that subject. Societies have been formed to cure the nation of the evils of civilization. A great English writer has written a work called *Civilization : Its Cause and Cure*. Therein he has called it a disease.

READER : Why do we not know this generally?

EDITOR : The answer is very simple. We rarely find people arguing against themselves. Those who are intoxicated by modern civilization are not likely to write against it. Their care will be to find out facts and arguments in support of it, and this they do unconsciously, believing it to be true. A man, whilst he is reaming, believes in his dream; he is undeceived only when he is awakened from his sleep. A man labouring under the bane of civilization is like a dreaming man. What we usually read are the works of defenders of modern civilization, which undoubtedly claims among its votaries very brilliant and even some very good men. Their writings hypnotize us. And so, one by one, we are drawn into the vortex.

READER : This seems to be very plausible. Now will you tell me something of what you have read and thought of this civilization?

EDITOR : Let us first consider what state of things is described by the word "civilization". Its true test lies in the fact that people living in it make bodily welfare the object of life. We will take some examples. The people of Europe today live in better-built houses than they did a hundred years ago. This is considered an emblem of civilization, and this is also a matter to promote bodily happiness. Formerly, they wore skins, and used spears as their weapons. Now, they wear long trousers, and, for embellishing their bodies, they wear a variety of clothing, and, instead of spears, they carry with them revolvers containing five or more chambers. If people of a certain country, who have hitherto not been in the habit of wearing much clothing, boots, etc., adopt European clothing, they are supposed to have become civilized out of savagery. Formerly, in Europe, people ploughed their lands mainly by manual labour. Now, one man can plough a vast tract by means of steam engines and can thus amass great wealth. This is called a sign of civilization. Formerly, only a few men wrote valuable books. Now, anybody writes and prints anything he likes and poisons people's minds. Formerly, men travelled in wagons. Now, they fly through the air and in trains at the rate of four hundred and more miles per day. This is considered the height of civilization. It has been stated that, as men progress, they shall be able to travel in airships and reach any part of the world in a few hour. Men will not need the use of their hands and feet. They will press a button, and they will have their clothing by their side. They will press another button, and they will have their newspaper. A third, and a motor-car will be in waiting for them. They will have a variety of delicately dished up food. Everything will be done by machinery. Formerly, when people wanted to fight with one another, they measured between them their bodily strength; now it is possible to take away thousands of lives by one man working behind a gun from a hill. This is civilization. Formerly, men worked in the open air only as much as they liked. Now thousands of workmen meet together and for the sake of maintenance work in factories or mines. Their condition is worse than that of beasts. They are obliged to work, at the risk of their lives, at most dangerous occupations, for the sake of millionaires. Formerly, men were made slaves under physical compulsion. Now they are enslaved by temptation of money and of the luxuries that money can buy. There are now diseases of which people never dreamt before, and an army of doctors is engaged in finding out their cures, and so hospitals have increased. This is a test of civilization. Formerly, special messengers were required and much expense was incurred in order to send letters; today, anyone can abuse his fellow by means of a letter for one penny. True, at the same cost, one can send one's thanks also. Formerly, people had two or three meals consisting of home-made bread and vegetables; now, they require something to eat every two hours so that they have hardly leisure for anything else. What more need I say? All this you can ascertain from several authoritative books. These are all true tests of civilization. And if anyone speaks to the contrary, know that he is ignorant. This civilization takes note neither of morality nor of religion. Its votaries calmly state that their business is not to teach religion. Some even consider it to be a superstitious growth. Others put on the cloak of religion, and prate about morality. But, after twenty years' experience, I have come to the conclusion that immorality is often taught in the name of morality. Even a child can understand that in all I have described above there can be no inducement to morality. Civilization seeks to increase bodily comforts, and it fails miserably even in doing so.

This civilization is irreligion, and it has taken such a hold on the people in Europe that those who are in it appear to be half mad. They lack real physical strength or courage. They keep up their energy by intoxication. They can hardly be happy in solitude. Women, who should be the queens of households, wander in the streets or they slave away in factories. For the sake of a pittance, half a million women in England alone are labouring under trying circumstances in factories or similar institutions. This awful fact is one of the causes of the daily growing suffragette movement.

This civilization is such that one has only to be patient and it will be self-destroyed. According to the teaching of Mahomed this would be considered a Satanic Civilization. Hinduism calls it the Black Age. I cannot give you an adequate conception of it. It is eating into the vitals of the English nation.

It must be shunned. Parliaments are really emblems of slavery. If you will sufficiently think over this, you will entertain the same opinion and cease to blame the English. They rather deserve our sympathy. They are a shrewd nation and I, therefore, believe that they will cast off the evil. They are enterprising and industrious, and their mode of thought is not inherently immoral. Neither are they bad at heart. I, therefore, respect them. Civilization is not an incurable disease, but it should never be forgotten that the English people are at present afflicted by it.

2.7

Why Was India Lost ?

READER : You have said much about civilization—enough to make me ponder over it. I do not now know what I should adopt and what I should avoid from the nations of Europe, but one question comes to my lips immediately. If civilization is a disease and if it has attacked England, why has she been able to take India, and why is she able to retain it?

EDITOR : Your question is not very difficult to answer, and we shall presently be able to examine the true nature of Swaraj; for I am aware that I have still to answer that question. I will, however, take up your previous question. The English have not taken India; we have given it to them. They are not in India because of their strength, but because we keep them. Let us now see whether these propositions can be sustained. They came to our country originally for purposes of trade. Recall the Company Bahadur. Who made it Bahadur? They had not the slightest intention at the time of establishing a kingdom.

Who assisted the Company's officers? Who was tempted at the sight of their silver? Who bought their goods? History testifies that we did all this. In order to become rich all at once we welcomed the Company's officers with open arms. We assisted them. If I am in the habit of drinking *bhang* and a seller thereof sells it to me, am I to blame him or myself? By blaming the seller, shall I be able to avoid the habit? And, if a particular retailer is driven away, will not another take his place? A true servant of India will have to go to the root of the matter. If an excess of food has caused me indigestion, I shall certainly not avoid it by blaming water. He is a true physician who probes the cause of disease, and if you pose as a physician for the disease of India, you will have to find out its true cause.

READER : You are right. Now I think you will not have to argue much with me to drive your conclusions home. I am impatient to know your further views. We are now on a most interesting topic. I shall, therefore, endeavour to follow your thought, and stop you when I am in doubt.

EDITOR : I am afraid that, in spite of your enthusiasm, as we proceed further, we shall have differences of opinion. Nevertheless, I shall argue only when you stop me. We have already seen that the English merchants were able to get a footing in India because we encouraged them. When our Princes fought among themselves, they sought the assistance of Company Bahadur. That corporation was versed alike in commerce and war. It was unhampered by questions of morality. Its object was to increase its commerce and to make money. It accepted our assistance, and increased the number of its warehouses. To protect the latter it employed an army which was utilized by us also. Is it not then useless to blame the English for what we did at that time? The Hindus and the Mahomedans were at daggers drawn. This, too, gave the Company its opportunity and thus we created the circumstances that gave the Company its control over India. Hence it is truer to say that we gave India to the English than that India was lost.

READER : Will you now tell me how they are able to retain India?

EDITOR : The causes that gave them India enable them to retain it. Some Englishmen state that they took and they hold India by the sword. Both these statements are wrong. The sword is entirely useless for holding India. We alone keep them. Napoleon is said to have described the English as a nation of shopkeepers. It is a fitting description. They hold whatever dominions they have for the sake of their commerce. Their army and their navy are intended to protect it. When the Transvaal offered no such attractions, the late Mr. Gladstone discovered that it was not right for the English to hold it.

When it became a paying proposition, resistance led to war. Mr. Chamberlain soon discovered that England enjoyed a suzerainty over the Transvaal. It is related that someone asked the late President Kruger whether there was gold in the moon. He replied that it was highly unlikely because, if there were, the English would have annexed it. Many problems can be solved by remembering that money is their God. Then it follows that we keep the English in India for our base self-interest. We like their commerce; they please us by their subtle methods and get what they want from us. To blame them for this is to perpetuate their power. We further strengthen their hold by quarrelling amongst ourselves. If you accept the above statements, it is proved that the English entered India for the purposes of trade. They remain in it for the same purpose and we help them to do so. Their arms and ammunition are perfectly useless. In this connection I remind you that it is the British flag which is waving in Japan and not the Japanese. The English have a treaty with Japan for the sake of their commerce, and you will see that if they can manage it, their commerce will greatly expand in that country. They wish to convert the whole world into a vast market for their goods. That they cannot do so is true, but the blame will not be theirs. They will leave no stone unturned to reach the goal.

2.8
The Condition of India

READER : I now understand why the English hold India. I should like to know your views about the condition of our country.

EDITOR : It is a sad condition. In thinking of it my eyes water and my throat gets parched. I have grave doubts whether I shall be able sufficiently to explain what is in my heart. It is my deliberate opinion that India is being ground down, not under the English heel, but under that of modern civilization. It is groaning under the monster's terrible weight. There is yet time to escape it, but everyday makes it more and more difficult. Religion is dear to me and my first complaint is that India is becoming irreligious. Here I am not thinking of the Hindu or the Mahomedan or the Zoroastrian religion but of that religion which underlies all religions. We are turning away from God.

READER : How so?

EDITOR : There is a charge laid against us that we are a lazy people and that Europeans are industrious and enterprising. We have accepted the charge and we, therefore, wish to change our condition. Hinduism, Islam, Zoroastrianism, Christianity and all other religions teach that we should remain passive about worldly pursuits and active about godly pursuits, that we should set a limit to our worldly ambition and that our religious ambition should be illimitable. Our activity should be directed into the latter channel.

READER : You seem to be encouraging religious charlatanism. Many a cheat has, by talking in a similar strain, led the people astray.

EDITOR : You are bringing an unlawful charge against religion. Humbug there undoubtedly is about all religions. Where there is light, there is also shadow. I am prepared to maintain that humbugs in worldly matters are far worse than the humbugs in religion. The humbug of civilization that I am endeavouring to show to you is not to be found in religion.

READER : How can you say that? In the name of religion Hindus and Mahomedans fought against one another. For the same cause Christians fought Christians. Thousands of innocent men have been murdered, thousands have been burned and tortured in its name. Surely, this is much worse than any civilization.

EDITOR : I certainly submit that the above hardships are far more bearable than those of civilization. Everybody understands that the cruelties you have named are not part of religion although they have been practised in its name, therefore, there is no aftermath to these cruelties. They will always happen so long as there are to be found ignorant and credulous people. But there is no end to the victims destroyed in the fire of civilization. Its deadly effect is that people come under its scorching flames believing it to be all good. They become utterly irreligious and, in reality, derive little advantage from the world. Civilization is like a mouse gnawing while it is soothing us. When its full effect is realized, we shall see that religious superstition is harmless compared to that of modern civilization. I am not pleading for a continuance of religious superstitions. We shall certainly fight them tooth and nail, but we can never do so by disregarding religion. We can only do so by appreciating and conserving the latter.

READER : Then you will contend that the Pax Britannica is a useless encumbrance ?

EDITOR : You may see peace if you like; I see none.

READER : You make light of the terror that the Thugs, the Pindaris and the Bhils were to the country.

EDITOR : If you give the matter some thought, you will see that the terror was by no means such a mighty thing. If it had been a very substantial thing, the other people would have died away before the English advent. Moreover, the present peace is only nominal, for by it we have become emasculated and cowardly. We are not to assume that the English have changed the nature of the Pindaris and the Bhils. It is, therefore, better to suffer the Pindari peril than that someone else should protect us from it and thus render us effeminate. I should prefer to be killed by the arrow of a Bhil than to seek unmanly protection. India without such protection was an India full of valour. Macaulay betrayed gross ignorance when he libelled Indians as being practically cowards. They never merited the charge. Cowards living in a country inhabited by hardy mountaineers and infested by wolves and tigers must surely find an early grave. Have you ever visited our fields? I assure you that our agriculturists sleep fearlessly on their farms even today; but the English and you and I would hesitate to sleep where they sleep. Strength lies in absence of fear, not in the quantity of flesh and muscle we may have on our bodies. Moreover, I must remind you who desire Home Rule that, after all, the Bhils, the Pindaris, and the Thugs are our own countrymen. To conquer them is your and my work. So long as we fear our own brethren, we are unfit to reach the goal.

2.9

The Condition of India (*continued*)

Railways

READER : You have deprived me of the consolation I used to have regarding peace in India.

EDITOR : I have merely given you my opinion on the religious aspect, but when I give you my views as to the poverty of India, you will perhaps begin to dislike me because what you and I have hitherto considered beneficial for India no longer appears to me to be so.

READER : What may that be ?

EDITOR : Railways, lawyers and doctors have impoverished the country so much so that, if we do not wake up in time, we shall be ruined.

READER : I do now, indeed, fear that we are not likely to agree at all. You are attacking the very institutions which we have hitherto considered to be good.

EDITOR : It is necessary to exercise patience. The true inwardness of the evils of civilization you will understand with difficulty. Doctors assure us that a consumptive clings to life even when he is about to die. Consumption does not produce apparent hurt—it even produces a seductive colour about a patient's face so as to induce the belief that all is well. Civilization is such a disease and we have to be very wary.

READER : Very well, then. I shall hear you on the railways.

EDITOR : It must be manifest to you that, but for the railways, the English could not have such a hold on India as they have. The railways, too, have spread the bubonic plague.

Without them, the masses could not move from place to place. They are the carriers of plague germs. Formerly, we had natural segregation. Railways have also increased the frequency of famines because, owing to facility of means of locomotion, people sell out their grain and it is sent to the dearest markets. People become careless and so the pressure of famine increases. Railways accentuate the evil nature of man. Bad men fulfil their evil designs with greater rapidity. The holy places of India have become unholy. Formerly, people went to these places with very great difficulty. Generally, therefore, only the real devotees visited such places. Nowadays rogues visit them in order to practise their roguery.

READER : You have given a one-sided account. Good men can visit these places as well as bad men. Why do they not take the fullest advantage of the railways?

EDITOR : Good travels at a snail's pace—it can, therefore, have little to do with the railways. Those who want to do good are not selfish, they are not in a hurry, they know that to impregnate people with good requires a long time. But evil has wings. To build a house takes time. Its destruction takes none. So the railways can become a distributing agency for the evil one only. It may be a debatable matter whether railways spread famines, but it is beyond dispute that they propagate evil.

READER : Be that as it may, all the disadvantages of railways are more than counterbalanced by the fact that it is due to them that we see in India the new spirit of nationalism.

EDITOR : I hold this to be a mistake. The English have taught us that we were not one nation before and that it will require centuries before we become one nation. This is without foundation. We were one nation before they came to India. One thought inspired us. Our mode of life was the same. It was because we were one nation that they were able to establish one kingdom. Subsequently they divided us.

READER : This requires an explanation.

EDITOR : I do not wish to suggest that because we were one nation we had no differences, but it is submitted that our leading men travelled throughout India either on foot or in bullock-carts. They learned one another's languages and there was no aloofness between them. What do you think could have been the intention of those farseeing ancestors of ours who established Setubandha (Rameshwar) in the South, Jagannath in the East and Hardwar in the North as places of pilgrimage ? You will admit they were no fools. They knew that worship of God could have been performed just as well at home. They taught us that those whose hearts were aglow with righteousness had the Ganges in their own homes. But they saw that India was one undivided land so made by nature. They, therefore, argued that it must be one nation. Arguing thus, they established holy places in various parts of India, and fired the people with an idea of nationality in a manner unknown in other parts of the world. And we Indians are one as no two Englishmen are. Only you and I and others who consider ourselves civilized and superior persons imagine that we are many nations. It was after the advent of railways that we began to believe in distinctions, and you are at liberty now to say that it is through the railways that we are beginning to abolish those distinctions. An opium-eater may argue the advantage of opium-eating from the fact that he began to understand the evil of the opium habit after having eaten it. I would ask you to consider well what I had said on the railways.

READER : I will gladly do so, but one question occurs to me even now. You have described to me the India of the pre-Mahomedan period, but now we have Mahomedans, Parsis and Christians. How can they be one nation? Hindus and Mahomedans are old enemies. Our very proverbs prove it. Mahomedans turn to the West for worship, whilst Hindus turn to the East. The former look down on the Hindus as idolaters. The Hindus worship the cow, the Mahomedans kill her. The Hindus believe in the doctrine of non-killing, the Mahomedans do not. We thus meet with differences at every step. How can India be one nation?

2.10

The Condition of India (*continued*)

The Hindus and the Mahomedans

EDITOR : Your last question is a serious one and yet, on careful consideration, it will be found to be easy of solution. The question arises because of the presence of the railways, of the lawyers and of the doctors. We shall presently examine the last two. We have already considered the railways. I should, however, like to add that man is so made by nature as to require him to restrict his movements as far as his hands and feet will take him. If we did not rush about from place to place by means of railways and such other maddening conveniences, much of the confusion that arises would be obviated. Our difficulties are of our own creation. God set a limit to man's locomotive ambition in the construction of his body. Man immediately proceeded to discover means of overriding the limit. God gifted man with intellect that he might know his Maker. Man abused it so that he might forget his Maker. I am so constructed that I can only serve my immediate neighbours, but in my conceit I pretend to have discovered that I must with my body serve every individual in the Universe. In thus attempting the impossible, man comes in contact with different natures, different religions, and is utterly confounded. According to this reasoning, it must be apparent to you that railways are a most dangerous institution. Owing to them, man has gone further away from his Maker.

READER : But I am impatient to hear your answer to my question. Has the introduction of Mahomedanism not unmade the nation?

EDITOR : India cannot cease to be one nation because people belonging to different religions live in it. The introduction of foreigners does not necessarily destroy the nation; they merge in it. A country is one nation only when such a condition obtains in it. That country must have a faculty for assimilation. India has ever been such a country. In reality, there are as many religions as there are individuals; but those who are conscious of the spirit of nationality do not interfere with one another's religion. If they do, they are not fit to be considered a nation. If the Hindus believe that India should be peopled only by Hindus, they are living in dreamland. The Hindus, the Mahomedans, the Parsis and the Christians who have made India their country are fellow countrymen, and they will have to live in unity, if only for their own interest. In no part of the world are one nationality and one religion synonymous terms; nor has it ever been so in India.

READER : But what about the inborn enmity between Hindus and Mahomedans?

EDITOR : That phrase has been invented by our mutual enemy. When the Hindus and Mahomedans fought against one another, they certainly spoke in that strain. They have long since ceased to fight. How, then, can there be any inborn enmity? Pray remember this too, that we did not cease to fight only after British occupation. The Hindus flourished under Moslem sovereigns and Moslems under the Hindu. Each party recognized that mutual fighting was suicidal, and that neither party would abandon its religion by force of arms. Both parties, therefore, decided to live in peace. With the English advent quarrels re-commenced. The proverbs you have quoted were coined when both were fighting; to quote them now is obviously harmful. Should we not remember that many Hindus and Mahomedans own the same ancestors and the same blood runs through their veins? Do people become enemies because they change their religion? Is the God of the Mahomedan different from the God of the Hindu? Religions are different roads converging to the same point. What does it matter that we take different roads so long as we reach the same goal? Wherein is the cause for quarrelling? Moreover, there are deadly proverbs as between the followers of Shiva and those of Vishnu, yet nobody suggests that these two do not belong to the same nation. It is said that the Vedic religion is different from Jainism, but the followers of the respective faiths are not different nations. The fact is that we have become enslaved and, therefore, quarrel and like to have our quarrels decided by a third party. There are Hindu iconoclasts as there are Mahomedan. The more we advance in true knowledge, the better we shall understand that we need not be at war with those whose religion we may not follow.

READER : Now I would like to know your views about cow protection.

EDITOR : I myself respect the cow, that is, I look upon her with affectionate reverence. The cow is the protector of India because, being an agricultural country, she is dependent on the cow. The cow is a most useful animal in hundreds of ways. Our Mahomedan brethren will admit this.

But, just as I respect the cow, so do I respect my fellow-men. A man is just as useful as a cow no matter whether he be a Mahomedan or a Hindu. Am I, then, to fight with or kill a Mahomedan in order to save a cow? In doing so, I would become an enemy of the Mahomedan as well as of the cow. Therefore, the only method I know of protecting the cow is that I should approach my Mahomedan brother and urge him for the sake of the country to join me in protecting her. If he would not listen to me I should let the cow go for the simple reason that the matter is beyond my ability. If I were overfull of pity for the cow, I should sacrifice my life to save her but not take my brother's. This, I hold, is the law of our religion.

When men become obstinate, it is a difficult thing. If I pull one way, my Moslem brother will pull another. If I put on superior airs, he will return the compliment. If I bow to him gently, he will do it much more so; and if he does not, I shall not be considered to have done wrong in having bowed. When the Hindus became insistent, the killing of cows increased. In my opinion, cow-protection societies may be considered cow-killing societies. It is a disgrace to us that we should need such societies. When we forgot how to protect cows, I suppose we needed such societies.

What am I to do when a blood-brother is on the point of killing a cow? Am I to kill him, or to fall down at his feet and implore him? If you admit that I should adopt the latter course, I must do the same to my Moslem brother.

Who protects the cow from destruction by Hindus when they cruelly ill-treat her? Whoever reasons with the Hindus when they mercilessly belabour the progeny of the cow with their sticks ? But this has not prevented us from remaining one nation.

Lastly, if it be true that the Hindus believe in the doctrine of non-killing and the Mahomedans do not, what, pray, is the duty of the former? It is not written that a follower of the religion of *ahimsa* (non-killing) may kill a fellow-man. For him the way is straight. In order to save one being, he may not kill another. He can only plead—therein lies his sole duty.

But does every Hindu believe in *ahimsa*? Going to the root of the matter, not one man really practises such a religion because we do destroy life. We are said to follow that religion because we want to obtain freedom from liability to kill any kind of life. Generally speaking, we may observe that many Hindus partake of meat and are not, therefore, followers of *ahimsa*. It is, therefore, preposterous to suggest that the two cannot live together amicably because the Hindus believe in *ahimsa* and the Mahomedans do not.

These thoughts are put into our minds by selfish and false religious teachers. The English put the finishing touch. They have a habit of writing history; they pretend to study the manners and customs of all peoples. God has given us a limited mental capacity, but they usurp the function of the Godhead and indulge in novel experiments. They write about their own researches in most laudatory terms and hypnotize us into believing them. We in our ignorance then fall at their feet.

Those who do not wish to misunderstand things may read up the *Koran*, and they will find therein hundreds of passages acceptable to the Hindus; and the *Bhagavad Gita* contains passages to which not a Mahomedan can take exception. Am I to dislike a Mahomedan because there are passages in the *Koran* I do not understand or like? It takes two to make a quarrel. If I do not want to quarrel with a Mahomedan, the latter will be powerless to foist a quarrel on me; and, similarly, I should be powerless if a Mahomedan refuses his assistance to quarrel with me. An arm striking the air will become disjointed. If everyone will try to understand the core of his own religion and adhere to it, and will not allow false teachers to dictate to him, there will be no room left for quarrelling.

READER : But will the English ever allow the two bodies to join hands ?

EDITOR : This question arises out of your timidity. It betrays our shallowness. If two brothers want to live in peace, is it possible for a third party to separate them? If they were to listen to evil counsels we would consider them to be foolish. Similarly, we Hindus and Mahomedans would have to blame our folly rather than the English, if we allowed them to put us asunder. A clay pot would breakthrough impact, if not with one stone, then with another. The way to save the pot is not to keep it away from the danger point but to bake it so that no stone would break it. We have then to make our hearts of perfectly baked clay. Then we shall be steeled against all danger. This can be easily done by the Hindus. They are superior in numbers; they pretend that they are more educated; they are, therefore, better able to shield themselves from attack on their amicable relations with the Mahomedans. There is mutual distrust between the two communities. The Mahomedans, therefore, ask for certain concessions from Lord Morley. Why should the Hindus oppose this? If the Hindus desisted, the English would notice it, the Mahomedans would gradually begin to trust the Hindus, and brotherliness would be the outcome. We should be ashamed to take our quarrels to the English. Everyone can find out for himself that the Hindus can lose nothing by desisting. That man who has inspired confidence in another has never lost anything in this world. I do not suggest that the Hindus and the Mahomedans will never fight. Two brothers living together often do so. We shall sometimes have our heads broken. Such a thing ought not to be necessary, but all men are not equitable. When people are in a rage, they do many foolish things. These we have to put up with. But when we do quarrel, we certainly do not want to engage counsel and resort to English or any law-courts. Two men fight; both have their heads broken, or one only. How shall a third party distribute justice amongst them? Those who fight may expect to be injured.

2.11

The Condition of India (*continued*)

Lawyers

READER : You tell me that when two men quarrel they should not go to a law-court. This is astonishing.

EDITOR : Whether you call it astonishing or not, it is the truth. And your question introduces us to the lawyers and the doctors. My firm opinion is that the lawyers have enslaved India, have accentuated Hindu-Mahomedan dissensions and have confirmed English authority.

READER : It is easy enough to bring these charges, but it will be difficult for you to prove them. But for the lawyers, who would have shown us the road to independence? Who would have protected the poor? Who would have secured justice? For instance, the late Manomohan Ghose defended many a poor man free of charge. The Congress, which you have praised so much, is dependent for its existence and activity upon the work of the lawyers. To denounce such an estimable class of men is to spell injustice, and you are abusing the liberty of the Press by decrying lawyers.

EDITOR : At one time I used to think exactly like you. I have no desire to convince you that they have never done a single good thing. I honour Mr. Ghose's memory. It is quite true that he helped the poor. That the Congress owes the lawyers something is believable. Lawyers are also men, and there is something good in every man. Whenever instances of lawyers having done good can be brought forward, it will be found that the good is due to them as men rather than as lawyers. All I am concerned with is to show you that the profession teaches immorality; it is exposed to temptation from which few are saved. The Hindus and the Mahomedans have quarrelled. An ordinary man will ask them to forget all about it; he will tell them that both must be more or less at fault, and will advise them no longer to quarrel. But they go to lawyers. The latter's duty is to side with their clients and to find out ways and arguments in favour of the clients, to which they (the clients) are often strangers. If they do not do so, they will be considered to have degraded their profession. The lawyers, therefore, will, as a rule, advance quarrels instead of repressing them. Moreover, men take up that profession, not in order to help others out of their miseries, but to enrich themselves. It is one of the avenues of becoming wealthy and their interest exists in multiplying disputes. It is within my knowledge that they are glad when men have disputes. Petty pleaders actually manufacture them. Their touts, like so many leeches, suck the blood of the poor people. Lawyers are men who have little to do. Lazy people, in order to indulge in luxuries, take up such professions. This is a true statement. Any other argument is a mere pretension. It is the lawyers who have discovered that theirs is an honourable profession. They frame laws as they frame their own praises. They decide what fees they will charge and they put on so much side that poor people almost consider them to be heaven-born. Why do they want more fees than common labourers? Why are their requirements greater? In what way are they more profitable to the country than the labourers? Are those who do good entitled to greater payment? And, if they have done anything for the country for the sake of money, how shall it be counted as good? Those who know anything of the Hindu-Mahomedan quarrels know that they have been often due to the intervention or lawyers. Some families have been ruined through them; they have made brothers enemies. Principalities, having come under the lawyers' power, have become loaded with debt. Many have been robbed of their all. Such instances can be multiplied. But the greatest injury they have done to the country is that they have tightened the English grip. Do you think that it would be possible for the English to carry on their Government without law courts? It is wrong to consider that courts are established for the benefit of the people. Those who want to perpetuate their power do so through the courts. If people were to settle their own quarrels, a third party would not be able to exercise any authority over them. Truly, men were less unmanly when they settled their disputes either by fighting or by asking their relatives to decide for them. They became more unmanly and cowardly when they resorted to the courts of law. It was certainly a sign of savagery when they settled their disputes by fighting. Is it any the less so, if I ask a third party to decide between you and me? Surely, the decision of a third party is not always right. The parties alone know who is right. We, in our simplicity and ignorance, imagine that a stranger, by taking our money, gives us justice. The chief thing, however, to be remembered is that without lawyers courts could not have been established or conducted and without the latter the English could not rule. Supposing that there were only English judges, English pleaders and English police, they could only rule over the English. The English could not do without Indian Judges and Indian pleaders. How the pleaders were made in the first instance and how they were favoured you should understand well. Then you will have the same abhorrence for the profession that I have. If pleaders were to abandon their profession, and consider it just as degrading as prostitution, English rule would break up in a day. They have been instrumental in having the charge laid against us that we love quarrels and courts as fish love water. What I have said with reference to the pleaders necessarily applies to the Judges; they are first cousins; and the one gives strength to the other.

2.12

The Condition of India (*continued*)

Doctors

READER : I now understand the lawyers; the good they may have done is accidental. I feel that profession is certainly hateful. You, however, drag in the doctors also, how is that?

EDITOR : The views I submit to you are those I have adopted.They are not original. Western writers have used stronger terms regarding both lawyers and doctors. One writer has likened the whole modern system to the Upas tree. Its branches are represented by parasitical professions, including those of law and medicine, and over the trunk has been raised the axe of true religion. Immorality is the root of the tree. So you will see that the views do not come right out of my mind but represent the combined experiences of many. I was at one time a great lover of the medical profession. It was my intention to become a doctor for the sake of the country. I no longer hold that opinion. I now understand why the medicine men (the *vaids*) among us have not occupied a very honourable status. The English have certainly effectively used the medical profession for holding us. English physicians are known to have used their profession with several Asiatic potentates for political gain. Doctors have almost unhinged us. Sometimes I think that quacks are better than highly qualified doctors. Let us consider : the business of a doctor is to take care of the body, or, properly speaking, not even that. Their business is really to rid the body of diseases that may afflict it. How do these diseases arise? Surely by our negligence or indulgence. I overeat, I have indigestion, I go to a doctor, he gives me medicine, I am cured. I overeat again, I take his pills again. Had I not taken the pills in the first instance, I would have suffered the punishment deserved by me and I would not have overeaten again. The doctor intervened and helped me to indulge myself. My body thereby certainly felt more at ease; but my mind became weakened. A continuance of a course of medicine must, therefore, result in loss of control over the mind. I have indulged in vice, I contract a disease, a doctor cures me, the odds are that I shall repeat the vice. Had the doctor not intervened, nature would have done its work, and I would have acquired mastery over myself, would have been freed from vice and would have become happy. Hospitals are institutions for propagating sin. Men take less care of their bodies and immorality increases. European doctors are the worst of all. For the sake of a mistaken care of the human body, they kill annually thousands of animals. They practise vivisection. No religion sanctions this. All say that it is not necessary to take so many lives for the sake of our bodies. These doctors violate our religious instinct. Most of their medical preparations contain either animal fat or spirituous liquors; both of these are tabooed by Hindus and Mahomedans. We may pretend to be civilized, call religious prohibitions a superstition and want only to indulge in what we like. The fact remains that the doctors induce us to indulge, and the result is that we have become deprived of self-control and have become effeminate. In these circumstances, we are unfit to serve the country. To study European medicine is to deepen our slavery. It is worth considering why we take up the profession of medicine. It is certainly not taken up for the purpose of serving humanity. We become doctors so that we may obtain honours and riches. I have endeavoured to show that there is no real service of humanity in the profession, and that it is injurious to mankind. Doctors make a show of their knowledge, and charge exorbitant fees. Their preparations, which are intrinsically worth a few pence, cost shillings. The populace, in its credulity and in the hope of ridding itself of some disease, allows itself to be cheated. Are not quacks then, whom we know, better than the doctors who put on an air of humaneness,

2.13

What is True Civilization ?

READER : You have denounced railways, lawyers and doctors. I can see that you will discard all machinery. What, then, is civilization?

EDITOR : The answer to that question is not difficult. I believe that the civilization India has evolved is not to be beaten in the world. Nothing can equal the seeds sown by our ancestors. Rome went, Greece shared the same fate; the might of the Pharaohs was broken; Japan has become westernized; of China nothing can be said; but India is still, somehow or other, sound at the foundation. The people of Europe learn their lessons from the writings of the men of Greece or Rome, which exist no longer in their former glory. In trying to learn from them, the Europeans imagine that they will avoid the mistakes of Greece and Rome. Such is their pitiable condition. In the midst of all this India remains immovable and that is her glory. It is a charge against India that her people are so uncivilized, ignorant and stolid, that it is not possible to induce them to adopt any changes. It is a charge really against our merit. What we have tested and found true on the anvil of experience, we dare not change. Many thrust their advice upon India, and she remains steady. This is her beauty : it is the sheet-anchor of our hope. Civilization is that mode of conduct which points out to man the path of duty. Performance of duty and observance of morality are convertible terms. To observe morality is to attain mastery over our mind and our passions. So doing, we know ourselves. The Gujarati equivalent for civilization means "good conduct". If this definition be correct, then India, as so many writers have shown, has nothing to learn from anybody else, and this is as it should be. We notice that the mind is a restless bird; the more it gets the more it wants, and still remains unsatisfied. The more we indulge our passions, the more unbridled they become. Our ancestors, therefore, set a limit to our indulgences. They saw that happiness was largely a mental condition. A man is not necessarily happy because he is rich, or unhappy because he is poor. The rich are often seen to be unhappy, the poor to be happy. Millions will always remain poor. Observing all this, our ancestors dissuaded us from luxuries and pleasures. We have managed with the same kind of plough as existed thousands of years ago. We have retained the same kind of cottages that we had in former times and our indigenous education remains the same as before. We have had no system of life-corroding competition. Each followed his own occupation or trade and charged a regulation wage. It was not that we did not know how to invent machinery, but our forefathers knew that, if we set our hearts after such things, we would become slaves and lose our moral fibre. They, therefore, after due deliberation decided that we should only do what we could with our hands and feet. They saw that our real happiness and health consisted in a proper use of our hands and feet. They further reasoned that large cities were a snare and a useless encumbrance and that people would not be happy in them, that there would be gangs of thieves and robbers, prostitution and vice flourishing in them and that poor men would be robbed by rich men. They were, therefore, satisfied with small villages. They saw that kings and their swords were inferior to the sword of ethics, and they, therefore, held the sovereigns of the earth to be inferior to the *rishis* and the *fakirs.* A nation with a constitution like this is fitter to teach others than to learn from others. This nation had courts, lawyers and doctors, but they were all within bounds. Everybody knew that these professions were not particularly superior; moreover, these *vakils* and *vaids* did not rob people; they were considered people's dependants, not their masters. Justice was tolerably fair. The ordinary rule was to avoid courts. There were no touts to lure people into them. This evil, too, was noticeable only in and around capitals. The common people lived independently and followed their agricultural occupation. They enjoyed true Home Rule. And where this cursed modern civilization has not reached, India remains as it was before. The inhabitants of that part of India will very properly laugh at your new-fangled notions. The English do not rule over them, nor will you ever rule over them. Those in whose name we speak we do not know, nor do they know us. I would certainly advise you and those like you who love the motherland to go into the interior that has yet been not polluted by the railways and to live there for six months; you might then be patriotic and speak of Home Rule. Now you see what I consider to be real civilization. Those who want to change conditions such as I have described are enemies of the country and are sinners.

READER : It would be all right if India were exactly as you have described it, but it is also India where there are hundreds of child widows, where two-year-old babies are married, where twelve-year-old girls are mothers and housewives, where women practise polyandry, where the practice of Niyoga1 obtains, where, in the name of religion, girls dedicate themselves to prostitution, and in the name of religion sheep and goats are killed. Do you consider these also symbols of the civilization that you have described?

EDITOR : You make a mistake. The defects that you have shown are defects. Nobody mistakes them for ancient civilization. They remain in spite of it. Attempts have always been made and will be made to remove them. We may utilize the new spirit that is born in us for purging ourselves of these evils. But what I have described to you as emblems of modern civilization are accepted as such by its votaries. The Indian civilization, as described by me, has been so described by its votaries. In no part of the world, and under no civilization, have all men attained perfection. The tendency of the Indian civilization is to elevate the moral being, that of the Western civilization is to propagate immorality. The latter is godless, the former is based on a belief in God. So understanding and so believing, it behoves every lover of India to cling to the old Indian civilization even as a child clings to the mother's breast.

2.14

How Can India Become Free ?

READER : I appreciate your views about civilization. I will have to think over them. I cannot take them in all at once. What, then, holding the views you do, would you suggest for freeing India?

EDITOR : I do not expect my views to be accepted all of a sudden. My duty is to place them before readers like yourself. Time can be trusted to do the rest. We have already examined the conditions for freeing India, but we have done so indirectly; we will now do so directly. It is a world-known maxim that the removal of the cause of a disease results in the removal of the disease itself. Similarly if the cause of India's slavery be removed, India can become free.

READER : If Indian civilization is, as you say, the best of all, how do you account for India's slavery?

EDITOR : This civilization is unquestionably the best, but it is to be observed that all civilizations have been on their trial. That civilization which is permanent outlives it. Because the sons of India were found wanting, its civilization has been placed in jeopardy. But its strength is to be seen in its ability to survive the shock. Moreover, the whole of India is not touched. Those alone who have been affected by Western civilization have become enslaved. We measure the universe by our own miserable foot-rule. When we are slaves, we think that the whole universe is enslaved. Because we are in an abject condition, we think that the whole of India is in that condition. As a matter of fact, it is not so, yet it is as well to impute our slavery to the whole of India. But if we bear in mind the above fact, we can see that if we become free, India is free. And in this thought you have a definition of *Swaraj*. It is *Swaraj* when we learn to rule ourselves. It is, therefore, in the palm of our hands. Do not consider this *Swaraj* to be like a dream. There is no idea of sitting still. The *Swaraj* that I wish to picture is such that, after we have once realized it, we shall endeavour to the end of our life-time to persuade others to do likewise. But such Swaraj has to be experienced, by each one for himself. One drowning man will never save another. Slaves ourselves, it would be a mere pretension to think of freeing others. Now you will have seen that it is not necessary for us to have as our goal the expulsion of the English. If the English become Indianized, we can accommodate them. If they wish to remain in India along with their civilization, there is no room for them. It lies with us to bring about such a state of things.

READER : It is impossible that Englishmen should ever become Indianized.

EDITOR : To say that is equivalent to saying that the English have no humanity in them. And it is really besides the point whether they become so or not. If we keep our own house in order, only those who are fit to live in it will remain. Others will leave of their own accord. Such things occur within the experience of all of us.

READER : But it has not occurred in history.

EDITOR : To believe that what has not occurred in history will not occur at all is to argue disbelief in the dignity of man. At any rate, it behaves us to try what appeals to our reason. All countries are not similarly conditioned. The condition of India is unique. Its strength is immeasurable. We need not, therefore, refer to the history of other countries. I have drawn attention to the fact that, when other civilizations have succumbed, the Indian has survived many a shock.

READER : I cannot follow this. There seems little doubt that we shall have to expel the English by force of arms. So long as they are in the country we cannot rest. One of our poets says that slaves cannot even dream of happiness. We are day by day becoming weakened owing to the presence of the English. Our greatness is gone; our people look like terrified men. The English are in the country like a blight which we must remove by every means.

EDITOR : In your excitement, you have forgotten all we have been considering. We brought the English, and we keep them. Why do you forget that our adoption of their civilization makes their presence in India at all possible? Your hatred against them ought to be transferred to their civilization. But let us assume that we have to drive away the English by fighting, how is that to be done?

READER : In the same way as Italy did it. What was possible for Mazzini and Garibaldi is possible for us. You cannot deny that they were very great men.

2.15

Italy and India

EDITOR : It is well that you have instanced Italy. Mazzini was a great and good man; Garibaldi was a great warrior. Both are adorable; from their lives we can learn much. But the condition of Italy was different from that of India. In the first instance, the difference between Mazzini and Garibaldi is worth noting. Mazzini's ambition was not and has not yet been realized regarding Italy. Mazzini has shown in his writings on the duty of man that every man must learn how to rule himself. This has not happened in Italy. Garibaldi did not hold this view of Mazzini. Garibaldi gave and every Italian took arms. Italy and Austria had the same civilization; they were cousins in this respect. It was a matter of tit for tat. Garibaldi simply wanted Italy to be free from the Austrian yoke. The machinations of Minister Cavour disgrace that portion of the history of Italy. And what has been the result? If you believe that because Italians rule Italy the Italian nation is happy, you are groping in darkness. Mazzini has shown conclusively that Italy did not become free. Victor Emmanuel [II] gave one meaning to the expression; Mazzini gave another. According to Emmanuel, Cavour and even Garibaldi, Italy meant the King of Italy and his henchmen. According to Mazzini, it meant the whole of the Italian people, that is, its agriculturists. Emmanuel was only its servant. The Italy of Mazzini still remains in a state of slavery. At the time of the so-called national war, it was a game of chess between two rival kings with the people of Italy as pawns. The working classes in that land are still unhappy. They, therefore, indulge in assassination, rise in revolt, and rebellion on their part is always expected. What substantial gain did Italy obtain after the withdrawal of the Austrian troops? The gain was only nominal. The reforms for the sake of which the war was supposed to have been undertaken have not yet been granted. The condition of the people in general still remains the same. I am sure you do not wish to reproduce such a condition in India. I believe that you want the millions of India to be happy, not that you want the reins of government in your hands. If that be so, we have to consider only one thing : how can the millions obtain self-rule? You will admit that people under several Indian princes are being ground down. The latter mercilessly crush them. Their tyranny is greater than that of the English, and if you want such tyranny in India, then we shall never agree. My patriotism does not teach me that I am to allow people to be crushed under the heel of Indian princes if only the English retire. If I have the power, I should resist the tyranny of Indian princes just as much as that of the English. By patriotism I mean the welfare of the whole people, and if I could secure it at the hands of the English, I should bow down my head to them. If any Englishman dedicated his life to securing the freedom of India, resisting tyranny and serving the land, I should welcome that Englishman as an Indian.

Again, India can fight like Italy only when she has arms. You have not considered this problem at all. The English are splendidly armed; that does not frighten me, but it is clear that, to pit ourselves against them in arms, thousands of Indians must be armed. If such a thing be possible, how many years will it take? Moreover, to arm India on a large scale is to Europeanize it. Then her condition will be just as pitiable as that of Europe. This means, in short, that India must accept European civilization, and if that is what we want, the best thing is that we have among us those who are so well trained in that civilization. We will then fight for a few rights, will get what we can and so pass our days. But the fact is that the Indian nation will not adopt arms, and it is well that it does not.

READER : You are over-stating the facts. All need not be armed. At first, we shall assassinate a few Englishmen and strike terror; then, a few men who will have been armed will fight openly. We may have to lose a quarter of a million men, more or less, but we shall regain our land. We shall undertake guerilla warfare, and defeat the English.

EDITOR : That is to say, you want to make the holy land of India unholy. Do you not tremble to think of freeing India by assassination? What we need to do is to sacrifice ourselves. It is a cowardly thought, that of killing others. Whom do you suppose to free by assassination? The millions of India do not desire it. Those who are intoxicated by the wretched modern civilization think these things. Those who will rise to power by murder will certainly not make the nation happy. Those who believe that India has gained by Dhingra's act and other similar acts in India make a serious mistake. Dhingra was a patriot, but his love was blind. He gave his body in a wrong way; its ultimate result can only be mischievous.

READER : But you will admit that the English have been frightened by these murders, and that Lord Morley's reforms are due to fear.

EDITOR : The English are both a timid and a brave nation. England is, I believe, easily influenced by the use of gunpowder. It is possible that Lord Morley has granted the reforms through fear, but what is granted under fear can be retained only so long as the fear lasts.

2.16

Brute Force

READER : This is a new doctrine, that what is gained through fear is retained only while the fear lasts. Surely, what is given will not be withdrawn?

EDITOR : Not so. The Proclamation of 1857 was given at the end of a revolt, and for the purpose of preserving peace. When peace was secured and people became simple-minded, its full effect was toned down. If I cease stealing for fear of punishment, I would recommence the operation as soon as the fear is withdrawn from me. This is almost a universal experience. We have assumed that we can get men to do things by force and, therefore, we use force.

READER : Will you not admit that you are arguing against yourself? You know that what the English obtained in their own country they obtained by using brute force. I know you have argued that what they have obtained is useless, but that does not affect my argument. They wanted useless things and they got them. My point is that their desire was fulfilled. What does it matter what means they adopted? Why should we not obtain our goal, which is good, by any means whatsoever, even by using violence? Shall I think of the means when I have to deal with a thief in the house? My duty is to drive him out anyhow. You seem to admit that we have received nothing, and that we shall receive nothing, by petitioning. Why, then, may we not do so by using brute force? And, to retain what we may receive, we shall keep up the fear by using the same force to the extent that it may be necessary. You will not find fault with a continuance of force to prevent a child from thrusting its foot into fire? Somehow or other we have to gain our end.

EDITOR : Your reasoning is plausible. It has deluded many. I have used similar arguments before now. But I think I know better now, and I shall endeavour to undeceive you. Let us first take the argument that we are justified in gaining our end by using brute force because the English gained theirs by using similar means. It is perfectly true that they used brute force and that it is possible for us to do likewise, but by using similar means we can get only the same thing that they got. You will admit that we do not want that. Your belief that there is no connection between the means and the end is a great mistake. Through that mistake even men who have been considered religious have committed grievous crimes. Your reasoning is the same as saying that we can get a rose through planting a noxious weed. If I want to cross the ocean, I can do so only by means of a vessel; if I were to use a cart for that purpose, both the cart and I would soon find the bottom. "As is the God, so is the votary", is a maxim worth considering. Its meaning has been distorted and men have gone astray. The means may be likened to a seed, the end to a tree; and there is just the same inviolable connection between the means and the end as there is between the seed and the tree. I am not likely to obtain the result flowing from the worship of God by laying myself prostrate before Satan. If, therefore, anyone were to say : "I want to worship God; it does not matter that I do so by means of Satan", it would be set down as ignorant folly. We reap exactly as we sow. The English in 1833 obtained greater voting power by violence. Did they by using brute force better appreciate their duty ? They wanted the right of voting, which they obtained by using physical force. But real rights are a result of performance of duty; these rights they have not obtained. We, therefore, have before us in England the force of everybody wanting and insisting on his rights, nobody thinking of his duty. And, where everybody wants rights, who shall give them to whom? I do not wish to imply that they do no duties. They don't perform the duties corresponding to those rights; and as they do not perform that particular duty, namely, acquire fitness, their rights have proved a burden to them. In other words, what they have obtained is an exact result of the means they adopted. They used the means corresponding to the end. If I want to deprive you of your watch, I shall certainly have to fight for it; if I want to buy your watch, I shall have to pay you for it; and if I want a gift I shall have to plead for it and, according to the means I employ, the watch is stolen property, my own property, or a donation. Thus we see three different results from three different means. Will you still say that means do not matter?

Now we shall take the example given by you of the thief to be driven out. I do not agree with you that the thief may be driven out by any means. If it is my father who has come to steal I shall use one kind of means. If it is an acquaintance I shall use another; and in the case of a perfect stranger I shall use a third. If it is a white man, you will perhaps say you will use means different from those you will adopt with an Indian thief. If it is a weakling, the means will be different from those to be adopted for dealing with an equal in physical strength; and if the thief is armed from top to toe, I shall simply remain quiet. Thus we have a variety of means between the father and the armed man. Again, I fancy that I should pretend to be sleeping whether the thief was my father or that strong armed man. The reason for this is that my father would also be armed and I should succumb to the strength possessed by either and allow my things to be stolen. The strength of my father would make me weep with pity; the strength of the armed man would rouse in me anger and we should become enemies. Such is the curious situation. From these examples we may not be able to agree as to the means to be adopted in each case. I myself seem clearly to see what should be done in all these cases, but the remedy may frighten you. I, therefore, hesitate to place it before you. For the time being I will leave you to guess it, and if you cannot, it is clear you will have to adopt different means in each case. You will also have seen that any means will not avail to drive away the thief. You will have to adopt means to fit each case. Hence, it follows that your duty is *not* to drive away the thief by any means you like.

Let us proceed a little further. That well-armed man has stolen your property; you have harboured the thought of his act; you are filled with anger; you argue that you want to punish that rogue, not for your own sake, but for the good of your neighbours; you have collected a number of armed men, you want to take his house by assault; he is duly informed of it, he runs away; he too is incensed. He collects his brother-robbers, and sends you a defiant message that he will commit robbery in broad daylight. You are strong, you do not fear him, you are prepared to receive him. Meanwhile, the robber pesters your neighbours. They complained before you. You reply that you are doing all for their sake, you do not mind that your own goods have been stolen. Your neighbours reply that the robber never pestered them before, and that he commenced his depredations only after you declared hostilities against him. You are between Scylla and Charybdis. You are full of pity for the poor men. What they say is true. What are you to do? You will be disgraced if you now leave the robber alone. You, therefore, tell the poor men : "Never mind. Come, my wealth is yours, I will give you arms, I will teach you how to use them; you should belabour the rogue; don't you leave him alone." And so the battle grows; the robbers increase in numbers; your neighbours have deliberately put themselves to inconvenience. Thus the result of wanting to take revenge upon the robber is that you have disturbed your own peace; you are in perpetual fear of being robbed and assaulted; your courage has given place to cowardice. If you will patiently examine the argument, you will see that I have not overdrawn the picture. This is one of the means. Now let us examine the other. You set this armed robber down as an ignorant brother; you intend to reason with him at a suitable opportunity : you argue that he is, after all, a fellow man; you do not know what prompted him to steal. You, therefore, decide that, when you can, you will destroy the man's motive for stealing. Whilst you are thus reasoning with yourself the man comes again to steal. Instead of being angry with him, you take pity on him. You think that this stealing habit must be a disease with him. Henceforth, you, therefore, keep your doors and windows open, you change your sleeping-place, and you keep your things in a manner most accessible to him. The robber comes again and is confused as all this is new to him; nevertheless, he takes away your things. But his mind is agitated. He inquires about you in the village, he comes to learn about your broad and loving heart, he repents, he begs your pardon, returns you your things, and leaves off the stealing habit. He becomes your servant, and you find for him honourable employment. This is the second method. Thus, you see, different means have brought about totally different results. I do not wish to deduce from this that robbers will act in the above manner or that all will have the same pity and love like you, but I only wish to show that fair means alone can produce fair results, and that, at least in the majority of cases, if not indeed in all, the force of love and pity is infinitely greater than the force of arms. There is harm in the exercise of brute force, never in that of pity.

Now we will take the question of petitioning. It is a fact beyond dispute that a petition, without the backing of force, is useless. However, the late Justice Ranade used to say that petitions served a useful purpose because they were a means of educating people. They give the latter an idea of their condition and warn the rulers. From this point of view, they are not altogether useless. A petition of an equal is a sign of courtesy; a petition from a slave is a symbol of his slavery. A petition backed by force is a petition from an equal and, when he transmits his demand in the form of a petition, it testifies to his nobility. Two kinds of force can back petitions. "We shall hurt you if you do not give this," is one kind of force; it is the force of arms, whose evil results we have already examined. The second kind of force can thus be stated : "If you do not concede our demand, we shall be no longer your petitioners. You can govern us only so long as we remain the governed; we shall no longer have any dealings with you." The force implied in this may be described as love-force, soul-force, or, more popularly but less accurately, passive resistance. This force is indestructible. He who uses it perfectly understands his position. We have an ancient proverb which literally means : "One negative cures thirty-six diseases." The force of arms is powerless when matched against the force of love or the soul.

Now we shall take your last illustration,\that of the child thrusting its foot into fire. It will not avail you. What do you really do to the child ? Supposing that it can exert so much physical force that it renders you powerless and rushes into fire, then you cannot prevent it. There are only two remedies open to you—either you must kill it in order to prevent it from perishing in the flames, or you must give your own life because you do not wish to see it perish before your very eyes. You will not kill it. If your heart is not quite full of pity, it is possible that you will not surrender yourself by preceding the child and going into the fire yourself. You, therefore, helplessly allow it to go into the flames. Thus, at any rate, you are not using physical force. I hope you will not consider that it is still physical force, though of a low order, when you would forcibly prevent the child from rushing towards the fire if you could. That force is of a different order and we have to understand what it is.

Remember that, in thus preventing the child, you are minding entirely its own interest, you are exercising authority for its sole benefit. Your example does not apply to the English. In using brute force against the English you consult entirely your own, that is the national interest. There is no question here either of pity or of love. If you say that the actions of the English, being evil, represent fire, and that they proceed to their actions through ignorance, and that, therefore, they occupy the position of a child and that you want to protect such a child, then you will have to overtake every evil action of that kind by whomsoever committed and, as in the case of the evil child, you will have to sacrifice yourself. If you are capable of such immeasurable pity, I wish you well in its exercise.

2.17

Passive Resistance

READER : Is there any historical evidence as to the success of what you have called soul-force or truth-force? No instance seems to have happened of any nation having risen through soul-force. I still think that the evil-doers will not cease doing evil without physical punishment.

EDITOR : The poet Tulsidas has said : "Of religion, pity, or love, is the root, as egotism of the body. Therefore, we should not abandon pity so long as we are alive." This appears to me to be a scientific truth. I believe in it as much as I believe in two and two being four. The force of love is the same as the force of the soul or truth. We have evidence of its working at every step. The universe would disappear without the existence of that force. But you ask for historical evidence. It is, therefore, necessary to know what history means. The Gujarati equivalent means : "It so happened." If that is the meaning of history, it is possible to give copious evidence. But, if it means the doings of kings and emperors, there can be no evidence of soul-force or passive resistance in such history. You cannot expect silver ore in a tin mine. History, as we know it, is a record of the wars of the world, and so there is a proverb among Englishmen that a nation which has no history, that is, no wars, is a happy nation. How kings played, how they became enemies of one another, how they murdered one another, is found accurately recorded in history, and if this were all that had happened in the world, it would have been ended long ago. If the story of the universe had commenced with wars, not a man would have been found alive today. Those people who have been warred against have disappeared as, for instance, the natives of

Australia of whom hardly a man was left alive by the intruders. Mark, please, that these natives did not use soul-force in self-defence, and it does not require much foresight to know that the Australians will share the same fate as their victims. "Those that take the sword shall perish by the sword." With us the proverb is that professional swimmers will find a watery grave.

The fact that there are so many men still alive in the world shows that it is based not on the force of arms but on the force of truth or love. Therefore, the greatest and most unimpeachable evidence of the success of this force is to be found in the fact that, in spite of the wars of the world, it still lives on. Thousands, indeed tens of thousands, depend for their existence on a very active working of this force. Little quarrels of millions of families in their daily lives disappear before the exercise of this force. Hundreds of nations live in peace. History does not and cannot take note of this fact. History is really a record of every interruption of the even working of the force of love or of the soul. Two brothers quarrel; one of them repents and re-awakens the love that was lying dormant in him; the two again begin to live in peace; nobody takes note of this. But if the two brothers, through the intervention of solicitors or some other reason take up arms or go to law—which is another form of the exhibition of brute force,—their doings would be immediately noticed in the Press, they would be the talk of their neighbours and would probably go down to history. And what is true of families and communities is true of nations. There is no reason to believe that there is one law for families and another for nations. History, then, is a record of an interruption of the course of nature. Soul-force, being natural, is not noted in history.

READER : According to what you say, it is plain that instances of this kind of passive resistance are not to be found in history. It is necessary to understand this passive resistance more fully. It will be better, therefore, if you enlarge upon it.

EDITOR : Passive resistance is a method of securing rights by personal suffering; it is the reverse of resistance by arms. When I refuse to do a thing that is repugnant to my conscience, I use soul-force. For instance, the Government of the day has passed a law which is applicable to me. I do not like it. If by using violence I force the Government to repeal the law, I am employing what may be termed bodyforce. If I do not obey the law and accept the penalty for its breach, I use soul-force. It involves sacrifice of self. Everybody admits that sacrifice of self is infinitely superior to sacrifice of others. Moreover, if this kind of force is used in a cause that is unjust, only the person using it suffers. He does not make others suffer for his mistakes. Men have before now done many things which were subsequently found to have been wrong. No man can claim that he is absolutely in the right or that a particular thing is wrong because he thinks so, but it is wrong for him so long as that is his deliberate judgment. It is, therefore, meet that he should not do that which he knows to be wrong, and suffer the consequence whatever it may be. This is the key to the use of soul-force.

READER : You would then disregard laws—this is rank disloyalty. We have always been considered a law-abiding nation. You seem to be going even beyond the extremists. They say that we must obey the laws that have been passed, but that if the laws be bad, we must drive out the law-givers even by force.

EDITOR : Whether I go beyond them or whether I do not is a matter of no consequence to either of us. We simply want to find out what is right and to act accordingly. The real meaning of the statement that we are a law-abiding nation is that we are passive resisters. When we do not like certain laws, we do not break the heads of law-givers but we suffer and do not submit to the laws. That we should obey laws whether good or bad is a new-fangled notion. There was no such thing in former days. The people disregarded those laws they did not like and suffered the penalties for their breach. It is contrary to our manhood if we obey laws repugnant to our conscience. Such teaching is opposed to religion and means slavery. If the Government were to ask us to go about without any clothing should we do so? If I were a passive resister, I would say to them that I would have nothing to do with their law. But we have so forgotten ourselves and become so compliant that we do not mind any degrading law.

A man who has realized his manhood, who fears only God, will fear no one else. Man-made laws are not necessarily binding on him. Even the Government does not expect any such thing from us. They do not say : "You must do such and such a thing," but they say : "If you do not do it, we will punish you." We are sunk so low that we fancy that it is our duty and our religion to do what the law lays down. If man will only realize that it is unmanly to obey laws that are unjust, no man's tyranny will enslave him. This is the key to self-rule or home rule.

It is a superstition and ungodly thing to believe that an act of a majority binds a minority. Many examples can be given in which acts of majorities will be found to have been wrong and those of minorities to have been right. All reforms owe their origin to the initiation of minorities in opposition to majorities. If among a band of robbers a knowledge of robbing is obligatory, is a pious man to accept the obligation? So long as the superstition that men should obey unjust laws exists, so long will their slavery exist. And a passive resister alone can remove such a superstition.

To use brute-force, to use gunpowder, is contrary to passive resistance, for it means that we want our opponent to do by force that which we desire but he does not. And if such a use of force is justifiable, surely he is entitled to do likewise by us. And so we should never come to an agreement. We may simply fancy, like the blind horse moving in a circle round a mill, that we are making progress. Those who believe that they are not bound to obey laws which are repugnant to their conscience have only the remedy of passive resistance open to them. Any other must lead to disaster.

READER : From what you say I deduce that passive resistance is a splendid weapon of the weak, but that when they are strong they may take up arms.

EDITOR : This is gross ignorance. Passive resistance, that is, soul force, is matchless. It is superior to the force of arms. How, then, can it be considered only a weapon of the weak? In physical-force men are strangers to the courage that is requisite in a passive resister. Do you believe that a coward can ever disobey a law that he dislikes? Extremists are considered to be advocates of brute force. Why do they, then, talk about obeying laws? I do not blame them. They can say nothing else. When they succeed in driving out the English and they themselves become governors, they will want you and me to obey their laws. And that is a fitting thing for their constitution. But a passive resister will say he will not obey a law that is against his conscience, even though he may be blown to pieces at the mouth of a cannon. What do you think? Wherein is courage required—in blowing others to pieces from behind a cannon, or with a smiling face to approach a cannon and be blown to pieces? Who is the true warrior— he who keeps death always as a bosom-friend, or he who controls the death of others? Believe me that a man devoid of courage and manhood can never be a passive resister.

This, however, I will admit : that even a man weak in body is capable of offering this resistance. One man can offer it just as well as millions. Both men and women can indulge in it. It does not require the training of an army; it needs no Jiu-Jitsu. Control over the mind is alone necessary, and when that is attained, man is free like the king of the forest and his very glance withers the enemy.

Passive resistance is an all-sided sword, it can be used anyhow; it blesses him who uses it and him against whom it is used. Without drawing a drop of blood it produces far-reaching results. It never rusts and cannot be stolen. Competition between passive resisters does not exhaust. The sword of passive resistance does not require a scabbard. It is strange indeed that you should consider such a weapon to be a weapon merely of the weak.

READER : You have said that passive resistance is a speciality of India. Have cannons never been used in India?

EDITOR : Evidently, in your opinion, India means its few princes. To me it means its teeming millions on whom depends the existence of its princes and our own.

Kings will always use their kingly weapons. To use force is bred in them. They want to command, but those who have to obey commands do not want guns : and these are in a majority throughout the world. They have to learn either body-force or soul-force. Where they learn the former, both the rulers and the ruled become like so many madmen; but where they learn soul-force, the commands of the rulers do not go beyond the point of their swords, for true men disregard unjust commands. Peasants have never been subdued by the sword, and never will be. They do not know the use of the sword, and they are not frightened by the use of it by others. That nation is great which rests its head upon death as its pillow. Those who defy death are free from all fear. For those who are labouring under the delusive charms of brute-force, this picture is not overdrawn. The fact is that, in India, the nation at large has generally used passive resistance in all departments of life. We cease to co-operate with our rulers when they displease us. This is passive resistance.

I remember an instance when, in a small principality, the villagers were offended by some command issued by the prince. The former immediately began vacating the village. The prince became nervous, apologized to his subjects and withdrew his command. Many such instances can be found in India. Real Home Rule is possible only where passive resistance is the guiding force of the people. Any other rule is foreign rule.

READER : Then you will say that it is not at all necessary for us to train the body?

EDITOR : I will certainly not say any such thing. It is difficult to become a passive resister unless the body is trained. As a rule, the mind, residing in a body that has become weakened by pampering, is also weak, and where there is no strength of mind there can be no strength of soul. We shall have to improve our physique by getting rid of infant marriages and luxurious living. If I were to ask a man with a shattered body to face a cannon's mouth, I should make a laughing stock of myself.

READER : From what you say, then, it would appear that it is not a small thing to become a passive resister, and, if that is so, I should like you to explain how a man may become one.

EDITOR : To become a passive resister is easy enough but it is also equally difficult. I have known a lad of fourteen years become a passive resister; I have known also sick people do likewise; and I have also known physically strong and otherwise happy people unable to take up passive resistance. After a great deal of experience it seems to me that those who want to become passive resisters for the service of the country have to observe perfect chastity, adopt poverty, follow truth, and cultivate fearlessness.

Chastity is one of the greatest disciplines without which the mind cannot attain requisite firmness. A man who is unchaste loses stamina, becomes emasculated and cowardly. He whose mind is given over to animal passions is not capable of any great effort. This can be proved by innumerable instances. What, then, is a married person to do is the question that arises naturally; and yet it need not. When a husband and wife gratify the passions, it is no less an animal indulgence on that account. Such an indulgence, except for perpetuating the race, is strictly prohibited. But a passive resister has to avoid even that very limited indulgence because he can have no desire for progeny. A married man, therefore, can observe perfect chastity. This subject is not capable of being treated at greater length. Several questions arise : How is one to carry one's wife with one, what are her rights, and other similar questions. Yet those who wish to take part in a great work are bound to solve these puzzles.

Just as there is necessity for chastity, so is there for poverty. Pecuniary ambition and passive resistance cannot well go together. Those who have money are not expected to throw it away, but they *are* expected to be indifferent about it. They must be prepared to lose every penny rather than give up passive resistance.

Passive resistance has been described in the course of our discussion as truth-force. Truth, therefore, has necessarily to be followed and that at any cost. In this connection, academic questions such as whether a man may not lie in order to save a life, etc., arise, but these questions occur only to those who wish to justify lying. Those who want to follow truth every time are not placed in such a quandary; and if they are, they are still saved from a false position.

Passive resistance cannot proceed a step without fearlessness. Those alone can follow the path of passive resistance who are free from fear, whether as to their possessions, false honour, their relatives, the government, bodily injuries or death.

These observances are not to be abandoned in the belief that they are difficult. Nature has implanted in the human breast ability to cope with any difficulty or suffering that may come to man unprovoked. These qualities are worth having, even for those who do not wish to serve the country. Let there be no mistake, as those who want to train themselves in the use of arms are also obliged to have these qualities more or less. Everybody does not become a warrior for the wish. A would-be warrior will have to observe chastity and to be satisfied with poverty as his lot. A warrior without fearlessness cannot be conceived of. It may be thought that he would not need to be exactly truthful, but that quality follows real fearlessness. When a man abandons truth, he does so owing to fear in some shape or form. The above four attributes, then, need not frighten anyone. It may be as well here to note that a physical-force man has to have many other useless qualities which a passive resister never needs. And you will find that whatever extra effort a swordsman needs is due to lack of fearlessness. If he is an embodiment of the latter, the sword will drop from his hand that very moment. He does not need its support. One who is free from hatred requires no sword. A man with a stick suddenly came face to face with a lion and instinctively raised his weapon in self-defence. The man saw that he had only prated about fearlessness when there was none in him. That moment he dropped the stick and found himself free from all fear.

2.18

Education

READER : In the whole of our discussion, you have not demonstrated the necessity for education; we always complain of its absence among us. We notice a movement for compulsory education in our country. The Maharaja Gaekwar has introduced it in his territories. Every eye is directed towards them. We bless the Maharaja for it. Is all this effort then of no use?

EDITOR : If we consider our civilization to be the highest, I have regretfully to say that much of the effort you have described is of no use. The motive of the Maharaja and other great leaders who have been working in this direction is perfectly pure. They, therefore, undoubtedly deserve great praise. But we cannot conceal from ourselves the result that is likely to flow from their effort. What is the meaning of education? It simply means a knowledge of letters. It is merely an instrument, and an instrument may be well used or abused. The same instrument that may be used to cure a patient may be used to take his life, and so may a knowledge of letters. We daily observe that many men abuse it and very few make good use of it; and if this is a correct statement, we have proved that more harm has been done by it than good. The ordinary meaning of education is a knowledge of letters. To teach boys reading, writing and arithmetic is called primary education. A peasant earns his bread honestly. He has ordinary knowledge of the world. He knows fairly well how he should behave towards his parents, his wife, his children and his fellow-villagers. He understands and observes the rules of morality. But he cannot write his own name. What do you propose to do by giving him a knowledge of letters? Will you add an inch to his happiness? Do you wish to make him discontented with his cottage or his lot? And even if you want to do that, he will not need such an education. Carried away by the flood of western thought we came to the conclusion, without weighing pros and cons, that we should give this kind of education to the people.

Now let us take higher education. I have learned Geography, Astronomy, Algebra, Geometry, etc. What of that? In what way have I benefited myself or those around me? Why have I learned these things? Professor Huxley has thus defined education :

> That man I think has had a liberal education who has been so trained in youth that his body is the ready servant of his will and does with ease and pleasure all the work that as a mechanism it is capable of; whose intellect is a clear, cold, logic[al] engine with all its parts of equal strength and in smooth working order . . . whose mind is stored with a knowledge of the fundamental truths of nature . . . whose passions are trained to come to heel by a vigorous will, the servant of a tender conscience . . . who has learnt to hate all vileness and to respect others as himself. Such a one and no other, I conceive, has had a liberal education, for he is in harmony with nature. He will make the best of her and she of him.

If this is true education, I must emphatically say that the sciences I have enumerated above I have never been able to use for controlling my senses. Therefore, whether you take elementary education or higher education, it is not required for the main thing. It does not make men of us. It does not enable us to do our duty.

READER : If that is so, I shall have to ask you another question. What enables you to tell all these things to me? If you had not received higher education, how would you have been able to explain to me the things that you have?

EDITOR : You have spoken well. But my answer is simple : I do not for one moment believe that my life would have been wasted, had I not received higher or lower education. Nor do I consider that I necessarily serve because I speak. But I do desire to serve and in endeavouring to fulfil that desire, I make use of the education I have received. And, if I am making good use of it, even then it is not for the millions, but I can use it only for such as you, and this supports my contention. Both you and I have come under the bane of what is mainly false education. I claim to have become free from its ill effect, and I am trying to give you the benefit of my experience and in doing so, I am demonstrating the rottenness of this education.

Moreover, I have not run down a knowledge of letters in all circumstances. All I have now shown is that we must not make of it a fetish. It is not our *Kamadhuk*. In its place it can be of use and it has its place when we have brought our senses under subjection and put our ethics on a firm foundation. And then, if we feel inclined to receive that education, we may make good use of it. As an ornament it is likely to sit well on us. It now follows that it is not necessary to make this education compulsory. Our ancient school system is enough. Character building has the first place in it and that is primary education. A building erected on that foundation will last.

READER : Do I then understand that you do not consider English education necessary for obtaining Home Rule?

EDITOR : My answer is yes and no. To give millions a knowledge of English is to enslave them. The foundation that Macaulay laid of education has enslaved us. I do not suggest that he had any such intention, but that has been the result. Is it not a sad commentary that we should have to speak of Home Rule in a foreign tongue?

And it is worthy of note that the systems which the Europeans have discarded systems in vogue among us. Their learned men continually make changes. We ignorantly adhere to their cast-off systems. They are trying each division to improve its own status. Wales is a small portion of England. Great efforts are being made to revive a knowledge of Welsh among Welshmen. The English Chancellor, Mr. Lloyd George, is taking a leading part in the movement to make Welsh children speak Welsh. And what is our condition? We write to each in faulty English, and from this even our M.A's. are not free; our best thoughts are expressed in English; the proceedings of our Congress are conducted in English; our best newspapers are printed in English. If this state of things continues for a long time, posterity will—it is my firm opinion—condemn and curse us.

It is worth noting that, by receiving English education, we have enslaved the nation. Hypocrisy, tyranny, etc., have increased; English knowing Indians have not hesitated to cheat and strike terror into the people. Now, if we are doing anything for the people at all, we are paying only a portion of the debt due to them.

Is it not a painful thing that, if I want to go to a court of justice, I must employ the English language as a medium, that when I become a barrister, I may not speak my mother tongue and that someone else should have to translate to me from my own language? Is not this absolutely absurd? Is it not a sign of slavery? Am I to blame the English for it or myself? It is we, the English-knowing Indians, that have enslaved India. The curse of the nation will rest not upon the English but upon us.

I have told you that my answer to your last question is both yes and no. I have explained to you why it is yes. I shall now explain why it is no.

We are so much beset by the disease of civilization, that we cannot altogether do without English education. Those who have already received it may make good use of it wherever necessary. In our dealings with the English people, in our dealings with our own people, when we can only correspond with them through that language, and for the purpose of knowing how disgusted they (the English) have themselves become with their civilization, we may use or learn English, as the case may be. Those who have studied English will have to teach morality to their progeny through their mother-tongue and to teach them another Indian language; but when they have grown up, they may learn English, the ultimate aim being that we should not need it. The object of making money thereby should be eschewed. Even in learning English to such a limited extent we shall have to consider what we should learn through it and what we should not. It will be necessary to know what sciences we should learn. A little thought should show you that immediately we cease to care for English degrees, the rulers will prick up their ears.

READER : Then what education shall we give ?

EDITOR : This has been somewhat considered above, but we will consider it a little more. I think that we have to improve all our languages. What subjects we should learn through them need not be elaborated here. Those English books which are valuable, we should translate into the various Indian languages. We should abandon the pretension of learning many sciences. Religious, that is ethical, education will occupy the first place. Every cultured Indian will know in addition to his own provincial language, if a Hindu, Sanskrit; if a Mahomedan, Arabic; if a Parsee, Persian; and all, Hindi. Some Hindus should know Arabic and Persian; some Mahomedans and Parsees, Sanskrit. Several Northerners and Westerners should learn Tamil. A universal language for India should be Hindi, with the option of writing it in Persian or Nagari characters. In order that the Hindus and the Mahomedans may have closer relations, it is necessary to know both the characters. And, if we can do this, we can drive the English language out of the field in a short time. All this is necessary for us, slaves. Through our slavery the nation has been enslaved, and it will be free with our freedom.

READER : The question of religious education is very difficult.

EDITOR : Yet we cannot do without it. India will never be godless. Rank atheism cannot flourish in this land. The task is indeed difficult. My head begins to turn as I think of religious education. Our religious teachers are hypocritical and selfish; they will have to be approached. The Mullas, the Dasturs and the Brahmins hold the key in their hands, but if they will not have the good sense, the energy that we have derived from English education will have to be devoted to religious education. This is not very difficult. Only the fringe of the ocean has been polluted and it is those who are within the fringe who alone need cleansing. We who come under this category can even cleanse ourselves because my remarks do not apply to the millions. In order to restore India to its pristine condition, we have to return to it. In our own civilization there will naturally be progress, retrogression, reforms, and reactions; but one effort is required, and that is to drive out Western civilization. All else will follow.

2.19

Machinery

READER : When you speak of driving out Western civilization, I suppose you will also say that we want no machinery.

EDITOR : By raising this question you have opened the wound I have received. When I read Mr. Dutt's *Economic History of India,* I wept; and as I think of it again my heart sickens. It is machinery that has impoverished India. It is difficult to measure the harm that Manchester has done to us. It is due to Manchester that Indian handicraft has all but disappeared.

But I make a mistake. How can Manchester be blamed ? We wore Manchester cloth and this is why Manchester wove it. I was delighted when I read about the bravery of Bengal. There were no cloth-mills in that Presidency. They were, therefore, able to restore the original hand-weaving occupation. It is true Bengal encourages the mill-industry of Bombay. If Bengal had proclaimed a boycott of *all* machine-made goods, it would have been much better.

Machinery has begun to desolate Europe. Ruination is now knocking at the English gates. Machinery is the chief symbol of modern civilization; it represents a great sin.

The workers in the mills of Bombay have become slaves. The condition of the women working in the mills is shocking. When there were no mills, these women were not starving. If the machinery craze grows in our country, it will become an unhappy land. It may be considered a heresy, but I am bound to say that it were better for us to send money to Manchester and to use flimsy Manchester cloth than to multiply mills in

India. By using Manchester cloth we only waste our money; but by reproducing Manchester in India, we shall keep our money at the price of our blood, because our very moral being will be sapped, and I call in support of my statement the very mill-hands as witnesses. And those who have amassed wealth out of factories are not likely to be better than other rich men. It would be folly to assume that an Indian Rockefeller would be better than the American Rockefeller. Impoverished India can become free, but it will be hard for any India made rich through immorality to regain its freedom. I fear we shall have to admit that moneyed men support British rule; their interest is bound up with its stability. Money renders a man helpless. The other thing which is equally harmful is sexual vice. Both are poison. A snakebite is a lesser poison than these two, because the former merely destroys the body but the latter destroy body, mind and soul. We need not, therefore, be pleased with the prospect of the growth of the mill-industry.

READER : Are the mills, then, to be closed down?

EDITOR : That is difficult. It is no easy task to do away with a thing that is established. We, therefore, say that the non-beginning of a thing is supreme wisdom. We cannot condemn millowners; we can but pity them. It would be too much to expect them to give up their mills, but we may implore them not to increase them. If they would be good they would gradually contract their business. They can establish in thousands of households the ancient and sacred handlooms and they can buy out the cloth that may be thus woven. Whether the millowners do this or not, people can cease to use machine-made goods.

READER : You have so far spoken about machine-made cloth, but there are innumerable machine-made things. We have either to import them or to introduce machinery into our country.

EDITOR : Indeed, our gods even are made in Germany. What need, then, to speak of matches, pins and glassware ? My answer can be only one. What did India do before these articles were introduced? Precisely the same should be done today. As long as we cannot make pins without machinery, so long will we do without them. The tinsel splendour of glassware we will have nothing to do with, and we will make wicks, as of old, with home-grown cotton and use hand-made earthen saucers or lamps. So doing, we shall save our eyes and money and support *Swadeshi* and so shall we attain Home Rule.

It is not to be conceived that all men will do all these things at one time or that some men will give up all machine-made things at once. But, if the thought is sound, we shall always find out what we can give up and gradually cease to use it. What a few may do, others will copy; and the movement will grow like the coconut of the mathematical problem. What the leaders do, the populace will gladly do in turn. The matter is neither complicated nor difficult. You and I need not wait until we can carry others with us. Those will be the losers who will not do it, and those who will not do it, although they appreciate the truth, will deserve to be called cowards.

READER : What, then, of the tram-cars and electricity?

EDITOR : This question is now too late. It signifies nothing. If we are to do without the railways we shall have to do without the tram-cars. Machinery is like a snake-hole which may contain from one to a hundred snakes. Where there is machinery there are large cities; and where there are large cities, there are tram-cars and railways; and there only does one see electric light. English villages do not boast of any of these things. Honest physicians will tell you that where means of artificial locomotion have increased, the health of the people has suffered. I remember that when in a European town there was a scarcity of money, the receipts of the tramway company, of the lawyers and of the doctors went down and people were less unhealthy. I cannot recall a single good point in connection with machinery. Books can be written to demonstrate its evils.

READER : Is it a good point or a bad one that all you are saying will be printed through machinery?

EDITOR : This is one of those instances which demonstrate that sometimes poison is used to kill poison. This, then, will not be a good point regarding machinery. As it expires, the machinery, as it were, says to us : "Beware and avoid me. You will derive no benefits from me and the benefit that may accrue from printing will avail only those who are infected with the machinery-craze." Do not, therefore, forget the main thing. It is necessary to realize that machinery is bad. We shall then be able gradually to do away with it. Nature has not provided any way whereby we may reach a desired goal all of a sudden. If, instead of welcoming machinery as a boon, we should look upon it as an evil, it would ultimately go.

2.20

Conclusion

READER : From your views I gather that you would form a third party. You are neither an extremist nor a moderate.

EDITOR : That is a mistake. I do not think of a third party at all. We do not all think alike. We cannot say that all the moderates hold identical views. And how can those who want only to serve have a party ? I would serve both the moderates and the extremists. Where I differ from them, I would respectfully place my position before them and continue my service.

READER : What, then, would you say to both the parties?

EDITOR : I would say to the extremists : "I know that you want Home Rule for India; it is not to be had for your asking. Everyone will have to take it for himself. What others get for me is not Home Rule but foreign rule; therefore, it would not be proper for you to say that you have obtained Home Rule if you have merely expelled the English. I have already described the true nature of Home Rule. This you would never obtain by force of arms. Brute force is not natural to Indian soil. You will have, therefore, to rely wholly on soul-force. You must not consider that violence is necessary at any stage for reaching our goal".

I would say to the moderates : "Mere petitioning is derogatory; we thereby confess inferiority. To say that British rule is indispensable is almost a denial of the Godhead. We cannot say that anybody or anything is indispensable except God. Moreover, commonsense should tell us that to state that, for the time being, the presence of the English in India is a necessity, is to make them conceited. "If the English vacated

India, bag and baggage, it must not be supposed that she would be widowed. It is possible that those who are forced to observe peace under their pressure would fight after their withdrawal. There can be no advantage in suppressing an eruption; it must have its vent. If, therefore, before we can remain at peace, we must fight amongst ourselves, it is better that we do so. There is no occasion for a third party to protect the weak. It is this so-called protection which has unnerved us. Such protection can only make the weak weaker. Unless we realize this, we cannot have Home Rule. I would paraphrase the thought of an English divine and say that anarchy under Home Rule were better than orderly foreign rule. Only, the meaning that the learned divine attached to Home Rule is different from Indian Home Rule according to my conception. We have to learn, and to teach others, that we do not want the tyranny of either English rule or Indian rule."

If this idea were carried out, both the extremists and the moderates could join hands. There is no occasion to fear or distrust one another.

READER : What, then, would you say to the English?

EDITOR : To them I would respectfully say : "I admit you are my rulers. It is not necessary to debate the question whether you hold India by the sword or by my consent. I have no objection to your remaining in my country, but although you are the rulers, you will have to remain as servants of the people. It is not we who have to do as you wish, but it is you who have to do as we wish. You may keep the riches that you have drained away from this land, but you may not drain riches henceforth. Your function will be, if you so wish, to police India; you must abandon the idea of deriving any commercial benefit from us. We hold the civilization that you support to be the reverse of civilization. We consider our civilization to be far superior to yours. If you realize this truth, it will be to your advantage and, if you do not, according to your own proverb, you should only live in our country in the same manner as we do. You must not do anything that is contrary to our religions. It is your duty as rulers that for the sake of the Hindus you should eschew beef, and for the sake of Mahomedans you should avoid bacon and ham. We have hitherto said nothing because we have been cowed down, but you need not consider that you have not hurt our feelings by your conduct. We are not expressing our sentiments either through base selfishness or fear, but because it is our duty now to speak out boldly. We consider your schools and law courts to be useless. We want our own ancient schools and courts to be restored. The common language of India is not English but Hindi. You should, therefore, learn it. We can hold communication with you only in our national language.

"We cannot tolerate the idea of your spending money on railways and the military. We see no occasion for either. You may fear Russia; we do not. When she comes we shall look after her. If you are with us, we may then receive her jointly. We do not need any European cloth. We shall manage with articles produced and manufactured at home. You may not keep one eye on Manchester and the other on India. We can work together only if our interests are identical.

"This has not been said to you in arrogance. You have great military resources. Your naval power is matchless. If we wanted to fight with you on your own ground, we should be unable to do so, but if the above submissions be not acceptable to you, we cease to play the part of the ruled. You may, if you like, cut us to pieces. You may shatter us at the cannon's mouth. If you act contrary to our will, we shall not help you; and without our help, we know that you cannot move one step forward.

"It is likely that you will laugh at all this in the intoxication of your power. We may not be able to disillusion you at once; but if there be any manliness in us, you will see shortly that your intoxication is suicidal and that your laugh at our expense is an aberration of intellect. We believe that at heart you belong to a religious nation. We are living in a land which is the source of religions. How we came together need not be considered, but we can make mutual good use of our relations.

"You, English, who have come to India are not good specimens of the English nation, nor can we, almost half-Anglicized Indians, be considered good specimens of the real

Indian nation. If the English nation were to know all you have done, it would oppose many of your actions. The mass of the Indians have had few dealings with you. If you will abandon your so-called civilization and search into your own scriptures, you will find that our demands are just. Only on condition of our demands being fully satisfied may you remain in India; and if you remain under those conditions, we shall learn several things from you and you will learn many from us. So doing we shall benefit each other and the world. But that will happen only when the root of our relationship is sunk in a religious soil."

READER : What will you say to the nation ?

EDITOR : Who is the nation ?

READER : For our purposes it is the nation that you and I have been thinking of, that is, those of us who are affected by European civilization, and who are eager to have Home Rule.

EDITOR : To these I would say : "It is only those Indians who are imbued with real love who will be able to speak to the English in the above strain without being frightened, and only those can be said to be so imbued who conscientiously believe that Indian civilization is the best and that the European is a nine days' wonder. Such ephemeral civilizations have often come and gone and will continue to do so. Those only can be considered to be so imbued who, having experienced the force of the soul within themselves, will not cower before brute-force, and will not, on any account, desire to use brute-force. Those only can be considered to have been so imbued who are intensely dissatisfied with the present pitiable condition, having already drunk the cup of poison.

"If there be only one such Indian, he will speak as above to the English and the English will have to listen to him.

"These are not demands, but they show our mental state. We shall get nothing by asking; we shall have to take what we want, and we need the requisite strength for the effort and that strength will be available to him only who will act thus :

1. He will only on rare occasions make use of the English language.

2. If a lawyer, he will give up his profession, and take up a handloom.
3. If a lawyer, he will devote his knowledge to enlightening both his people and the English.
4. If a lawyer, he will not meddle with the quarrels between parties but will give up the courts, and from his experience induce the people to do likewise.
5. If a lawyer, he will refuse to be a judge, as he will give up his profession.
6. If a doctor, he will give up medicine, and understand that rather than mending bodies, he should mend souls.
7. If a doctor, he will understand that no matter to what religion he belongs, it is better that bodies remain diseased rather than that they are cured through the instrumentality of the diabolical vivisection that is practised in European schools of medicine.
8. Although a doctor, he will take up a handloom, and if any patients come to him, will tell them the cause of their diseases, and will advise them to remove the cause rather than pamper them by giving useless drugs; he will understand that if by not taking drugs, perchance the patient dies, the world will not come to grief and that he will have been really merciful to him.
9. Although a wealthy man, yet regardless of his wealth, he will speak out his mind and fear no one.
10. If a wealthy man, he will devote his money to establishing handlooms, and encourage others to use hand-made goods by wearing them himself.
11. Like every other Indian, he will know that this is a time for repentance, expiation and mourning.
12. Like every other Indian, he will know that to blame the English is useless, that they came because of us, and remain also for the same reason, and that they will either go or change their nature only when we reform ourselves.
13. Like others, he will understand that at a time of mourning, there can be no indulgence, and that, whilst we are in a fallen state, to be in gaol or in banishment is much the best.

14. Like others, he will know that it is superstition to imagine it necessary that we should guard against being imprisoned in order that we may deal with the people.
15. Like others, he will know that action is much better than speech; that it is our duty to say exactly what we think and face the consequences and that it will be only then that we shall be able to impress anybody with our speech.
16. Like others, he will understand that we shall become free only through suffering.
17. Like others, he will understand that deportation for life to the Andamans is not enough expiation for the sin of encouraging European civilization.
18. Like others, he will know that no nation has risen without suffering; that, even in physical warfare, the true test is suffering and not the killing of others, much more so in the warfare of passive resistance.
19. Like others, he will know that it is an idle excuse to say that we shall do a thing when the others also do it; that we should do what we know to be right, and that others will do it when they see the way; that when I fancy a particular delicacy, I do not wait till others taste it; that to make a national effort and to suffer are in the nature of delicacies; and that to suffer under pressure is no suffering".

READER : This is a large order. When will all carry it out?

EDITOR : You make a mistake, You and I have nothing to do with the others. Let each do his duty. If I do my duty, that is, serve myself, I shall be able to serve others. Before I leave you, I will take the liberty of repeating :

1. Real home-rule is self-rule or self-control.
2. The way to it is passive resistance : that is soul-force or love-force.
3. In order to exert this force, *Swadeshi* in every sense is necessary.

4. What we want to do should be done, not because we object to the English or because we want to retaliate but because it is our duty to do so. Thus, supposing that the English remove the salt-tax, restore our money, give the highest posts to Indians, withdraw the English troops, we shall certainly not use their machine-made goods, nor use the English language, nor many of their industries. It is worth noting that these things are, in their nature, harmful; hence, we do not want them. I bear no enmity towards the English but I do towards their civilization.

In my opinion, we have used the term *"Swaraj"* without understanding its real significance. I have endeavoured to explain it as I understand it, and my conscience testifies that my life henceforth is dedicated to its attainment.

2.21

Appendices

SOME AUTHORITIES AND TESTIMONIES BY EMINENT MEN

I. Some Authorities

The following books are recommended for perusal to follow up the study of the foregoing :

The Kingdom of God Is within You (Tolstoy)
What is Art? (Tolstoy)
The Slavery of Our Times (Tolstoy)
The First Step (Tolstoy)
How Shall We Escape? (Tolstoy)
Letter to a Hindoo (Tolstoy)
The White Slaves of England (Sherard)
Civilization—Its Cause and Cure (Carpenter)
The Fallacy of Speed (Taylor)
A New Crusade (Blount)
On the Duty of Civil Disobedience (Thoreau)
Life without Principle (Thoreau)
Unto This Last (Ruskin)
A Joy for Ever (Ruskin)
Duties of Man (Mazzini)
Defence and Death of Socrates (from Plato)
Paradoxes of Civilization (Max Nordau)
Poverty and Un-British Rule in India (Naoroji)
Economic History of India (Dutt)
Village Communities (Maine)

II. Testimonies by Eminent Men

The following extracts from Mr. Alfred Webb's valuable collection show that the ancient Indian civilization has little to learn from the modern :

J. Seymour Keay, M. P.

Banker in India and India Agent (Writing in 1883)

It cannot be too well understood that our position in India has never been in any degree that of civilians bringing civilization to savage races. When we landed in India we found there a hoary civilization, which, during the progress of thousands of years, had fitted into the character and adjusted itself to the wants of highly intellectual races. The civilization was not perfunctory, but universal and all-pervading—furnishing the country not only with political systems, but with social and domestic institutions of the most ramified description. The beneficent nature of these institutions as a whole may be judged from their effects on the character of the Hindu race. Perhaps there are no other people in the world who show so much in their character the advantageous effects of their own civilization. They are shrewd in business, acute in reasoning, thrifty, religious, sober, charitable, obedient to parents, reverential to old age, amiable, law abiding, compassionate towards the helpless and patient under suffering.

Victor Cousin (1792-1867)

Founder of Systematic Eclecticism in Philosophy

On the other hand when we read with attention the poetical and philosophical movements of the East, above all, those of India, which are beginning to spread in Europe, we discover there so many truths, and truths, so profound, and which make such a contrast with the meanness of the results at which the European genius has sometimes stopped, that we are constrained to bend the knee before that of the East, and do see in this cradle of the human race the native land of the highest philosophy.

Friedrich Max Muller

If I were to ask myself from what literature we here in Europe, we who have been nurtured almost exclusively on the thoughts of Greeks and Romans, and of one Semitic race, the Jewish, may draw that corrective which is most wanted in order to make our inner life more perfect, more comprehensive, more universal, in fact more truly human, a life, not for this life only, but a transfigured and eternal life—again I should point to India.

Frederick von Schlegel

It cannot be denied that the early Indians possessed a knowledge of the true God; all their writings are replete with sentiments and expressions, noble, clear, and severely grand, as deeply conceived and reverently expressed as in any human language in which men have spoken of their God. . . . Among nations possessing indigenous philosophy and metaphysics together with an innate relish for these pursuits, such as at present characterizes Germany, and, in olden times was the proud distinction of Greece, Hindustan holds the first rank in point of time.

Abbe J.A. Dubois

Missionary in Mysore

Extracts from a letter dated December 15, 1820, Seringapatam : December, 1820, Seringapatam :

The authority of married women within their houses is chiefly exerted in preserving good order and peace among the persons who compose their families; and a great many among them discharge this important duty with a prudence and a discretion which have scarcely a parallel in Europe. I have known families composed of between thirty and forty persons, or more, consisting of grown-up sons and daughters, all married and all having children, living together under the superintendence of an old matron—their mother or mother-in-law. The latter, by good management, and by accommodating herself to the temper of the daughters-in-law, by using, according to circumstances, firmness or forbearance, succeeded in preserving peace and harmony during many years amongst so many females, who had all jarring tempers. I ask you whether it would be possible to attain the same end, in the same circumstances, in our countries, where it is scarcely possible to make two women living under the same roof to agree together. In fact, there is perhaps no kind of honest employment in a civilized country in which the Hindu females have not a due share. Besides the management of the household, and the care of the family which (as already noticed is under their control) the wives and daughters of husbandmen attend and assist their husbands and fathers in the labours of agriculture. Those of tradesmen assist theirs in carrying on their trade. Merchants are attended and assisted by theirs in their shops. Many females are shopkeepers on their own account; and *without a knowledge of the alphabet* or of the decimal scale, they keep by other means their accounts in excellent order, and are considered as still shrewder than the males themselves in their commercial dealings.

J. Young

Secretary, Savon Mechanics Institutes within Recent Years

Those races (the Indian viewed from a moral aspect) are perhaps the most remarkable people in the world. They breathe in an atmosphere of moral purity, which cannot but excite admiration, and this is especially the case with the poorer classes, who, notwithstanding the privations of their humble lot, appear to be happy and contented. True children of nature, they live on from day to day, taking no thought for the morrow and thankful for the simple fare which Providence has provided for them. It is curious to witness the spectacle of coolies of both sexes returning home at nightfall after a hard day's work often lasting from sunrise to sunset. In spite of fatigue from the effects of the unremitting toil, they are, for the most part, gay and animated, conversing cheerfully together and occasionally breaking into snatches of light-hearted song. Yet what awaits them on their return to the hovels which they call home? A dish of rice for food, and the floor for a bed. Domestic felicity appears to be the rule among the Natives, and this is the more strange when the customs of marriage are taken into account, parents arranging all such matters. Many Indian households afford examples of the married state in its highest degree of perfection. This may be due to the teachings of the *Shastras*, and to the strict injunctions which they inculcate with regard to marital obligation; but it is no exaggeration to say that husbands are generally devotedly attached to their wives, and in many instances the latter have the most exalted conception of their duties towards their husbands.

Colonel Thomas Munro

Thirty-Two Years' Service in India

If a good system of agriculture, unrivalled manufacturing skill, a capacity to produce whatever can contribute to convenience or luxury; schools established in every village for teaching reading, writing and arithmetic; the general practice of hospitality and charity among each other; and, above all, a treatment of the female sex, full of confidence, respect and delicacy, are among the signs which denote a civilized people, then the Hindus are not inferior to the nations of Europe; and if civilization is to become an article of trade between the two countries, I am convinced that this country [England] will gain by the import cargo.

Sir William Wedderburn, Bart

The Indian village has thus for centuries remained a bulwark against political disorder, and the home of the simple domestic and social virtues. No wonder, therefore, that philosophers and historians have always dwelt lovingly on this ancient institution which is the natural social unit and the best type of rural life : self-contained, industrious, peace-loving, conservative in the best sense of the word. . . . I think you will agree with me that there is much that is both picturesque and attractive in this glimpse of social and domestic life in an Indian village. It is a harmless and happy form of human existence. Moreover, it is not without good practical outcome.

PART TWO

HISTORICAL SPEECHES OF MAHATMA GANDHI

3.1

Role of Asiatic and the Coloured Races in British Empire

GANDHI AT Y.M.C.A.

[Johannesburg, *May 18, 1908*]

The following address was given by Mr. M.K. Gandhi, Bar-at-Law, before the Y.M.C.A., Johannesburg, in moving the negative in a debate on the question, "Are Asiatics and the Coloured races a menace to the Empire?"

It seems to me somewhat remarkable that a question of this description should arise at all, or that there should be any debate whatsoever as to whether Coloured races are a menace to the Empire. I think that a question of that description could arise only in the Colonies or, better still, only in some of the Colonies. In a well-ordered society industrious and intelligent men can never be a menace. If they have any defects, the very order of the society corrects them. At the same time, we, as practical men and women living in this very practical age, have to face facts as they are and, seeing that questions of this description arise in the Colonies, it is undoubtedly well that we should discuss them and debate upon them; and, to my mind, it is a very happy augury for the future that your humble servant can be called upon to give his views on the question before an audience like this, and I think it is also a happy augury that this hall is so well filled, showing the keen interest taken in the subject.

By the term "Coloured people" generally, I think we understand only offspring of mixed marriages, but in connection with the question before us this evening, the term "Coloured people" has been taken more comprehensively, and has been made to include the Coloured people proper—the

Africans and the Asiatics. My own observations and experience, as you know, are confined very largely to British Indians, my own fellow-countrymen, but in studying the Indian question, I have endeavoured to study the question as it affects the Africans and the Chinese. It seems to me that both the Africans and the Asiatics have advanced the Empire as a whole; we can hardly think of South Africa without the African races. And who can think of the British Empire without India? South Africa would probably be a howling wilderness without the Africans. I do not think that the white man would have come to South Africa at all if there had been no Native races.

This brings me to the White Man's Burden as Kipling has called it. His writings, to my mind, have been very much misunderstood. We know now also that he himself has very considerably, with extended experience, revised his views, and he no longer thinks that the Coloured people are a menace to the Empire, or that the white man may not coexist with the Coloured man. Be that as it may, he has certainly shown in some of his writings that it was really a responsibility thrown on the white people, more particularly on the British people, to act as trustees for the Coloured races. But have the white people acted as trustees? Would you consider that your own wards were a menace to yourselves? The majority of people in South Africa, the majority of people in most of the Colonies, have become impatient of colour, and it behoves every right-minded man and woman to think twice before he or she jumps to the conclusion that the Coloured people are a menace and that, therefore, they ought to be got rid of with the greatest possible despatch.

We hear nowadays a great deal of the segregation policy, as if it were possible to put people in water-tight compartments. Captain Cooke has written to the papers and has taken the trouble of discussing the same question with me, and has propounded a policy of segregation. I had no hesitation in telling him that, in my own opinion, based now on 14 years' observation and study, such a scheme, if it was meant to people some portions of East Africa with Coloured people only or, better still, with Asiatics only, was not possible of fulfilment. How are you going to restrict Asiatics to some parts of the earth only? Will they be content to have those portions of the earth which may be apportioned to them and which are unfit for white occupation? I have certainly never been able to find any justification for the colourbarrier. In the words of Mr. Chamberlain, it is possible to make distinctions on the ground of want of education, on the ground of criminality, or some such ground. Then there will be no cry of segregation. But from the present civilisation, or, rather, from western civilization, there flow two propositions which have almost become maxims to live by—I call them fallacious maxims.

They are "might is right" and "survival of the fittest". Those who have propounded these two maxims have given a meaning to them. I am not going into the meaning that might be attached in our minds to them, but they have said undoubtedly, by [saying] "might is right", that physical might is right, that physical strength is right and supreme. Some of them have also combined intellectual strength with physical strength, but I would replace both these with heart-strength, and I say that nobody with merely physical might and intellectual might can ever enjoy that strength that can proceed from the heart. It never can be that mere intellectual or mere physical strength can ever supersede the heart-strength or, as Ruskin would say, social affections. A quickening and quickened soul responds only to the springs of the heart.

That is the difference between western and eastern civilization? I know that I am treading on very dangerous and delicate ground. We had the distinction given to us by so great an authority as Lord Selborne only a short time ago, and I have very humbly and very respectfully to differ from His Excellency's views.

It appears that western civilization is destructive, eastern civilisation is constructive. Western civilization is centrifugal, eastern civilization is centripetal. Western civilisation, therefore, is naturally disruptive, whereas eastern civilization combines. I believe also that western civilization is without a goal, eastern civilization has always had the goal before it. I do not mix up or confuse western civilization with Christian progress. I decline to believe that it is a symbol of Christian progress that we have covered a large part of the globe with the telegraph system, that we have got telephones and ocean greyhounds, and that we have trains running at a velocity of 50 or even 60 miles per hour. I refuse to believe that all this activity connotes Christian progress, but it does connote western civilization. I think western civilization also represents tremendous activity, eastern civilization represents contemplativeness, but it also sometimes represents lethargy. The people in India, the people in China—I leave Japan for the time being—having been sunk in their contemplative mood, have forgotten the essence of the thing, they have forgotten that, in transferring their activity from one sphere of life to another sphere of life, they had not to be idle, they had not to be lazy. The result is that immediately they find an obstacle in their way, they simply sit down. It is necessary that that civilization should come in contact with that of the West, it is necessary that civilization should be quickened with the western spirit. Immediately that fact is accomplished, I have no doubt also that the eastern civilization will become predominant, because it has a goal. I think you will see easily that a civilization or a condition in which all the forces fly away from the centre must necessarily be without a goal, whereas those which converge to a point have always a goal. It is then necessary for these two civilizations to meet and we shall have a different force altogether, by no means a menacing force, by no means a force that disunites, but a force that unites. The two forces are undoubtedly opposing forces, but perhaps in the economy of nature both are necessary. Only we, as intelligent human beings with heart and soul, have to see what those forces are, and have to use them, not blindly but intelligently, not anyhow and haphazard, but with a goal in view. Immediately that is done, there is no difficulty whatsoever in [the] two civilizations meeting and meeting for a good purpose.

I have said that the African races have undoubtedly served the Empire, and I believe so have the Asiatic races or, rather, British Indians. Have not the British Indians fought on many a battle field? A people, moreover, who have religion as the basis of life, cannot be a menace. And how can the African races be a menace? They are still in the history of the world's learners. Able-bodied and intelligent men as they are, they cannot but be an asset to the Empire. I believe with Mr. Creswell that they ought not to be protected. We do not want protection for them in any shape or form, but I do believe this—that they are entitled to justice, a fair field and no favour. Immediately you give that to them, you will find no difficulty.

Whilst, therefore, Asiatics and other Coloured people cannot be a menace, Asiatics at least have been made a menace in some Colonies. We have been told that Natal and Mauritius are awful examples to every white man throughout the world. I do not know that they are such awful countries, but I, at the same time, believe that, if what happened in Natal had not happened, it would have been different—whether better or worse, we are not for the present discussing; but, if these countries have been ruined, they have been ruined purposely by white men, or, rather, by a few of them who were in a hurry to get rich. If they had only bid their time and opportunity, no such thing need, would, have happened. They did not hesitate to import indentured labour, which might be called semislave labour, from India. Posterity has to pay for it. If, therefore, Natal or Mauritius has suffered, it has suffered not from Asiatics as such, but from a system of labour of which Asiatics happened to form part. Had there been white indentured labour instead, the result would have been the same. It is not the free Indian population that can ever do any harm whatsoever to the Colonies.

But I do also admit that there are some reasonable complaints with reference to British Indians. I venture, however, to submit that these complaints have no real basis. It is complained that they live in dirty hovels. Yes, some of them do. They are said to live very cheaply. But if you were to examine these complaints, I think, you would come to the conclusion that they could be dealt with very easily and very effectively by municipal regulations. There are many complaints against the people living in the East End of London by the people living in the West End, but no one has suggested that, therefore, the people in the East End should be swept away. Sweep away the rack-rent and the conditions prevailing in the East End, and its inhabitants will be just as good as those in the West End. Similarly also, sweep away the conditions under which British Indians are called upon to live, sweep away the condition that they cannot own a patch of land which they can call their own, that they cannot live, and move, and have their being on God's earth in South Africa with any degree of freedom, self-respect and manliness, and they will realize that in Rome they must live as the Romans do, and will respond to every real and reasonable call that can be made upon them by the white man; but I ask you to be patient with them just as you would be patient with any fellow-man. Treat him as a real, live human being, and you will have no such thing as the Indian question in the country. Please do not forget I do not advocate that there should be absolutely free immigration. On the contrary, I have always said, and British Indians admit, that there may be regulation of immigration, but never based on colour. Anyone who is accepted as an immigrant ought to be entitled to all the rights that a man who lives in the country should possess. Whether he should have political rights or not is another question. I am not here today to discuss the political question at all. But there should be no two opinions as to whether he may live freely without being restricted, move freely without being restricted, own land, or trade honestly. British Indians and Englishmen have come together by Divine Providence. I may add, and I believe it is true, that, when the British occupied India, it was not owing to humanitarian grounds, but that the act was selfish and often tinged with dishonesty. But Nature's ways are inscrutable. She often unmakes what man makes and produces good out of evil. Such is, in my opinion, the case with the British connection with India. I believe that the two races, the British and the Indian, have been brought together, not only for their own mutual advantage, but to leave an impress on the history of the world. Believing that, I also believe that it is well for me to be a loyal subject of the Empire, but not I hope a member of a subject race. I trust it is the mission of the English race, even where there are subject races, to raise them to equality with themselves, to give them free institutions and make them absolutely free men. If that be the mission of the Empire, the mission of the British race, then is it not as well that the millions of human beings should be trained for self-government? If we look into the future, is it not a heritage we have to leave to posterity, that all the different races commingle and produce a civilization that perhaps the world has not yet seen? There are difficulties and misunderstandings, but I do believe, in the words of the sacred hymn, "We shall know each other better when the mists have rolled away."

Indian Opinion, 6-6-1908
13-6-1908

3.2

At Benares Hindu University

February 4, 1916

The following is the full text of the speech delivered on February 4th on the occasion of the opening of the Benares Hindu University. Gandhiji, who edited the report for G. A. Natesan, wrote :

I have merely removed some of the verbiage which in cold print would make the speech bad reading : Friends, I wish to tender my humble apology for the long delay that took place before I was able to reach this place. And you will readily accept the apology when I tell you that I am not responsible for the delay nor is any human agency responsible for it. (Laughter.) The fact is that I am like an animal on show and lay keepers in their over-kindness always manage to neglect a necessary chapter in this life and that is pure accident. In this case, they did not provide for the series of accidents that happened to us—to me, my keepers ! and my carriers. Hence this delay.

Friends, under the influence of the matchless eloquence of the lady (Mrs. Besant) who has just sat down, pray, do not believe that our University has become a finished product and that all the young men who are to come to the University that has yet to rise and come into existence, have also come and returned from it finished citizens of a great empire. Do not go away with any such impression and if you, the student world to which my remarks are supposed to be addressed this evening, consider for one moment that the spiritual life, for which this country is noted and for which this country has no rival, can be transmitted through the lip, pray, believe me you are wrong. You will never be able merely through the lip to give the message that India, I hope, will one day deliver to the world. I myself have been "fed up" with speeches and lectures. I except the lectures that have been delivered here during the last two days from this category, because they were necessary. But I do venture to suggest to you that we have now reached almost the end of our resources in speech-making, and it is not enough that our ears are feasted, that our eyes are feasted, but it is necessary that our hearts have got to be touched and that our hands and feet have got to be moved. We have been told during the last two days how necessary it is, if we are to retain our hold upon the simplicity of Indian character, that our hands and feet should move in unison with our hearts. But this is only by way of preface, I wanted to say it is a matter of deep humiliation and shame for us that I am compelled this evening under the shadow of this great college, in this sacred city, to address my countrymen in a language that is foreign to me. I know that if I was appointed an examiner to examine all those who have been attending during these two days this series of lectures most of those who might be examined upon these lectures would fail. And why? Because they have not been touched. I was present at the sessions of the great Congress in the month of December. There was a much vaster audience, and will you believe me when I tell you that the only speeches that touched that huge audience in Bombay were the speeches that were delivered in Hindustani? In Bombay, mind you, not in Benares where everybody speaks Hindi. But between the vernaculars of the Bombay Presidency on the one hand; and Hindi on the other, no such great dividing line exists as there does between English and the sister-languages of India; and the Congress audience was better able to follow the speakers in Hindi. I am hoping that this University will see to it that the youths who come to it will receive their instruction through the medium of their vernaculars. Our language is the reflection of ourselves, and if you tell me that our languages are too poor to express the best thought, then I say that the sooner we are wiped out of existence, the better for us. Is there a man who dreams that English can ever become the national language of India? (Cries of "Never".) Why this handicap on the nation? Just consider for one moment what an unequal race our lads have to run with every English lad. I had the privilege of a close conversation with some Poona professors. They assured me that every Indian youth, because he reached his knowledge through the English language, lost at least six precious years of life. Multiply that by the number of students turned out by our schools and colleges and find out for yourselves how many thousand years have been lost to the nation. The charge against us is, that we have no initiative. How can we have any if we are to devote the precious years of our life to the mastery of a foreign tongue? We fail in this attempt also. Was it possible for any speaker yesterday and today to impress his audience as was possible for Mr. Higginbotham? It was not the fault of the previous speakers that they could not engage the audience. They had more than substance enough for us in their addresses. But their addresses could not go home to us. I have heard it said that after all it is English-educated India which is leading and which is doing all the things for the nation. It would be monstrous if it were otherwise. The only education we receive is English education. Surely we must show something for it. But suppose that we had been receiving during the past fifty years education through our vernaculars, what should we have had today? We should have today a free India, we should have our educated men, not as if they were foreigners in their own land but speaking to the heart of the nation; they would be working amongst the poorest of the poor, and whatever they would have gained during the past 50 years would be a heritage for the nation. (applause) Today even our wives are not the sharers in our best thought. Look at Professor Bose and Professor Ray and their brilliant researches. Is it not a shame that their researches are not the common property of the masses?

Let us now turn to another subject.

The Congress has passed a resolution about self-government and I have no doubt that the All-India Congress Committee and the Moslem League will do their duty and come forward with some tangible suggestions. But I, for one, must frankly confess that I am not so much interested in what they will be able to produce as I am interested in anything that the student world is going to produce or the masses are going to produce. No paper contribution will ever give us self-government. No amount of speeches will ever make us fit for self-government. It is only our conduct that will fit us for it. (applause.) And how are we trying to govern ourselves? I want to think audibly this evening. I do not want to make a speech and if you find me this evening speaking without reserve, pray, consider that you are only sharing the thoughts of a man who allows himself to think audibly, and if you think that I seem to transgress the limits that courtesy imposes upon me, pardon me for the liberty I may be taking. I visited the Viswanath Temple last evening and as I was walking through those lanes, these were the thoughts that touched me. If a stranger dropped from above on to this great temple and he had to consider what we as Hindus were, would he not be justified in condemning us? Is not this great temple a reflection of our own character? I speak feelingly as a Hindu. Is it right that the lanes of our sacred temple should be as dirty as they are? The houses round about are built anyhow. The lanes are tortuous and narrow. If even our temples are not models of roominess and cleanliness, what can our self-government be? Shall our temples be abodes of holiness, cleanliness and peace as soon as the English have retired from India, either of their own pleasure or by compulsion, bag and baggage?

I entirely agree with the President of the Congress that before we think of self-government, we shall have to do the necessary plodding. In every city there are two divisions, the cantonment and the city proper. The city mostly is a stinking den. But we are a people unused to city life. But if we want city life, we cannot reproduce the easy-going hamlet life. It is not comforting to think that people walk about the streets of Indian Bombay under the perpetual fear of dwellers in the storeyed buildings spitting upon them. I do a great deal of railway travelling. I observe the difficulty of third-class passengers. But the Railway Administration is by no means to blame for all their hard lot. We do not know the elementary his followers or subordinates will be rated as 'very good' because he then is motivating his employees or people by his example.

The leader who works himself utmost but is not able to motivate his team fully will be graded as 'good' with 8 marks. The leader is one who himself performs and sees that others also perform.

The leader who is routinely doing work during office hours without making the work interesting for his organization, will be valued as 'average' whereas the leadership which is only engaged in planning and idle gossiping will be 'below average'.

A leader who just shows alibi for work, is not respected by his workforce and is ultimately rejected by his people and he faces his downfall and causes gradual but certain failure of the organization, he is heading. He will, therefore, be given 'zero' marking.

(f) Energy

The leaders discover energy to achieve their goal. Unless there is a fire or an urgent urge to achieve, leader cannot be born. According to Debashis Chatterjee, leader see their world within themselves. This is close to the Indian thinking which says that every being has infinite source of energy because God himself is seated within it. There is no difference between the God and men's inner master or controller called *atman*. The followers expect infinite energy in their leaders. Sometimes leaders grow old yet the followers expect God sent energy in them. They talk a lot of about their leaders how he works tirelessly for hours more than any worker. His time management is the talk of the organization including his leisure and hobbies. Therefore, leadership is a very cautious path which one has to trace, if one chooses to be the leader. At least his 50 per cent personal life is off. He has to sacrifice his privacy and personal whims and fancies for the sake of success of the organization, he is working with. His one bad example can have lot of repercussions on the people working in his organization.

One has to pursue one's goal stubbornly. One has not to retreat after failures. One has to try hard and should finish the work whatsoever has been started.

The Japanese people have attained the highest rate of economic growth in the World. This is due to their commitment to their daily work which they regard as sacred. Consider the following song which workers in the Matsushita factories sing before starting their work everyday:

cannot be much spirit of self-government about us if we take away or allow others to take away from them almost the whole of the results of their labour. Our salvation can only come through the farmer. Neither the lawyers, nor the doctors, nor the rich landlords are going to secure it.

Now, last but not the least, it is my bounden duty to refer to what agitated our minds during these two or three days. All of us have had many anxious moments while the Viceroy was going through the streets of Benares. There were detectives stationed in many places. We were horrified. We asked ourselves : "Why this distrust? Is it not better that even Lord Hardinge should die than live a living death"? But a representative of a mighty Sovereign may not. He might find it necessary even to live a living death. But why was it necessary to impose these detectives on us? We may foam, we may fret, we may resent but let us not forget that India of today in her impatience has produced an army of anarchists. I myself am an anarchist, but of another type. But there is a class of anarchists amongst us, and if I was able to reach this class, I would say to them that their anarchism has no room in India if India is to conquer the conqueror. It is a sign of fear. If we trust and fear God, we shall have to fear no one, not Maharajahs, not Viceroys, not the detectives, not even King George. I honour the anarchist for his love of the country. I honour him for his bravery in being willing to die for his country; but I ask him : Is killing honourable? Is the dagger of an assassin a fit precursor of an honourable death? I deny it. There is no warrant for such methods in any scriptures. If I found it necessary for the salvation of India that the English should retire, that they should be driven out, I would not hesitate to declare that they would have to go, and I hope I would be prepared to die in defence of that belief. That would, in my opinion, be an honourable death. The bomb-thrower creates secret plots, is afraid to come into the open, and when caught pays the penalty of misdirected zeal. I have been told : "Had we not done this, had some people not thrown bombs, we should never have gained what we have got with reference to the partition movement." (Mrs. Besant : "Please stop it.")

This was what I said in Bengal when Mr. Lyons presided at the meeting. I think what I am saying is necessary. If I am told to stop, I shall obey. (Turning to the Chairman) I await your orders. If you consider that by my speaking as I am, I am not serving the country and the Empire, I shall certainly stop. (Cries of "Go on".) (The Chairman : "Please explain your object.") I am explaining my object. 1 am simply (Another interruption.) My friends, please do not resent this interruption. If Mrs. Besant this evening suggests that I should stop, she does so because she loves India so well, and she considers that I am erring in thinking audibly before you young men. But even so, I simply say this that I want to purge India of the atmosphere of suspicion on either side; if we are to reach our goal, we should have an empire which is to be based upon mutual love and mutual trust. Is it not better that we talk under the shadow of this college than that we should be talking irresponsibly in our homes? I consider that it is much better that we talk these things openly. I have done so with excellent results before now. I know that there is nothing that the students are not discussing. There is nothing that the students do not know. I am, therefore, turning the searchlight towards ourselves. I hold the name of my country so dear to me that I exchange these thoughts with you and submit to you that there is no reason for anarchism in India. Let us frankly and openly say whatever we want to say to our rulers and face the consequences if what we have to say does not please them. But let us not abuse. I was talking the other day to a member of the much-abused Civil Service. I have not very much in common with the members of that Service, but I could not help admiring the manner in which he was speaking to me. He said : "Mr. Gandhi, do you for one moment suppose that all we, Civil Servants, are a bad lot, that we want to oppress the people whom we have come to govern?" "No", I said. "Then, if you get an opportunity, put in a word for the much-abused Civil Service.", And I am here to put in that word. Yes, many members of the Indian Civil Service are most decidedly overbearing, they are tyrannical, at times thoughtless. Many other adjectives may be used. I grant all these things and I grant also that after having lived in

India for a certain number of years, some of them become somewhat degraded. But what does that signify? They were gentlemen before they came here, and if they have lost some of the moral fibre, it is a reflection upon ourselves. (Cries of "No".) Just think out for yourselves, if a man who was good yesterday has become bad after having come in contact with me, is he responsible that he has deteriorated or am I? The atmosphere of sycophancy and falsity that surrounds them on their coming to India demoralises them as it would many of us. It is well to take the blame sometimes. If we are to receive self-government, we shall have to take it. We shall never be granted self-government. Look at the history of the British Empire and the British nation; freedom loving as it is, it will not be a party to give freedom to a people who will not take it themselves. Learn your lesson if you wish to from the Boer War. Those who were enemies of that Empire only a few years ago have now become friends.

[At this point there was an interruption and there was a movement on the platform to leave; the speech, therefore, ended here abruptly.]

3.3

On Swadeshi at Missionary Conference, Madras

February 14, 1916

It was not without much diffidence that I undertook to speak to you at all. And I was hard put to it in the selection of my subject. I have chosen a very delicate and difficult subject. It is delicate because of the peculiar views I hold upon *swadeshi,* and it is difficult because I have not that command of language which is necessary for giving adequate expression to my thoughts. I know that I may rely upon your indulgence for the many shortcomings you will no doubt find in my address, the more so when I tell you that there is nothing in what I am about to say, that I am not either already practising or am not preparing to practise to the best of my ability. It encourages me to observe that last month you devoted a week to prayer in the place of an address. I have earnestly prayed that what I am about to say may bear fruit and I know that you will bless my words with a similar prayer.

After much thinking, I have arrived at a definition of *swadeshi* that perhaps best illustrates my meaning. *Swadeshi* is that spirit in us which restricts us to the use and service of our immediate surroundings to the exclusion of the more remote. Thus, as for religion, in order to satisfy the requirements of the definition, I must restrict myself to my ancestral religion. That is the use of my immediate religious surroundings. If I find it defective, I should serve it by purging it of its defects. In the domain of politics, I should make use of the indigenous institutions and serve them by curing them of their proved defects. In that of economics, I should use only things that are produced by my immediate neighbours and serve those industries by making them efficient and complete where they might be found wanting. It is suggested that such *swadeshi,* if reduced to practice, will lead to the millennium. And as we do not abandon our pursuit after the millennium because we do not expect quite to reach it within our time, so may we not abandon *swadeshi* even though it may not be fully attained for generations to come.

Let us briefly examine three branches of *swadeshi* as sketched above. Hinduism has become a conservative religion and, therefore, a mighty force because of the *swadeshi* spirit underlying it. It is the most tolerant because it is non-proselytising, and it is as capable of expansion today as it has been found to be in the past. It has succeeded not in driving, as I think it has been erroneously held, but in absorbing Buddhism. By reason of the *swadeshi* spirit, a Hindu refuses to change his religion not necessarily because he considers it to be the best, but because he knows that he can complement it by introducing reforms. And what I have said about Hinduism is, I suppose, true of the other great faiths of the world, only it is held that it is specially so in the case of Hinduism. But here comes the point I am labouring to reach. If there is any substance in what I have said, will not the great missionary bodies of India, to whom she owes a deep debt of gratitude for what they have done and are doing, do still better and serve the spirit of Christianity better, by dropping the goal of proselytising but continuing their philanthropic work? I hope you will not consider this to be an impertinence on my part. I make the suggestion in all sincerity and with due humility. Moreover, I have some claim upon your attention. I have endeavoured to study the *Bible.* I consider it as part of my scriptures. The spirit of the Sermon on the Mount competes almost on equal terms with the *Bhagavad Gita* for the domination of my heart. I yield to no Christian in the strength of devotion with which I sing, "Lead, kindly Light" and several other inspired hymns of a similar nature. I have come under the influence of noted Christian missionaries belonging to different denominations. And I enjoy to this day the privilege of friendship with some of them. You will perhaps, therefore, allow that I have offered the above suggestion not as a biased Hindu but as a humble and impartial student of religion with great leanings towards Christianity. May it not be that the "Go Ye unto All the World" message has been somewhat narrowly interpreted and the spirit of it missed? It will not be denied, I speak from experience, that many of the conversions are only so called. In some cases, the appeal has gone not to the heart but to the stomach. And in every case, a conversion leaves a sore behind it which, I venture to think, is avoidable. Quoting again from experience, a new birth, a change of heart, is perfectly possible in every one of the great faiths. I know I am now treading upon thin ice. But I do not apologise, in closing this part of my subject, for saving that the frightful outrage that is just going on in Europe, perhaps, shows that the message of Jesus of Nazareth, the Son of Peace, has been little understood in Europe, and that light upon it may have to be thrown from the East.

I have sought your help in religious matters, which it is yours to give in a special sense. But I make bold to seek it even in political matters. I do not believe that religion has nothing to do with politics. The latter divorced from religion is like a corpse only fit to be buried. As a matter of fact, in your own silent manner, you influence politics not a little. And I feel that if the attempt to separate politics from religion had not been made, as it is even now made, they would not have degenerated, as they often appear to do. No one considers that the political life of the country is in a happy state. Following out the *swadeshi* spirit, I observe the indigenous institutions and the village panchayats hold me. India is really a republican country, and it is because it is that that it has survived every shock hitherto delivered. Princes and potentates, whether they were Indian-born or foreigners, have hardly touched the vast masses except for collecting revenue. The latter in their turn seem to have rendered unto Caesar what was Caesar's and for the rest have done much as they have liked. The vast organisation of caste answered not only the religious wants of the community, but it answered too its political needs. The villagers managed their internal affairs through the caste system, and through it they dealt with any oppression from the ruling power or powers. It is not possible to deny of a nation that was capable of producing the caste system its wonderful power of organisation. One had but to attend the great Kumbha Mela at Hardwar last year to know how skilful that organisation must have been, which without any seeming effort, was able effectively to cater for more than a million pilgrims. Yet is it the fashion to say that we lack organising ability. This is true, I fear, to a certain extent, of those who have been nurtured in the new tradition's. We have laboured under a terrible handicap owing to an almost fatal departure from the *swadeshi* spirit. We the educated classes have received our education through a foreign tongue. We have, therefore, not reacted upon the masses. We want to represent the masses, but we fail. They recognise us not much more than they recognise the English officers. Their hearts are an open book to neither. Their aspirations are not ours. Hence, there is a break. And you witness not in reality failure to organise, but want of correspondence between the representatives and the represented. If during the last fifty years we had been educated through the vernaculars, our elders and our servants and our neighbours would have partaken of our knowledge; the discoveries of a Bose or a Ray would have been household treasure as are the *Ramayan* and the *Mahabharat*. As it is, so far as the masses are concerned, those great discoveries might as well have been made by foreigners. Had instruction in all the branches of learning been given through the vernaculars, I make bold to say that they would have been enriched wonderfully. The question of village sanitation, etc., would have been solved long ago. The village panchayats would be now a living force in a special way, and India would almost be enjoying self-government suited to its requirements and would have been spared the humiliating spectacle of organised assassination on its sacred soil. It is not too late to mend. And you can help if you will, as no other body or bodies can.

And now for the last division of *swadeshi*. Much of the deep poverty of the masses is due to the ruinous departure from *swadeshi* in the economic and industrial life. If not an article of commerce had been brought from outside India, she would be today a land flowing with milk and honey. But that was not to be. We were greedy and so was England. The connection between England and India was based clearly upon an error. But she (England) does not remain in India in error. It is her declared policy that India is to be held in trust for her people. If this be true, Lancashire must stand aside. And if the *swadeshi* doctrine is a sound doctrine, Lancashire can stand aside without hurt, though it may sustain a shock for the time being. I think of *swadeshi* not as a boycott movement undertaken by way of revenge. I conceive it as a religious principle to be followed by all. I am no economist, but I have read some treatises which show that England could easily become a self-sustained country, growing all the produce she needs. This may be an utterly ridiculous proposition, and perhaps the best proof that it cannot be true is that England is one of the largest importers in the world. But India cannot live for Lancashire or any other country before she is able to live for herself. And she can live for herself only if she produces and is helped to produce everything for her requirements within her own borders. She need not be, she ought not to be, drawn into the vortex of mad and ruinous competition which breeds fratricide, jealousy and many other evils.

But who is to stop her great millionaires from entering into the world competition? Certainly, not legislation. Force of public opinion, proper education, however, can do a great deal in the desired direction. The handloom industry is in a dying condition. I took special care during my wanderings last year to see as many weavers as possible, and my heart ached to find how they had lost, how families had retired from this once-flourishing and honourable occupation. If we follow the *swadeshi* doctrine, it would be your duty and mine to find out neighbours who can supply our wants and to teach them to supply them where they do not know how to, assuming that there are neighbours who are in want of healthy occupation. Then every village of India will almost be a self-supporting and self-contained unit exchanging only such necessary commodities with other villages where they are not locally producible. This may all sound nonsensical. Well, India is a country of nonsense. It is nonsensical to parch one's throat with thirst when a kindly Mahomedan is ready to offer pure water to drink. And yet thousands of Hindus would rather die of thirst than drink water from a Mahomedan household. These nonsensical men can also, once they are convinced that their religion demands that they should wear garments manufactured in India only and eat food only grown in India, decline to wear any other clothing or eat any other food. Lord Curzon set the fashion for tea-drinking. And that pernicious drug now bids fair to overwhelm the nation. It has already undermined the digestive apparatus of hundreds of thousands of men and women and constitutes an additional tax upon their slender purses. Lord Hardinge can set the fashion for *swadeshi* and almost the whole of India will foreswear foreign goods. There is a verse in the *Bhagavad Gita*, which, freely rendered, means masses follow the classes. It is easy to undo the evil if the thinking portion of the community were to take the *swadeshi* vow even though it may for a time cause considerable inconvenience. I hate interference in any department of life. At best, it is the lesser evil. But I would tolerate, welcome, indeed plead for, stiff protective duty upon foreign goods. Natal, a British colony, protected its sugar by taxing the sugar that came from another British colony, Mauritius. England has sinned against India by forcing free trade upon her. It may have been food for her, but it has been poison for this country. It has often been urged that India cannot adopt *swadeshi* in the economic life at any rate. Those who advance this objection do not look upon *swadeshi* as a rule of life. With them, it is a mere patriotic effort not to be made if it involved any self-denial. *Swadeshi,* as defined here, is a religious discipline to be undergone in utter disregard of the physical discomfort it may cause to individuals. Under its spell, the deprivation of pin or a needle, because these are not manufactured in India need cause no terror. A *swadeshi* will learn to do without hundreds of things which today he considers necessary. Moreover, those who dismiss *swadeshi* from their minds by arguing the impossible forget that *swadeshi,* after all, is a goal to be reached by steady effort. And we would be making for the goal even if we confined *swadeshi* to a given set of articles, allowing ourselves as a temporary measure to use such things as might not be procurable in the country.

There now remains for me to consider one more objection that has been raised against *swadeshi.* The objectors consider it to be a most selfish doctrine without any warrant in the civilized code of morality. With them, to practise *swadeshi* is to revert to barbarism. I cannot enter into a detailed analysis of the proposition. But I would urge that *swadeshi* is the only doctrine consistent with the law of humility and love. It is arrogance to think of launching out to serve the whole of India when I am hardly able to serve even my own family. It were better to concentrate my effort upon the family and consider that through them I was serving the whole nation and, if you will, the whole of humanity. This is humility and it is love. The motive will determine the quality of the act. I may serve my family regardless of the sufferings I may cause to others, as, for instance, I may accept an employment which enables me to extort money from people. I enrich myself thereby and then satisfy many unlawful demands of the family. Here I am neither serving the family nor the State. Or I may recognise that God has given me hands and feet only to work with for my sustenance and for that of those who may be dependent upon me. I would then at once simplify my life and that of those whom I can directly reach. In this instance, I would have served the family without causing injury to anyone else. Supposing that everyone followed this mode of life, we would have at once an ideal State. All will not reach that state at the same time. But those of us who, realising its truth, enforce it in practice will clearly anticipate and accelerate the coming of that happy day. Under this plan of life, in seeming to serve India to the exclusion of every other country, I do not harm any other country. My patriotism is both exclusive and inclusive. It is exclusive in the sense that in all humility I confine my attention to the land of my birth, but it is inclusive in the sense that my service is not of a competitive or antagonistic nature. *Sic utere tuo ut alienum non Laedas* is not merely a legal maxim, but it is a grand doctrine of life. It is the key to a proper practice of *ahimsa* or love. It is for you, the custodians of a great faith, to set the fashion and show by your preaching, sanctified by practice, that patriotism based on hatred "killeth" and that patriotism based on love "giveth life".

[*The Hindu*, 28-2-1916]

3.4

At Gurukul Anniversary

March 20, 1916

The following is the text of Mr. Gandhi's speech at the anniversary of the Gurukul, as written out by himself :

I propose to reproduce only as much of it as in my opinion is worth placing on record with additions where they may be found necessary. The speech, it may be observed, was delivered in Hindi. After thanking Mahatmaji Munshi Ram for his great kindness to my boys to whom he gave shelter on two occasions and acted as father to them and after stating that the time for action had arrived rather than for speeches, I proceeded :

I owe a debt of gratitude to the Arya Samaj. I have often derived inspiration from its activity. I have noticed among the members of the Samaj much self-sacrifice. During my travels in India, I came across many Arya Samajists who were doing excellent work for the country. I am, therefore, grateful to Mahatmaji, that I am enabled to be in your midst. At the same time, it is but fair to state that I am frankly a Sanatanist. For me Hinduism is all-sufficing. Every variety of belief finds protection under its ample fold. And though the Arya Samajists and the Sikhs and the Brahmo Samajists may choose to be classed differently from the Hindus, I have no doubt that at no distant future they will be all merged in Hinduism and find in it their fullness. Hinduism, like every other human institution, has its drawbacks and its defects. Here is ample scope for any worker to strive for reform, but there is little cause for secession.

Spirit of Fearlessness

Throughout my travels, I have been asked about the immediate need for India. And, perhaps, I would not do better than repeat this afternoon the answer I have given elsewhere. In general terms, a proper religious spirit is the greatest and most immediate need. But I know that this is too general an answer to satisfy anybody. And it is an answer true for all time. What, therefore, I desire to say is, that owing to the religious spirit being dormant in us, we are living in a state of perpetual fear. We fear the temporal as well as the spiritual authority. We dare not speak out our minds before our priests and our *pandits*. We stand in awe of the temporal power. I am sure that in so doing we do a disservice to them and us. Neither the spiritual teachers nor our political governors could possibly desire that we should hide the truth from them. Lord Wellington, speaking to a Bombay audience, has been saying recently that he had observed that we hesitated to say 'No' when we really meant it and advised his audience to cultivate a fearless spirit. Of course, fearlessness should never mean want of due respect or regard for the feelings of others. In my humble opinion, fearlessness is the first thing indispensable before we could achieve anything permanent and real. This quality is unattainable without religious consciousness. Let us fear God and we shall cease to fear man. If we grasp the fact that there is a divinity within us which witnesses everything we think or do and which protects us and guides us along the true path, it is clear that we shall cease to have any other fear on the face if the earth, save the fear of God. Loyalty to the Governor of governors supersedes all other loyalty and gives an intelligent basis to the latter.

Meaning of *Swadeshi*

And when we have sufficiently cultivated this spirit of fearlessness, we shall see that there is no salvation for us without true *swadeshi*, not the *swadeshi* which can be conveniently put off. *Swadeshi* for me has a deeper meaning. I would like us to apply it in our religious, political and economic life. It is not, therefore, merely confined to wearing on occasion *swadeshi* cloth. That we have to do for all time, not out of a spirit of jealousy or revenge, but because it is a duty we owe to our dear country. We commit a breach of the *swadeshi* spirit certainly if we wear foreign-made cloth, but we do so also if we adopt the foreign cut. Surely, the style of our dress has some correspondence with our environment. In elegance and tastefulness, it is immeasurably superior to the trousers and the jacket. An Indian, wearing a shirt flowing over his pyjamas with a waist-coat on it without a necktie and its flaps hanging loose behind, is not a very graceful spectacle. *Swadeshi* in religion teaches one to measure the glorious past and re-enact it in the present generation. The pandemonium that is going on in Europe shows that modern civilization represents forces of evil and darkness, whereas the ancient, i. e., Indian, civilization represents in its essence the divine force. Modern civilization is chiefly materialistic, as ours is chiefly spiritual. Modern civilization occupies self in the investigation of the laws of matter, and employs human ingenuity in inventing of discovering means of production and weapons of destruction; ours is chiefly occupied in exploring spiritual laws. Our *shastras* lay down unequivocally that a proper observance of truth, chastity, scrupulous regard for all life, abstention from coveting others' possessions and refusal to hoard anything but what is necessary for our daily wants is indispensable for a right life; that without it a knowledge of the divine element is an impossibility. Our civilization tells us with daring certainty that a proper and perfect cultivation of the quality of *ahimsa* which, in its active form means purest love and pity, brings the whole world to our feet. The author of this discovery gives a wealth of illustration which carries conviction with it.

The Doctrine of *Ahimsa*

Examine its result in the political life. There is no gift so valued by our *shastras* as the gift of life. Consider what our relations would be with our rulers if we gave absolute security of life to them. If they could but feel that, no matter what we might feel about their acts, we would hold their bodies as sacred as our own, there would immediately spring up an atmosphere of mutual trust, and there would be such frankness on either side as to pave the way for an honourable and just solution of many problems that worry us today. It should be remembered that in practising *ahimsa,* there need not be any reciprocation, though, as a matter of fact, in its final stages, it commands reciprocation. Many of us believe, and I am one of them, that through our civilization we have a message to deliver to the world. I render my loyalty to the British Government quite selfishly. I would like to use the British race for transmitting this mighty message of *ahimsa* to the whole world. But that can only be done when we have conquered our so-called conquerors; and you, my Arya Samaj friends, are perhaps specially elected for this mission. You claim to examine our scriptures critically; you take nothing for granted and you claim not to fear to reduce your belief to practice. I do not think that there is any room for trifling with or limiting the doctrine of *ahimsa.* You dare, then, to reduce it to practice regardless of immediate consequences which would certainly test the strength of your convictions. You would not only produce salvation for India, but you would render the noblest service that a man can render to humanity—a service moreover, which you would rightly assert the great *Swami* was born for. This *swadeshi* is to be considered as a very active force to be ceaselessly employed with an ever-increasing vigilance, searching self-examination. It is not meant for the lazy, but it is essentially meant for them who would gladly lay down their lives for the sake of truth. It is possible to dilate upon several other phases of *swadeshi,* but I think I have said enough to enable you to understand what I mean. I only hope that you, who represent a school of reformers in India, will not reject what I have said without thorough examination. And, if my word has commended itself to you, your past record entitles me to expect you to enforce in your own lives the things of eternity about which I have ventured to speak to you this afternoon, and cover the whole of India with your activity.

Work of the Arya Samaj

In concluding my report of the above speech, I would like to state what I did not in speaking to that great audience and it is this. I have now twice visited the Gurukul. In spite of some vital difference with my brethren of the Arya Samaj, I have a sneaking regard for them, and it, and perhaps the best result of the activity of the Arya Samaj is to be seen in the establishment and the conduct of the Gurukul. Though it depends for its vitality entirely upon the inspiring presence of Mahatmaji Munshi Ram, it is truly a national and self-governing and self-governed institution. It is totally independent of Government aid or patronage. Its war chest is filled not out of monies received from the privileged few, but from the poor many who make it a point of honour from year to year to make a pilgrimage to Kangri and willingly give their mite for maintaining this National College. Here at every anniversary a huge crowd gathers and the manner in which it is handled, housed and fed evinces no mean power of organisation. But the most wonderful thing about it all is that the crowd consisting of about the thousand men, women and children is managed without the assistance of a single policeman and without any fuss or semblance of force, the only force that subsists between the crowd and the managers of the institution is that of love and mutual esteem. Fourteen years are nothing in the life of a big institution like this. What the collegiates who have been just turned out during the last two or three years will be able to show, remains to be seen. The public will not and cannot judge men or institutions except through the results that they show. It makes no allowance for failures, it is a most exacting judge. The final appeal of the Gurukul as of all popular institutions must be to this judge. Great responsibility, therefore, rests upon the shoulders of the students who have been discharged from the college and who have entered upon the thorny path of life. Let them beware. Meanwhile those who are well-wishers of this great experiment may derive satisfaction from the fact that we have it as an indisputable rule of life, that as the tree is, so will the fruit be.

The tree looks lovely enough. He who waters it is a noble soul. Why worry about what the fruit is likely to be ?

Industrial Training

As a lover of the Gurukul, I may be permitted to offer one or two suggestions to the Committee and the parents. The Gurukul boys need a thorough industrial training if they are to become self-reliant and self-supporting. It seems to me that in our country in which 85 per cent of the population is agricultural and perhaps 10 per cent occupied in supplying the wants of the peasantry, it must be part of the training of every youth that he has a fair practical knowledge of agriculture and hand-weaving. He will lose nothing if he knows a proper use of tools, can saw a piece of board straight and build a wall that will not come down through a faulty handling of the plumber's line. A boy who is thus equipped will never feel helpless in battling with the world and never be in want of employment. A knowledge of the laws of hygiene and sanitation as well as the art of rearing children should also form a necessary part of [the training of] the Gurukul lads. The sanitary arrangements at the fair left much to be desired. The plague of flies told its own tale. These irrepressible sanitary inspectors incessantly warned us that in point of sanitation all was not well with us. They plainly suggested that the remains of our food and excreta needed to be properly buried. It seemed to me to be such a pity that a golden opportunity was being missed of giving to the annual visitors practical lessons on sanitation. But the work must begin with the boys. Then the management would have at the annual gathering three hundred practical sanitary teachers. Last but not least, let the parents and the Committee not spoil their lads by making them ape European dress or modern luxuries. These will hinder them in their afterlife and are antagonistic to *brahmacharya*. They have enough to fight against in the evil inclinations common to us all. Let us not make their fight more difficult by adding to their temptations.

3.5

At Muir College Economic Society, Allahabad

December 22, 1916

(Mr. M.K. Gandhi delivered an instructive lecture on 'Does economic progress clash with real progress?' at a meeting of the Muir Central College Economic Society held on Friday evening in the physical science theatre. The Hon. Pandit Madan Mohan Malaviya presided. There was a good gathering of ladies and gentlemen, European and Indian, besides a large number of students. Among those present were Dr. E.G. Hill, the Hon. Dr. Sundar Lal, the Hon. Mr. A.W. Pim, the Hon. Mr. H.C. Ferard, the Hon. Dr. Tej Bahadur Sapru, the Hon. Mr. E.H. Ashworth, Mr. H.S.L. Polak, Prof. Gidwani, Prof. Stanley Jevons, Prof. Higginbottom, the Hon. Mr. C.Y. Chintamani, Mr. B.H. Bourdillon, Mr. Mackenzie, Prof. Moody, Prof. Dunn, Prof. Redford, Pandit Baldeo Ram Dave, Mr. Lalit Mohan Banerji, Pandit Rama Kant Malaviya, Pandit Radha Kant Malaviya, Rai Braj Narain Gurtu, Mr. Kichlu, Mr. Shamnath Mushran, Mr. Iswar Saran, Babu Shiva Prasad Gupta, Prof. Sri Prakash, Prof. Ojha, Prof. Karwell, Prof. Thompson, Dr. M.C. Tandon, Mr. Purushottam Das Tandon, Mr. Jagjivan Nath Takru.)

Dr. Hill proposed the Hon. Pandit Malaviya to the chair and welcomed Mr. Gandhi in their midst.

The Hon. Pandit Malaviya in introducing Mr. Gandhi said that his was a name honoured throughout India and wherever Indians lived. His name was also appreciated by a large number of Europeans who understood his character. It was always an instruction to him to read of the work he had done and of the life he had led.

Mr. Gandhi then delivered the following lecture :

When I accepted Mr. Kapildeva Malaviya's invitation to speak to you upon the subject of this evening, I was painfully conscious of my limitations. You are an economic society. You have chosen distinguished specialists for the subjects included in your syllabus for this year and the next. I seem to be the only speaker ill-fitted for the task set before him. Frankly and truly, I know very little of economics, as you naturally understand them. Only the other day, sitting at an evening meal, a civilian friend deluged me with a series of questions on my crankisms. As he proceeded in his cross-examination, I being a willing victim, he found no difficulty in discovering my gross ignorance of the matters. I appeared to him to be handling with a cocksureness worthy only of a man who knows not that he knows not. To his horror and even indignation, I suppose, he found that I had not even read books on economics by such well-known authorities as Mill, Marshall, Adam Smith and a host of such other authors. In despair, he ended by advising me to read these works before experimenting in matters economic at the expense of the public. He little knew that I was a sinner past redemption. My experiments continue at the expense of trusting friends. For, there come to us moments in life when about some things we need no proof from without. A little voice within us tells us, "You are on the right track, move neither to your left nor right, but keep to the straight and narrow way." With such help we march forward slowly indeed, but surely and steadily. That is my position. It may be satisfactory enough for me, but it can in no way answer the requirements of a society such as yours. Still it was no use my struggling against Mr. Kapildeva Malaviya. I knew that he was intent upon having me to engage your attention for one of your evenings. Perhaps you will treat my intrusion as a welcome diversion from the trodden path. An occasional fast after a series of sumptuous feasts is often a necessity. And as with the body, so, I imagine, is the case with the reason. And if your reason this evening is found fasting instead of feasting, I am sure it will enjoy with the greater avidity the feast that Rao Bahadur Pandit Chandrika Prasad has in store for you for the 12th of January.

Before I take you to the field of my experiences and experiments, it is perhaps best to have a mutual understanding about the title of this evening's address : *Does economic progress clash with real progress*? By economic progress, I take it, we mean material advancement without limit and by real progress we mean moral progress, which again is the same thing as progress of the permanent element in us. The subject may, therefore, be stated thus : "Does not moral progress increase in the same proportion as material progress?" I know that this is a wider proposition than the one before us. But I venture to think that we always mean the larger one even when we lay down the smaller. For we know enough of science to realise that there is no such thing as perfect rest or repose in this visible universe of ours. If, therefore, material progress does not clash with moral progress, it must necessarily advance the latter. Nor can we be satisfied with the clumsy way in which sometimes those who cannot defend the larger proposition put their case. They seem to be obsessed with the concrete case of thirty millions of India stated by the late Sir William Wilson Hunter to be living on one meal a day. They say that before we can think or talk of their moral welfare, we must satisfy their daily wants. With these, they say, material progress spells moral progress. And then is taken a sudden jump : what is true of thirty millions is true of the universe. They forget that hard cases make bad law. I need hardly say to you how ludicrously absurd this deduction would be. No one has ever suggested that grinding pauperism can lead to anything else than moral degradation. Every human being has a right to live and, therefore, to find the wherewithal to feed himself and where necessary to clothe and house himself. But, for this very simple performance, we need no assistance from economists or their laws.

"Take no thought for the morrow" is an injuction which finds an echo in almost all the religious scriptures of the world. In well-ordered society, the securing of one's livelihood should be and is found to be the easiest thing in the world. Indeed, the test of orderliness in a country is not the number of millionaires it owns, but the absence of starvation among its masses. The only statement that has to be examined is whether it can be laid down as a law of universal application that material advancement means moral progress.

Now let us take a few illustrations. Rome suffered a moral fall when it attained high material affluence. So did Egypt and so perhaps most countries of which we have any historic record. The decendants, kinsmen of the royal and divine Krishna, too, fell when they were rolling in riches. We do not deny to the Rockefellers and the Carnegies possession of an ordinary measure of morality but we gladly judge them indulgently. I mean that we do not even expect them to satisfy the highest standard of morality. With them material gain has not necessarily meant moral gain. In South Africa, where I had the privilege of associating with thousands of our countrymen on most intimate terms, I observed almost invariably that the greater the possession of riches, the greater was their moral turpitude. Our rich men, to say the least, did not advance the moral struggle of passive resistance as did the poor. The rich men's sense of self-respect was not so much injured as that of the poorest. If I were not afraid of treading on dangerous ground, I would even come nearer home and show you that possession of riches has been a hindrance to real growth. I venture to think that the scriptures of the world are far safer and sounder treatises on laws of economics than many of the modern text-books. The question we are asking ourselves this evening is not a new one. It was addressed to Jesus two thousand years ago. St. Mark has vividly described the scene. Jesus is in his solemn mood; he is earnest. He talks of eternity. He knows the world about him. He is himself the greatest economist of his time. He succeeded in economising time and space—he transcended them. It is to him at his best that one comes running, kneels down, and asks : "Good Master, what shall I do that I may inherit eternal life?" And Jesus said unto him : "Why callest thou me good? There is none good but one, that is God. Thou knowest the commandments. Do not commit adultery, Do not kill, Do not steal, Do not bear false witness, Defraud not, Honour thy father and mother." And he answered and said unto him : "Master, all these have I observed from my youth." Then Jesus beholding him, loved him and said unto him : "One thing thou lackest. Go thy way, sell whatever thou hast and give to the poor, and thou shalt have treasure in heaven—come take up the cross and follow me." And he was sad at that saying and went away grieved—for he had great possessions. And Jesus looked round about and said unto his disciples : "How hardly shall they that have riches enter into the kingdom of God." And the disciples were astonished at his words. But Jesus answereth again and saith unto them : "Children, how hard it is for them that trust in riches to enter into the kindgom of God. It is easier for a camel to go through the eye of a needle than for a rich man to enter into the kingdom of God !" Here you have an eternal rule of life stated in the noblest words the English language is capable of producing. But the disciples nodded unbelief as we do even to this day. To him they said as we say today : "But look how the law fails in practice. If we sell all and have nothing, we shall have nothing to eat. We must have money or we cannot even be reasonably moral." So they state their case thus. "And they were astonished out of measure saying among themselves : 'Who then can be saved?' " And Jesus looking upon them saith : "With men it is impossible but not with God, for with God all things are possible." Then Peter began to say unto him : "Lo, we have left all, and have followed thee." And Jesus answered and said : "Verily I say unto you there is no man that has left house or brethren or sisters; or father or mother, or wife or children or lands for my sake and the Gospels, but he shall receive one hundred fold, now in this time houses and brethren and sisters and mothers and children and lands with persecutions and in the world to come eternal life. But many that are first shall be last and then last first." You have here the result or reward, if you prefer the term, of following the law. I have not taken the trouble of copying similar passages from the other non-Hindu scriptures and I will not insult you by quoting in support of the law stated by Jesus passages from the writings and sayings of our own sages, passages even stronger if possible than the Biblical extracts I have drawn your attention to. Perhaps the strongest of all the testimonies in favour of the affirmative answer to the question before us are the lives of the greatest teachers of the world. Jesus, Mahomed, Buddha, Nanak, Kabir, Chaitanya, Shankara, Dayanand,

Ramakrishna were men who exercised an immense influence over and moulded the character of thousands of men. The world is the richer for their having lived in it. And they were all men who deliberately embraced poverty as their lot.

I should not have laboured my point as I have done, if I did not believe that, insofar as we have made the modern materialistic craze our goal, insofar are we going downhill in the path of progress. I hold that economic progress in the sense I have put it is antagonistic to real progress. Hence, the ancient ideal has been the limitation of activities promoting wealth. This does not put an end to all material ambition. We should still have, as we have always had, in our midst people who make the pursuit of wealth their aim in life. But we have always recognised that it is a fall from the ideal. It is a beautiful thing to know that the wealthiest among us have often felt that to have remained voluntarily poor would have been a higher state for them. That you cannot serve God and Mammon is an economic truth of the highest value. We have to make our choice. Western nations today are groaning under the heel of the monster-god of materialism. Their moral growth has become stunted. They measure their progress in £ S d. American wealth has become the standard. She [*sic*] is the envy of the other nations. I have heard many of our countrymen say that we will gain American wealth but avoid its methods. I venture to suggest that such an attempt if it were made is foredoomed to failure. We cannot be 'wise, temperate and furious' in a moment. I would have our leaders to teach us to be morally supreme in the world. This land of ours was once, we are told, the abode of the gods. It is not possible to conceive gods inhabiting a land which is made hideous by the smoke and the din of null chimneys and factories and whose roadways are traversed by rushing engines dragging numerous cars crowded with men mostly who know not what they are after, who are often absent-minded, and whose tempers do not improve by being uncomfortably packed like sardines in boxes and finding themselves in the midst of utter strangers who would oust them if they could and whom they would in their turn oust similarly. I refer to these things because they are held to be symbolical of material progress. But they add not an atom to our happiness. This is what Wallace, the great scientist, has said as his deliberate Judgement. In the earliest records which have come down to us from the past, we find ample indications that general ethical considerations and conceptions, the accepted standard of morality, and the conduct resulting from these were in no degree inferior to those which prevail today.

In a series of chapter, he then proceeds to examine the position of the English nation under the advance in wealth it has made. He says :

This rapid growth of wealth and increase of our power over nature put too great a strain upon our crude civilization, on our superficial Christianity, and it was accompanied by various forms of social immorality almost as amazing and unprecedented.

He then shows how factories have risen on the corpses of men, women and children, how as the country has rapidly advanced in riches, it has gone down in morality. He shows this by dealing with insanitation, life-destroying trades, adulteration, bribery and gambling. He shows how, with the advance of wealth, justice has become immoral, deaths from alcoholism and suicide have increased. the average of premature births and congenital defects has increased, and prostitution has become an institution. He concludes his examination by these pregnant remarks :

> The proceedings of the divorce courts show other aspects of the result of wealth and leisure, while a friend who had been good deal in London society assured me that both in country houses and in London various kinds of orgies were occasionally to be met with which would hardly have been surpassed in the period of the most dissolute emperors. Of war, too, I need say nothing. It has always been more or less chronic since the rise of the Roman Empire; but there is now undoubtedly a disinclination for war among all civilized peoples. Yet the vast burden of armaments, taken together with the most pious declarations in favour of peace, must be held to show an almost total absence of morality as a guiding principle among the governing classes.

Under the British aegis, we have learnt much, but it is my firm belief that there is little to gain from Britain in intrinsic morality, that if we are not careful, we shall introduce all the vices that she has been a prey to, owing to the disease of materialism. We can profit by that connection only if we keep our civilization, and our morals, straight, i.e., if instead of boasting of the glorious past, we express the ancient moral glory in our own lives and let our lives bear witness to our past. Then we shall benefit her and ourselves. If we copy her because she provides us with rulers, both they and we shall suffer degradation. We need not be afraid of ideals or of reducing them to practice even to the uttermost. Ours will only then be a truly spiritual nation when we shall show more truth than gold, greater fearlessness than pomp of power and wealth, greater charity than love of self. If we will but clean town houses, our palaces and temples of the attributes of wealth and show in them the attributes of morality, we can offer battle to any combinations of hostile forces without having to carry the burden of a heavy militia. Let us seek first the kingdom of God and His righteousness and the irrevocable promise is that everything will be added with us. These are real economics. May you and I treasure them and enforce them in our daily life.

3.6

At Gujarati Political Conference–I

GODHRA, *November 3, 1917*

(Lokamaṇya B.G. Tilak having arrived late for the opening session, Gandhiji remarked :

I am not responsible for his being late. We demand *swaraj.* If one does not mind arriving late by three-quarters of an hour at a conference summoned for the purpose, one should not mind if *swaraj* too comes correspondingly late.

Gandhiji then read his speech) :

Brothers and Sisters,

I am thankful to you all for the exalted position to which you have called me. I am but a baby of two years and a half in Indian politics. I cannot trade here on my experience in South Africa. I know that, in these circumstances, acceptance of the position is to certain extent impertinence. I have accepted it, all the same, unable to resist the pressure of your overwhelming affection.

I am conscious of my responsibility. This Conference is the first of its kind in Gujarat. The time is most critical for the whole of India. The Empire is labouring under a strain never before experienced. My views do not quite take the general course. I feel that some of them run in the opposite direction. Under the circumstances, I am hardly qualified for this privileged position. The President of a meeting is usually its spokesman. I cannot pretend to lay any such claim. It is your kindness that gives me such a unique opportunity of placing my thoughts before the Gujarat public. I do not see anything wrong in these views being subjected to criticism, dissent and even emphatic protest. I would like them to be freely discussed. I will only say with regard to them that they were not formed today or yesterday. But they were formed years ago. I am enamoured of them, and my Indian experience of two years and a half has not altered them.

I congratulate the originators of the proposal to hold this conference as also those friends who have given practical shape to it. It is a most important event for Gujarat. It is possible for us to make it yield very valuable results. This conference is in the nature of a foundation, and if it is well and truly laid, we need have no anxiety as to the superstructure. Being in the nature of a foundation, it carries a heavy responsibility. I pray that God may bless us with wisdom and that our deliberations will benefit the people.

This is a political conference. Let us pause a moment over the word "political". It is, as a rule, used in a restricted sense, but I believe it is better to give it a wider meaning. If the work of such a conference were to be confined to a consideration of the relations between the rulers and the ruled, it would not only be incomplete, but we should even fail to have an adequate conception of those relations. For instance, the question of *mahua* flowers is of great importance for a part of Gujarat. If it is considered merely as a question between the Government and the people, it might have unhappy consequences or we might fail in our aim. If we considered the genesis of the law on *mahua* flowers and also appreciated our duty as individuals in this matter, we would, very probably, succeed sooner in our fight with the Government than otherwise and easily discover the key to successful agitation. You will more clearly perceive my interpretation of the word "political" in the light of the views I shall place before you.

Conferences do not, as a rule at the end of their deliberations, leave behind them an executive body, and even when such a body is appointed; it is, to use the language of the late Mr. Gokhale composed of men who are amateurs. What we need is men who would make it their business to give effect to the resolutions of such conferences. If such men come forward in great numbers, then and then only will such conferences be a credit to the country and produce lasting results. At present there is much waste of energy. It is desirable that there should be many institutions of the type of the Servants of India Society. Only when men, fired with the belief that service is the highest religion, come forward in great numbers, could we hope to see great results. Fortunately, India is richly endowed with the religious spirit, and if it is realized that in the present age service of the motherland is the best religion, religiously inclined men and women would take part in public life in larger numbers. When sages and saints take up this work, I believe India will achieve her cherished aims quite easily. At all events, it is incumbent on us that, for the purposes of this conference, we form an executive committee whose business it would be to enforce its resolutions.

The air in the country is thick with cries of *swaraj.* It is due to Mrs. Besant that *swaraj* is on the lips of hundreds of thousands of men and women. What was unknown to most men and women only two years ago, has, by her consummate tact and her indefatigable efforts, become common property for them. There cannot be the slightest doubt that her name will take the first rank in history among those who inspired us with the hope that *swaraj* was attainable at no distant date. *swaraj* was, and is, the goal of the Congress. The idea did not originate with her. But the credit of presenting it to us as a goal realizable in the immediate future belongs to that lady alone. For that we could hardly thank her enough. By releasing her and her associates, Messrs Arun Date and Wadia, Government have laid us under an obligation, and at the same time acknowledged the just and reasonable nature of the agitation for *swaraj.* It is to be wished that the Government extend the same generosity towards our brothers, Mahomed Ali and Shaukat Ali. It is not necessary to inquire how much of what Sir William Vincent has said about them needs to be looked into. It is to be hoped that the Government will accede to the people's desire for their release and leave it to them to see that no untoward results follow. This will place the people under a still greater obligation. The act of generosity will be incomplete so long as these brothers are not released. The grant of freedom to the brothers will gladden the people's hearts and endear the Government to them.

Mr. Montagu will shortly be in our midst. The work of taking signatures to the petition to be submitted to him is going on apace. The chief object of this petition is to educate the people about *swaraj.* To say that literacy is essential for achieving *swaraj* betrays ignorance of history. It is not necessary for the purpose of inculcating among people the idea that we ought to manage our own affairs. What is essential is the idea, the desire itself. Hundreds of unlettered kings have ruled kingdoms with great success. To see how far such an idea exists in the minds of the people and to try to create it where it is absent is the object of this petition. It is desirable that millions of men and women should sign it with the fullest understanding of what it means. That such a largely signed petition will naturally have its due weight with Mr. Montagu is its natural result.

No one has the right to alter the scheme of reforms approved by the Congress and the Moslem League, and one need not, therefore, go into the merits thereof. For our present purposes, we have to understand thoroughly the scheme formulated most thoughtfully by our leaders and, putting our faith in them, do whatever is necessary to get it implemented.

This scheme is not *swaraj,* but is a great step towards *swaraj.* Some English critics tell us that we are not fit to enjoy *swaraj,* because the class that demands it is incapable of defending India. "Is the defence of India to rest with the British alone?" they ask, "and are the reins of Government to be in the hands of the Indians?" Now this is a question which is both amusing and painful. It is amusing because our British friends fancy that they are not of us, whilst our plan of *swaraj* is based upon retention of the British connection. We do not want the Englishmen who have settled here to leave this country. They will be our partners in *swaraj.* And they will have nothing to complain about if, in such a scheme, the burden of the defence of the country falls on them. They are, however, hasty in assuming that we shall not do our share of defending the country. When India decides to acquire military strength, she will attain it in no time. We have but to harden our feelings to be able to strike. To cultivate a hardened feeling does not take ages. It grows like weeds. The question is painful, because it puts in mind the fact that the Government have up to now debarred us from military training. Had they been so minded, they would have had at their disposal today, from among the educated classes, quite a large army. Government have to accept a larger measure of blame than the educated classes for the latter having taken little part in the War. Had the Government policy been shaped differently from the very beginning, they would have today an unconquerable army. But let no one be blamed for the present situation. At the time the British rule was established, it was considered a wise policy for the governance of crores of men to deprive them of arms and military training. But it is never too late to mend, and both the rulers and the ruled must immediately repair the omission.

In offering these views I have assumed the propriety of the current trend of thought. To me, however, it does not appear to be tending altogether in the right direction. Our agitation is based on the Western model. The *swaraj* we desire is of a Western type. As a result of it, India will have to enter into competition with the Western nations. Many believe that there is no escape from this. I do not think so. I cannot forget that India is not Europe, India is not Japan, India is not China. The divine word that "India alone is the land of *karma* the rest is the land of *bhoga* (enjoyment)," is indelibly imprinted on my mind. I feel that India's mission is different from that of other countries. India is fitted for the religious supremacy of the world. There is no parallel in the world for the *tapascharya* that this country has voluntarily gone through. India has little use for steel weapons; it has fought with divine weapons; it can still do so. Other nations have been votaries of brute force. The terrible war going on in Europe furnishes an irrefutable proof of this. India can conquer all by soul-force. History supplies numerous instances to prove that brute force is nothing before soul-force. Poets have sung of this and men of wisdom have said so. A thirty-year-old youth behaves like a lamb before his eighty-year-old father. This is an instance of love-force. Love is *atman* it is the very property of *atman*. If we have faith enough, we can wield that force over the whole world. Religion having lost its hold on us, we are without an anchor to keep us firm amidst the storm of modern civilization, and are, therefore, being tossed to and fro. I shall return to this idea at a later stage.

These views of mine notwithstanding, I have joined the *swaraj* movement, for India is being governed at present under a modern system. The Government themselves believe that the "Parliament" is the best form of that system. Without such a Parliament, we should have neither the modern nor the ancient form. Mrs. Besant is only too true when she says that we shall soon be facing a hunger strike, if we do not have Home Rule. I do not want to go into statistics. The evidence of my eyes is enough for me. Poverty in India is deepening day by day. No other result is possible. A country that exports its raw produce and imports it back as finished goods, a country which, though growing its own cotton, has to pay crores of rupees to outsiders for its cloth, cannot be otherwise than poor. A country, in which it is considered extravagance to spend on marriages, etc., can only be described as poor. It must be a terribly poor country that cannot afford to spend enough in carrying out improvements for stamping out epidemics like the plague. In a country whose officials spend most of their earnings outside, the people are bound to grow poorer day by day. What are we to say of the poverty of a country whose people, during cold weather, burn their precious manure for want of woollen clothing in order to warm themselves? Throughout my wanderings in India I have rarely, seen a face exuding strength and joy. The middle classes are groaning under the weight of awful distress. The lowest orders have nothing but the earth below and the sky above. They do not know a bright day. It is pure fiction to say that India's riches are buried underground, or are to be found in her ornaments. What there is of such riches is of no consequence. The nation's expenditure has increased, not so its income. Government have not deliberately brought about this state of things. I believe that their intentions are sincere. It is their honest opinion that the nation's prosperity is daily growing. Their faith in their Blue books is immovable. It is only too true that statistics can be made to prove anything. The economists deduce India's prosperity from statistics. People like me who follow rough and ready ways of reckoning shake their heads over Blue-book statistics. If the gods were to come down and testify otherwise, I would insist on saying that I see India growing poorer.

What then would our Parliament do if we had one? When we have it, we would have a right to commit blunders and to correct them. In the early stages we are bound to make blunders. But, we, being children of the soil, won't lose time in setting ourselves right. We shall, therefore, soon find out remedies against poverty. Then our existence won't be dependent on Lancashire goods. Then we shall not be found spending untold riches on building Imperial Delhi. It will, then, be in keeping with the cottages of India. There will be some proportion observed between that cottage and our Parliament House. *The nation today is in a helpless condition; it does not possess even the right to err. He who has no right to err can never go forward.* The history of the Commons is a history of blunders. Man, says an Arabian proverb, is error personified. *The freedom to err and the power to correct errors is one definition of Swaraj.* Having a Parliament means such *swaraj.*

We ought to have Parliament this very day. We are quite fit for it. We shall, therefore, get it on demand. It rests with us to define "this very day".

Swaraj is not to be attained through an appeal to the British democracy, the British people. They cannot appreciate such an appeal. Its reply will be : "We never sought outside help to obtain *swaraj.* We achieved it with our own strength. You have not received it because you do not deserve it. When you do, nobody can withhold it from you".

How then shall we fit ourselves for it? We have to demand *swaraj* from our own people. Our appeal must be to them. When the peasantry of India understands what *swaraj* is, the demand will become irresistible.

The late Sir W.W. Hunters said that, in the British system, victory on the battle-field was the shortest way to one's goal. If educated India had, silently, taken its full share in the present War, I am certain that we would not only have reached our goal already, but the manner of it would have been altogether unique.

We often refer to the fact that many sepoys of Hindustan have lost their lives on the battle-fields of France and Mesopotamia. The educated classes cannot claim the credit for this. They were not sent out by us, nor did they join up through patriotism. They know nothing of *swaraj*. At the end of the War they will not ask for it. They have gone to demonstrate that they are faithful to the salt they eat. In asking for *swaraj*, I feel that it is not possible for us to bring into account their services. The only thing we can say is that we are not to blame for not being able to take a big part in the prosecution of the War.

That we have been loyal at a time of stress is no test of fitness for *swaraj*. Loyalty is no merit. It is a necessity of national existence all the world over. That loyalty can be no passport to *swaraj* is a self-demonstrated maxim.

Our fitness lies in that we now keenly desire *swaraj*, and in our clearly realizing that bureaucracy, although it has served India with best intentions, has had its day. And this kind of fitness is sufficient for our purpose. Without *swaraj* there is now no possibility of peace in India.

But if we confine our activities for advancing *swaraj* only to holding meetings, the nation is likely to suffer harm. Meetings and speeches have their own place and time. *But they cannot make a nation.*

In a nation fired with the zeal for *swaraj*, we should observe an awakening in all departments of life. The first step to *swaraj* lies in the individual. The great truth, "As with the individual, so with the Universe," is applicable here as elsewhere. If we are ever torn by conflict from within, if we are ever going astray, and if instead of ruling our passions we allow them to rule us, *swaraj* can have no meaning for us. Government of self, then, is the first step.

Then the family. If dissensions reign supreme in our families, if brothers fight among themselves, if members of a family cannot live together; if joint families, i.e., families enjoying self-government, become divided through family quarrels, how can we be considered fit for *swaraj* ?

Now for caste. If caste-fellows become jealous of one another, if the castes cannot manage their affairs in an orderly manner, if the elders claim especial importance, if the members become self-opinionated and thus show their unfitness for self-government in this limited sphere, how can they be fit for national government?

After caste, the city. If we cannot regulate the affairs of our cities, if our streets are not kept clean, if our homes are dilapidated and if our roads are crooked, if we cannot command the services of selfless citizens for civic government, and those who are in charge of affairs are neglectful or selfish, how shall we claim larger powers?

The way to national life lies through the cities. It is, therefore, necessary to linger a little longer on this subject. The plague has found a home in India. Cholera has been always with us. Malaria takes an annual toll of thousands. The plague has been driven out from every other part of the world. Glasgow stamped it out the moment it made its appearance there. In Johannesburg it could appear but once. Its municipality made a great effort and stamped it out within a month, whereas we are able to do nothing about it. We cannot blame the Government for this state of things. To tell the truth, we cannot even blame it on our poverty. None can stand in our way in any remedies that we may wish to adopt.

Ahmedabad, for instance, cannot evade responsibility by pleading poverty. I am afraid that in regard to the plague, we must shoulder the entire responsibility. It is very significant that when the plague is working havoc in our rural quarters, cantonments as a rule remain free. The reasons are obvious. In the cantonments the air is a pure, house detached, roads are wide and clean and the sanitary habits of the residents wholesome, whereas ours are as unhygienic as they well could be. Our closets are as filthy as hell. In a country in which ninety per cent of the populations go barefoot, people spit anywhere and perform natural functions anywhere and we are obliged to walk on roads and paths thus dirtied. It is no wonder that the plague has found a home in our midst.

Unless we alter the conditions in our cities, rid ourselves of our dirty habits and have improved latrines, *swaraj* can have no value for us.

It will not be out of place here to refer to another matter. We regard men who render us most useful service, *Bhangis*, as untouchables. The result has been that we let them clean only a part of our closets. In the name of religion, we ourselves would not clean the places for fear of pollution and so, despite our reputation for personal cleanliness, a portion of our houses remains the dirtiest in the world, with the result that we grow up in an air which is laden with disease germs. We were safe so long as we kept to our villages. But in the cities we are ever committing suicide by reason of our insanitary habits.

Where large numbers suffer living death, it is very likely that people know neither true religion nor right action and conduct. I believe that it ought not to be beyond us to banish the plague from India, and if we can do so, we shall have so increased our fitness for *swaraj*, as it cannot be by any agitation, howsoever powerful. This is a question meriting the serious consideration of our doctors and *vaidyas*.

Not far from here is the holy centre of pilgrimage, Dakor. I have visited it. Its unholiness is limitless. I consider myself a devout *Vaishnava*. I claim, therefore, a special privilege of criticising the condition of Dakorji. The insanitation of that place is so great that one used to hygienic conditions can hardly bear to pass even twenty-four hours there. The pilgrims pollute the tank and the streets as they choose. The keepers of the shrine quarrel among themselves and, to add insult to injury, a receiver has been appointed to take charge of the jewellery and costly robes of the idol. It is our clear duty to set matters right. How shall we, Gujaratis, out to have *swaraj*, fare as soldiers in the army fighting for it, if we cannot put our own house in order?

To think of the state of education in our cities also fills us with despair. It is plainly our duty by our own effort to provide education to the masses. But our gaze is fixed upon Government, whilst thousands of children go without education.

In the cities the drink-evil is on the increase, tea-shops are multiplying, gambling is rampant. If we cannot remedy these evils, how can we attain *swaraj* ? *Swaraj* means managing our own affairs.

We are approaching a time when we and our children may have to go without milk altogether. Dairies, here in Gujarat, are doing us infinite harm. They buy out practically the whole milk-supply and produce butter, cheese, etc., for sale. How can a nation whose nourishment is chiefly derived from milk permit itself to be deprived of this important article of food? How can men be so selfish as to be heedless of the national health and think of enriching themselves through commercial exploitation of an article of diet ? Milk and its products are of such paramount value to the nation that they deserve to be controlled by the municipalities. What are we doing about them?

I have just returned from the scene of *Bakr-i-Id* riots. For a trivial cause, the two communities fell out with each other, mischievous men joined in the fray and a mere spark became a blaze. We found ourselves helpless. We have been obliged to depend entirely upon Government assistance. This shows how crippled we are.

It will not be inopportune to dwell for a moment on the question of cow-protection. It is an important question. And yet it is left to be solved by cow-protection societies. Protecting the cows seems to be an ancient practice. It originated in the special needs of this country. Protection of its cows is incumbent upon a country, whose 90 per cent population lives upon agriculture and needs bullocks for it. In such a country, even meat-eaters should abstain from beef eating. These natural causes should be enough justification for not killing cows. But here we have to face a peculiar situation. The chief meaning of cow-protection seems to be to prevent cows from falling into the hands of our Muslim brethren and being used as food. The rulers need beef. On their account thousands of cows are slaughtered daily. We do nothing to prevent this slaughter. We hardly make any attempt to prevent the cruel torture of cows by certain Hindus of Calcutta, who subject them to a practice known as "blowing" and make them yield the last drop of milk. In Gujarat, Hindu cart-drivers use sharp goads to drive bullocks. We say nothing about this. The condition of bullocks in our cities is pitiable. Indeed, protection of the cow and her progeny is a very great problem. By making it a pretext for quarrelling with the Muslims, we have only ensured greater slaughter of cows. It is not religion, but want of it, to kill a Muslim brother in order to save a cow. I feel sure that if we were to discuss the matter with our Muslim brethren in the spirit of love, they also would appreciate the peculiar condition of India and readily co-operate with us in the protection of cows. By courtesy and through *satyagraha*, we can bring them to join that mission. But, in order to be able to do this, we shall have to understand the question in its true bearing. Instead of killing our brethren, we should be ready to die ourselves. But we shall be able to do this only when we understand the real value of the cow and have pure love for her. Success in this will ensure several things simultaneously. Hindus and Muslims will live in peace, the cow will be safe, milk and its products will be available in a pure condition and will be cheaper than now, and our bullocks will become the envy of the world. If our *tapascharya* is pure, we shall succeed in stopping slaughter of cows, whether by the British, Muslims or Hindus. Even this one achievement will bring *swaraj* nearer.

Many of these issues arise out of civic government. We can clearly see from this that our running the Government of India is dependent upon our upright management of civic affairs.

It will not be incorrect to say that practically there is no *swadeshi* movement in the country. We do not realize that this movement almost holds the key to *swaraj*. If we have no regard for our own language, if we feel aversion to cloth made in our country, if our dress repels us, if we are ashamed to wear the sacred *shikha* if our food is distasteful to us, even our climate is not good enough, our people uncouth and unfit for our company, our civilization ugly and the foreign attractive, in short, if everything native is bad and everything foreign pleasing to us, I do not know what *swaraj* can mean for us. If everything foreign is to be adopted, surely it will be necessary for us to continue long under foreign tutelage, for so far foreign ways have touched the masses but little. It seems to me that, before we can appreciate *swaraj*, we should have not only love but passion for *swadeshi*. Every act of ours should bear the *swadeshi* stamp. *Swaraj* can only be built upon the assumption that most of what is national is, on the whole, sound. If the view here put forth be correct, we should have a big movement in our country for *swadeshi*. Every country that has carried on a movement for *swaraj* has fully appreciated the *swadeshi* spirit. Scottish Highlanders hold on to their kilts even at the risk of their lives. We humorously call them the "petticoat brigade". But the whole world testifies to the strength that lies behind that "petticoat" and the Highlanders of Scotland will not abandon it, even though it is an inconvenient dress, and an easy target for the enemy. I don't wish to suggest that we should treasure our faults, but that what is national, even though not rich in excellences, should be adhered to, and that what is foreign should be avoided though one may succeed well enough in adopting it. That which is wanting in our civilization can be supplied by proper effort on our part. I do hope that the *swadeshi* spirit will possess every member in this assembly; if they all take the vow of *swadeshi* and observe it in the face of any difficulty or inconvenience, *swaraj* will be easy of attainment.

The foregoing illustrations go to show that our movement should be two-fold. We may petition the Government, we may agitate in the Imperial Council for our rights; but for a real awakening of the people, the more important thing is activities directed inwards. There is a possibility of hypocrisy and selfishness tainting activities directed outwards. There is very much less danger of this in activities of the other kind. Not only will the former not be justified unless balanced by the latter, they may even be barren of results. It is not my contention that we have no activities at all directed inward, but I submit that we do not lay enough stress upon them.

One sometimes hears it said, "Let us get the Government of India in our own hands; everything will be all right afterwards". There could be no greater superstition than this. No nation has gained its independence in this manner. The splendour of the spring is reflected in every tree, the whole earth is then filled with the freshness of youth. Similarly, when the spring of *swaraj* is on us, a stranger suddenly arriving in our midst will observe the freshness of youth in every walk of life and find servants of the people engaged, each according to his own abilities, in all manner of public activities.

If we admit that our progress has not been what it might have been, we should also admit two reasons for this. We have kept our women away from these activities of ours and have thus become victims of a kind of paralysis. The nation walks with one leg only. All its work appears to be only half or incompletely done. Moreover, the educated section, having received its education through a foreign tongue, has become enervated and is unable to give the nation the benefit of such ability as it acquires. I need not reiterate my views on this subject, as I have elaborated them in my address at the Gujarat Educational Conference. It is a wise decision, that of conducting the proceedings of this conference in Gujarati, and I hope that nothing will induce the people of Gujarat to change it.

The educated class, lovers of *swaraj*, must freely mix with the masses. We dare not turn away from a single section of the community or disown any. We shall make progress only if we carry all with us. Had the educated class identified itself with the masses, *Bakr-i- Id* riots would have been an impossibility.

Before coming to the last topic, it remains for me to refer to certain events as a matter of duty and to make one or two suggestions.

Every year the god of death exacts his toll from among our leaders. I do not intend to mention the victims claimed by this god all over India during the last 12 months. But it is impossible to omit reference to the sage-like Grand Old Man of India. Who am I to estimate the value of his services to the country? I am no more than one who sat at his feet. I paid my respects to him when I went to London as a mere lad. I came to revere him from the very moment I waited upon him with a letter of introduction. Dadabhai's flawless and uninterrupted service to the country, his impartiality, his spotless character, will always furnish India with an ideal to follow. May God give him peace ! May He grant his family and the Nation the ability to bear the loss? We can immortalize him by making his character our own, by copying his manner of service and by enthroning him forever in our hearts. May the great soul of Dadabhai watch over our deliberations !

It is our duty to express our thanks to His Excellency the Viceroy for having announced the decision of the Government of India to abolish the customs levy on the border [between Saurashtra and British Indian territory] at Viramgam. This step should have been taken earlier. The people were groaning under the weight of this impost. It cost large number of their trade. It has caused much suffering to many women. The decision does not seem to have been brought into effect. It is to be hoped that it will soon be.

I have submitted through the Press my experiences about the hardships of third-class railway passengers. They are, indeed, past endurance. The people of India are docile and trained in silent suffering. Thousands, therefore, put up with the hardships, but they remain unredressed. There is, indeed, merit in such suffering, but it must have its limits. Submission out of weakness is unmanliness. That we tamely put up with the hardships of railway travelling is a sign of our unmanliness. These hardships are of two kinds, those which are due to the remissness of railway administration and those occasioned by the carelessness of the travelling public. The remedies are also, therefore, two-fold. Where the railway administration is to blame, complaints should be addressed to it by everyone who suffers. This may be done even in Gujarati. The matter should be ventilated in the Press. Secondly, where the public are to blame, the wiser among passengers should inculcate manners upon their ignorant companions and enlighten them on their carelessness and dirty habits. This will require volunteers. Everyone can do his share according to his ability, and leaders might, in order to appreciate the difficulties of third-class travelling, resort to it from time to time without making themselves known and bring their unhappy experiences to the notice of the administration. If these remedies are adopted, we should, in a short time, see great changes.

A committee had been appointed in London to consider certain measures about the supply of indentured labour to Fiji and the other sister islands. The views of that committee have been officially published and the Government of India have invited the opinion of the public upon them. I need not dwell at length upon the matter as I have submitted my views already through the Press. I have given it as my opinion that the recommendations of the committee, if adopted, will result in a kind of indenture. We can, therefore, only come to one conclusion. We do not want to see labourers emigrating under bondage in any shape or form. There is no need for such emigration. The only thing required is a complete repeal of the law of indenture. It is no part of our duty to look to the convenience of the Colonies.

I come now to the last subject. There are two methods of attaining one's goal. *Satyagraha* and *duragraha*. In our scriptures, they have been described, respectively, as divine and devilish modes of action. In *satyagraha,* there is always unflinching adherence to truth. It is never to be forsaken on any account. Even for the sake of one's country, it does not permit resort to falsehood. It proceeds on the assumption of the ultimate triumph of truth. A *satyagrahi* does not abandon his path, even though at times it seems impenetrable and best with difficulties and dangers, and a slight departure from that straight path may appear full of promise. Even in these circumstances, his faith shines resplendent like the midday sun and he does not despond. With truth for sword, he needs neither a steel sword nor gun-powder. Even an inveterate enemy he conquers by the force of the soul, which is love. Love for a friend is not put to the test. There is nothing surprising in a friend loving a friend; there is no merit in it and it costs no effort. When love is bestowed on the so-called enemy, it is tested, it becomes a virtue and requires an effort, and hence it is an act of manliness and real bravery. We can cultivate such an attitude even towards the Government and, doing so, we shall be able to appreciate their beneficial activities and, as for their errors, rather than feel bitter on their account, point them out in love and so get them rectified. Love does not act through fear. Weakness there certainly cannot be. A coward is incapable of bearing love, it is the prerogative of the brave. Looking at everything with love, we shall not regard the Government with suspicion, nor believe that all their actions are inspired with bad motives. And our examination of their actions being directed by love, will be unerring and is bound, therefore, to carry conviction with them.

Love can fight; often, it is obliged to. In the intoxication of power, man fails to see his error. When that happens, a *satyagrahi* does not sit still. He suffers. He disobeys the ruler's orders and his laws in a civil manner, and willingly submits to the penalties of such disobedience, for instance, imprisonment and gallows. Thus is the soul disciplined. In this, one never finds that one's time has been wasted and, if it is subsequently realized that such respectful disobedience was an error, the consequences are suffered merely by the *satyagrahi* and his co-workers. In the event, no bitterness develops between the *satyagrahi* and those in power; the latter, on the contrary, willingly yield to him. *They discover that they cannot command the* satyagrahi's *obedience. They cannot make him do anything against his will. And this is the consummation of* swaraj, *because it means complete independence*. It need not be assumed that such resistance is possible only against civilized rulers. Even a heart of flint will melt in the fire kindled by the power of the soul. Even a Nero becomes a lamb when he faces love. This is no exaggeration. It is as true as an algebraic equation. This *satyagraha* is India's distinctive weapon. It has had others but *satyagraha* has been in greater use. It is an unfailing source of strength, and is capable of being used at all times and under all circumstances. It requires no stamp of approval from the Congress or any other body. He who knows its power cannot but use it. Even as the eyelashes automatically protect the eyes, so does *satyagraha*, when kindled, automatically protect the freedom of the soul.

But *duragraha* is a force with the opposite attributes. As we saw earlier, the terrible War going on in Europe is a case in point. Why should a nation's cause be considered right and another's wrong because it overpowers the latter by sheer brute force? The strong are often seen preying upon the weak. The wrongness of the latter's cause is not to be inferred from their defeat in a trial of brute strength, nor is the rightness of the strong to be inferred from their success in such a trial. The wielder of brute force does not scruple about the means to be used. He does not question the propriety of means, if he can somehow achieve his purpose. This is not *dharma* but the opposite of it. In *dharma,* there can be no room for even a particle of untruth or cruelty, and no injury to life. The measure of *dharma* is love, compassion, truth. Heaven itself, if attained through sacrifice of these, is to be despised. *Swaraj* is *useless at the sacrifice of truth*. Such *swaraj* will ultimately ruin the people. The man who follows the path of *duragraha* becomes impatient and wants to kill the so-called enemy. There can be but one result of this. Hatred increases. The defeated party vows vengeance and simply bides its time. The spirit of revenge thus descends from father to son. It is much to be wished that India never gives predominance to this spirit of *duragraha*. If the members of this assembly deliberately accept *satyagraha* and chalk out its programme accordingly, they will reach their goal all the more easily for doing so. They may have to face disappointment in the initial stages. They may not see results for a time. But *satyagraha* will triumph in the end. The *duragrahi,* like the oilman's ox, moves in a circle. His movement is only motion but it is not progress. The *satyagrahi* is ever moving forward.

A superficial critic of my views may find some contradiction in them. On the one hand, I appeal to the Government to give military training to the people. On the other, I put *satyagraha* on the pedestal. Surely, there can be no room for the use of arms in *satyagraha*. Of course there is none. But military training is intended for those who do not believe in *satyagraha*. That the whole of India will ever accept *satyagraha* is beyond my imagination. A cowardly refusal to defend the nation, or the weak, is ever to be shunned. In order to protect an innocent woman from the brutal design of a man, we ought to offer ourselves a willing sacrifice and by the force of love conquer the brute in the man. Lacking such strength, we should employ all our physical strength to frustrate those designs. The *satyagrahi* and the *duragrahi* are both warriors. The latter, bereft of his arms, acknowledges defeat, the former never. He does not depend upon the perishable body and its weapons, but he fights on with the strength of the unconquerable and immortal *atman*. Anyone who is neither of the two is not a man, for he does not recognize the *atman*. If he did, he would not take fright and run away from danger. Like a miser his wealth, he tries to save his body and loses all; such a one does not know how to die. But the armoured soldier always has death by him as a companion. There is hope of his becoming one day a *satyagrahi*. The right thing to hope from India is that this great and holy Aryan land will ever give the predominant place to the divine force and employ the weapon of *satyagraha*, that it will never accept the supremacy of armed strength. India will never respect the principle of might being right. She will ever reserve her allegiance to the principle : "Truth alone triumphs".

On reflection, we find that we can employ *satyagraha* even for social reform. We can rid ourselves of the many defects of our caste system. We can resolve Hindu-Muslim differences and can solve political problems. It is all right that, for the sake of convenience, we speak of these things as separate subjects. But it should never be forgotten that they are all closely inter-related. It is not true to say that neither religion nor social reform has anything to do with politics. The result obtained by bringing religion into play in the field of politics will be different from that obtained otherwise. When thinking of political matters, we cannot ignore 56,000 ignorant *sadhus* living as wandering mendicants. Our Muslim brethren cannot lose sight of their *fakirs*. Nor can we be unmindful of the condition of our widows and the custom of child marriage and the Muslims of the custom of *purdah*. The two communities cannot, likewise, shut their eyes to scores of questions that arise between them.

Indeed, our difficulties are Himalayan. But we have equally potent means at our disposal for overcoming them. We are children of an ancient nation. We have witnessed the burial of civilizations : those of Rome, Greece and Egypt. Our civilization abides even as the ocean in spite of its ebbs and flows. We have all we need to keep ourselves independent. We have great mountains and rivers. We have the matchless beauty of nature, and the sons and daughters of this land have handed down to us a heritage of deeds of valour. This country is the treasure house of *tapascharya*. In this country alone do people belonging to different religions live together in amity and the gods of all are venerated. If, despite all this bounty, we fail to work a miracle, bring peace to the world and conquer the British through the play of moral force in our life, we shall have disgraced our heritage. The English nation is full of adventure, the religious spirit guides it, it has unquenchable faith in itself, it is a nation of great soldiers, it treasures its independence; but it has given the place of honour to its commercial instinct, it has not always narrowly examined the means adopted for seeking wealth. It worships modern civilization. The ancient ideals have lost their hold upon it. If, therefore, instead of imitating that nation, we cherish our past and sincerely value our strength, trust firmly in its supremacy, we shall know how to take the best advantage of our connection with the British and so make it profitable to us, to them and to the entire world. I pray to the Almighty that this assembly may play its part in this great work and thereby shed lustre upon itself, upon Gujarat, and upon the whole of India.

[*From Gujarati*]

3.7

On Regeneration of Women

February 2, 1918

The largest part of our effort in promoting the regeneration of women should be directed towards removing those blemishes which are represented in our *shastras* as the necessary and ingrained characteristics of women. Who will attempt this and how? In my humble opinion, in order to make the attempt we will have to produce women, pure, firm and self-controlled as Sita, Damayanti and Draupadi. If we do produce them, such modern sisters will receive the same homage from Hindu society as is being paid to their prototypes of yore. Their words will have the same authority as the *shastras*. We will feel ashamed of the stray reflections on them in our *smritis* and will soon forget them. Such revolutions have occurred in Hinduism in the past and will still take place in the future, leading to the stability of our faith.

We have considered the ideals by the realization of which the present condition of our women can be improved. The number of women who can realize those ideals will be necessarily very few and, therefore, we will now consider what ordinary women can accomplish if they will try. Their first attempt should be directed towards awakening in the minds of as many women as possible a proper sense of their present condition. I am not among those who believe that such an effort can be made through literary education only. To work on that basis would be to postpone indefinitely the accomplishment of our aims; I have experienced at every step that it is not at all necessary to wait so long. We can bring home to our women the sad realities of their present condition without, in the first instance, giving them any literary education. Many of our movements stop half way because of the condition of our women. Much of our work does not yield appropriate results; our lot is like that of the penny wise and pound foolish trader who does not invest enough capital in his business.

But although much good and useful work can be done without a knowledge of reading and writing, yet it is my firm belief that you cannot always do without a knowledge thereof. It develops and sharpens one's intellect and it stimulates our power of doing good. I have never placed an unnecessarily high value on the knowledge of reading and writing. I am only attempting to assign its proper place to it. I have pointed out from time to time [that] there is no justification for men to deprive women or to deny to them equal rights on the grounds of their illiteracy ; but education is essential for enabling women to uphold these natural rights, to improve them and to spread them; again, the true knowledge of self is unattainable by the millions who are without such education. Many a book is full of innocent pleasure and this will be denied to us without education. It is no exaggeration to say that a human being without education is not far removed from an animal. Education, therefore, is necessary for women as it is for men. Not that the methods of education should be identical in both cases. In the first place, our State system of education is full of error and productive of harm in many respects. It should be eschewed by men and women alike. Even if it were free from its present blemishes, I would not regard it as proper for women from all points of view.

In framing any scheme of women's education, this cardinal truth must be constantly kept in mind. Man is supreme in the outward activities of a married pair and, therefore, it is in the fitness of things that he should have a greater knowledge thereof. On the other hand, home life is entirely the sphere of woman and, therefore, in domestic affairs, in the upbringing and education of children, women ought to have more knowledge. Not that knowledge should be divided into watertight compartments or that some branches of knowledge should be closed to any one; but unless courses of instruction are based on a discriminating appreciation of these basic principles, the fullest life of man and woman cannot be developed.

I should like to say a word or two as to whether English education is or is not necessary for our women. I have come to the conclusion that, in the ordinary course of our lives, neither our men nor our women need necessarily have any knowledge of English. True, English is necessary for making a living and for active association in our political movements. The few women who may require or desire to have English education can very easily have their way by joining the schools for men. To introduce English education in schools meant for women could only lead to a prolongation of our helplessness. I have often read and heard people saying that the rich treasures of English literature should be opened alike to men and women. I submit in all humility that there is some misapprehension in assuming such an attitude. No one intends to close these treasures against women while keeping them open for men. There is none on earth able to prevent you from studying the literature of the whole world if you are fond of literary tastes. But when courses of education have been framed with the needs of a particular society in view, you cannot supply the requirements of the few who have cultivated a literary taste. In asking our men and women to spend less time in the study of English than they are doing now, my object is not to deprive them of the pleasure which they are likely to derive from it, but I hold that the same pleasure can be obtained at less cost and trouble if we follow a more natural method. The world is full of many a gem of priceless beauty; but then those gems are not all of English setting. Other languages can well boast of productions of similar excellence; all these should be made available to our common people and that can only be done if our own learned men will undertake to translate them for us in our own languages.

Merely to have outlined a scheme of education as above is not to have removed the bane of child marriage from our society or to have conferred on our women an equality of rights.

Let us now consider the case of our girls who disappear, so to say, from view after marriage. They are not likely to return to our schools. Conscious of the unspeakable and unthinkable sin of the child-marriage of their daughters, their mothers cannot think of educating them or of otherwise making their dry life a cheerful one. The man who marries a young girl does not do so out of any altruistic motives, but through sheer lust. Who is to rescue these girls? A proper answer to this question will also be a solution of the woman's problem. The answer is *albeit* difficult, but it is the only one. There is, of course, none to champion her cause but her husband. It is useless to expect a child-wife to be able to bring round the man who has married her. The difficult work must, therefore, for the present at least, be left to man. If I could, I would take a census of child-wives and would find the friends of their husbands and through such friends, as well as through moral and polite exhortations, I will attempt to bring home to them the enormity of their crimes in linking their fortunes with child-wives and will warn them that there is no expiation for that sin unless and until they have by education made their wives fit not only to bear children but also to bring them up properly, and unless, in the meantime, they live a life of absolute celibacy.

When printing presses were non-existent and scope for speech-making very limited, when one could hardly travel twenty-four miles in the course of a day instead of a thousand miles as now, we had only one agency for propagating our ideals and that was our 'acts'; and acts had immense potency. We are now rushing to and fro with the velocity of air, delivering speeches, writing newspaper articles, and yet we fall short of our accomplishments and the cry of despair fills the air. I for one am of opinion that, as in old days, our acts will have a more powerful influence on the public than any number of speeches and writings. (Therefore we) should give prominence to quiet and unobtrusive work.

(From a speech at the annual gathering of the Bombay Bhagini Samaj held on February 20, 1918)

3.8

To Ahmedabad Mill-Hands

March 15, 1918

You must have heard what happened this morning. Some were shocked, others wept. I do not feel that there was anything wrong, or anything of which I need be ashamed, in this morning's development. I do not feel angry at the criticism made by the residents of Jugaldas Chawl. Rather, I, and others as well who want to serve India, have much to learn from it. I have always believed that, if our capacity for *tapascharya* or voluntary suffering is real enough, we are bound to reap the fruit. You took an oath relying on my advice. In this age the oath has lost its value. Men break their oath at any time and for any reason and I am grieved to have been instrumental in thus lowering the value of an oath. There is nothing else that will bind a man as effectively as an oath does. The meaning of an oath is that we decide to do a particular thing with God in whom we believe as our witness. People who are on a higher plane can perhaps do without oaths, but we who are on a lower one cannot. We who fall a thousand times cannot raise ourselves without oaths. You will admit that, had we not taken the oath and repeated it daily, many of us would have fallen long ago. You yourselves have said that never before have you known a strike as peaceful as this. The reason why some have fallen is that they are faced with starvation. I would advice you to keep your oath even if you have to starve, though it is our pledge, mine and my co-workers', that we will not allow you to starve. If we look on unconcernedly while you are starving, you may give up your pledge by all means. There is one more thing we should have mentioned along with these two. It is that if, while not allowing you to starve, we ask you to beg, we would be guilty in the eyes of God and would prove no better than thieves. But what should I do to persuade you to maintain yourselves with manual labour? I can do manual work, I have been doing it, and would do so even now; but I do not get the opportunity for it. I have a number of things to attend to, and can, therefore, do some manual work only by way of exercise. Will it behave you to tell me that you have worked on looms, but cannot do other physical labour ? This notion has taken deep root in India. It is good as a principle that a man should specialize in one type of work only; but it would be improper to use this as an excuse. I have thought much about this. When I came to know of your bitter criticism of me, I felt that, if I wanted to keep you to the path of *dharma* and show you the worth of an oath and the value of labour, I must set a concrete example before you. We are not out to have fun at your cost or to act a play. How can I prove to you that we are prepared to carry out whatever we tell you? I am not God that I can demonstrate this to you in some way [other than by fasting]. I should very much like to do something which would convince you that you would have to be plain with me, that it would not do for you merely to act a part. Nobody can be induced or coerced to keep his oath. Love is the only inducement that can be offered. You must understand that he alone, who loves his religion, loves his honour and country, will refuse to give up his resolve . . . . . .

I am used to taking such pledges. For fear that people may wrongly imitate me, I would rather not take one at all. But I am dealing with hundreds of thousands of workers. I must, therefore, see that my conscience is clean. I wanted to show you that I was not playing with you.

I have attempted to show you by example that you should value your oath in the same manner as I have done. You have already done one thing. You could have said : "What have we to do with your oath, we cannot continue the fight, we must go back"; but you did not do so. You decided to accept our service. And I thought of you the more highly for that. It seemed a beautiful thing to me to sink or swim with you.

[From Gujarati]
Ek Dharmayuddha

3.9

On Hindi

Indore
March 29, 1918

[Gandhiji's Presidential Speech at the Eighth Session of the Hindi Sahitya Sammelan, Indore, *1918*]

Brothers and Sisters,

Our most venerable and selfless leader Pandit Madan Mohan Malaviya has not found it possible to attend this conference. I had requested him to come if he could and he promised to do so. But though he has not been able to come he has sent us a letter. I was sure that in case he did not come, he would send a letter stating his views, and it would be possible for me to read it out to you. I have received the letter today. I had asked the reception committee to secure views of scholars on two questions in regard to Hindi. Panditji in his letter has replied to these two questions.

(After reading out Malaviyaji's letter, Gandhiji said :)

The question of language presents a big and indeed a very important problem. Even if all the leaders were to devote themselves entirely to this task turning away from everything else, they well may. If on the other hand, we were to regard it as of secondary importance only and to direct our attention away from it then all the enthusiasm which people now feel for it and the keen interest they are taking in it at present would be in vain.

Language is like our mother. In fact I have no real interest in this sort of a conference. It will be a three days' pageant after which we shall disperse, go away to our respective places and forget all that we said or heard. What is needed is the urge and the resolve to do things. The President's speech cannot give you that urge. It is something which you have to create for yourselves. One of the charges made against us is that our language lacks spirit. Where there is no knowledge there is no spirit. We have neither the urge to know nor to do things. It is only when we acquire dynamic energy that our people and our language also will acquire it. We cannot get the freedom we want through a foreign language for the simple reason that we are not able to use it effectively. I am pleased to know that in Indore you carry on all your dealings through Hindi. But—excuse me please—the letter I have received from your Chief Minister is in English. The people of Indore perhaps do not know—but I will tell them—that here the courts entertain petitions written in English. I ask why it should be so in Indore. I admit that this movement—the movement for the adoption of Hindi—cannot yet succeed in British India, but there is no reason why it should not succeed in the Indian States. The educated classes, as Pandit Malaviyaji has pointed out in his letter, have unfortunately fallen under the spell of English and have developed a distaste for their own mother tongue. The milk one gets from the former is adulterated with water and contaminated with poison, while that from the latter is pure. It is impossible to make any advance without this pure milk. But a blind person cannot see and a slave does not know how to break his fetters. We have been living under the spell of the English now for the past fifty years. In the result our people have remained steeped in ignorance. The conference must give special attention to this part of the problem. We should see that within a year conditions are created when not a word of English will be heard in any of our political or social conferences, in the Congress, in the provincial assemblies and the like. Let us abandon the use of English entirely. English has attained the position of a universal language. But that is because the English have spread and established themselves throughout the world. As soon as they lose that position,

English will shrink in its extent. We should no more neglect and thus destroy our own language. The English insist on speaking their mother tongue and using it for all their purposes. Let us do the same and thus raise Hindi to the high status of a national language. Only thus shall we discharge our duty to it. Now I will read out my written speech.

Mr. President, Delegates, Brothers and Sisters,

You have done me great honour in conferring on me the Presidentship of this conference. I know only too well that from the point of view of the knowledge of Hindi, my qualifications for this honour are almost nil. The only thing which may be said to qualify me for it is my boundless love of Hindi. I hope that I would always be able to pass this test of love.

The extent of a particular literature can only be reckoned on the basis of the region where that language is spoken. If the region of Hindi remains confined to the Northern part of India, the extent of its literature must remain limited. But in case it becomes a national language, the expanse of its literature will become as wide as the country. As the people speaking a particular language, so the language. If we want that high-souled men from the East and the West, from the North and the South, should come to take a dip in the sea of this language, it is obvious that the sea must acquire sufficient importance. Therefore the place of Hindi from the point of view of developing a national literature needs to be considered.

It is necessary to give some thought to the definition of the Hindi language. I have often said that Hindi is that language which is spoken in the North by both Hindus and Muslims and which is written either in the Nagari or the Persian script. This Hindi is neither too Sanskritized nor too Persianized. The sweetness which I find in the village Hindi is found neither in the speech of the Muslims of Lucknow nor in that of the Hindu *pandits* of Prayag. The language which is easily understood by the masses is the best. All can easily follow the village Hindi. The source of the river of language lies in the Himalayas of the people. It will always be so. The Ganga arising with the village Hindi which will flow on for ever, while the Sanskritized and Persianized Hindi will dry up and fade away, as does a rivulet springing from a small hillock.

The distinction made between Hindus and Muslims is unreal. The same unreality is found in the distinction between Hindi and Urdu. It is unnecessary for Hindus to reject Persian words and for Muslims to reject Sanskrit words from their speech. A harmonious blend of the two will be as beautiful as the confluence of the Ganga and Yamuna and last for ever. I hope that we will not waste our energy and weaken our strength by entering into the Hindi-Urdu controversy. There is, no doubt, difficulty in regard to script. As things are, Muslims will patronize the Arabic script, while Hindus will mostly use the Nagari script. Both scripts will, therefore, have to be accorded their due places. Officials must know both scripts. There is no difficulty in this. In the end, the script which is the easier of the two will prevail. There is no doubt that there ought to be a common language for mutual intercourse between the different parts of India. Once we forget the Hindi-Urdu controversy, we shall realize that for Muslims throughout India Urdu is the *lingua franca.* This proves that since Moghul times, Hindi or Urdu was well on its way to becoming the national language of India.

Even today, there is no language to rival Hindi in this respect. The question of national language becomes quite easy of solution once we give up the Hindi-Urdu controversy. Hindus will have to learn some Persian words while Muslims will have to learn some Sanskrit words. This exchange will enrich and strengthen the Islamic language and provide a very fruitful means for bringing Hindus and Muslims closer together. In fact we have to work so hard for dispelling the present fascination for the English language that we must not raise the Hindu-Urdu controversy. Nor must we fight over the script.

Why English cannot become our national language, what harm results from the imposition of English on our people, how our people have suffered and their development has been retarded by the adoption of English as the medium of education—I have dealt with in my speeches at Broach and

Bhagalpur. I will not, therefore, repeat myself here. Indeed there is no doubt that Sir Rabindranath Tagore, Smt. Besant, Lokamanya Tilak and other respected and influential persons entertain similar views regarding this question. There will certainly be difficulties in the way of the achievement of our purpose but it will be for this body to tackle them. Lokamanya Tilak has indeed expressed his views in this regard not only in words but also in action by starting a Hindi section in his papers the *Kesari* and *The Mahratta*. The views of Bharat Ratna Pandit Madan Mohan Malaviya on this question are well known. Still, unfortunately, some of our learned leaders hold that for at least some years to come English must remain the national language. We will respectfully request these leaders to consider that this unreasonable attraction for English is causing much hardship to our people, as they get little benefit out of the knowledge of their English-educated countrymen between whom and them a wide gulf has been created through English.

It is unnecessary to say that I do not hate the English language. I myself have benefited from many of the precious gems of the great treasure of English Literature. We have also to acquire a knowledge of science and such like through the English Language. Knowledge of English is therefore necessary for us. But it is one thing to give it its due place and quite another to make a fetish of it.

It is clear that our purpose will not be achieved merely by accepting that Hindi-Urdu should be our national language. We have to consider how we may achieve this goal. The scholars who have graced this assembly by their presence will certainly have something to say on this point. I will make a few suggestions on how we may spread this language. There must first be a handy book—sort of a "Hindi Teacher" which will meet the needs of those who want to learn Hindi. I have seen a small book of this type for those who want to learn Hindi through Bengali. There is one in Marathi also. But I have not seen any such books for other regional languages. This is as easy to do as it is necessary. I hope that this Sammelan will soon take up this work. Of course, these books should be written by learned and experienced writers.

The greatest difficulty will be felt in the case of the Southern languages. No effort whatever in this direction has yet been made there. We must train good Hindi teachers to take up the work. There is a great scarcity of such teachers. I have secured one such teacher from Prayag through your popular secretary, Bhai Purushottamdasji Tandon.

Similarly, I have not yet seen a single complete grammar of the Hindi language. Such as exist in English and have been written by foreigners. One of these grammars is by Dr. Kellog. There must be a good Hindi grammar which can compare favourably with similar grammars of other Indian languages. It is my humble request to scholars who love Hindi to make up this deficiency.

In our national Councils Hindi alone should be used. Congress workers and leaders can and should do much in this respect. I would suggest that this Conference should make a request to this effect to the Congress at its next session.

In our legislative bodies too the entire proceedings should be conducted through the national language. Our people cannot have training in political affairs so long as this is not done. Our Hindi newspapers are doing something in this respect but the education we want to be imparted to our people cannot be given through translations. Similarly in our courts too the national and provincial languages must be used. Under the existing set-up people are being deprived of the education which they can easily receive from those who administer justice.

The Princes can promote the national language in a way in which the English Government cannot. In the Holkar State, for example, in the Council and in the courts, Hindi and the provincial language alone can be used. The encouragement they thus give to the national language will go a long way in helping its progress. In the schools of this State the entire education from the beginning to the end should be imparted through the mother tongue. In this way our Princes can render much service to the language. I hope that Maharaja Holkar and his officials will take up this work enthusiastically.

It will be a sad delusion to think that we can achieve our objective merely through conferences. Single-minded devotion and constant application alone will bring success. Only when hundreds of selfless scholars regard this work as their own can it be accomplished.

What I regret is that even the provinces which have Hindi for their mother tongue do not seem to show any enthusiasm for its promotion and propagation. The educated classes in these provinces continue to use English for purposes of conversation and correspondence. A friend has written to me that our newspaper proprietors do all their work in English; they keep their accounts, too, in English. Englishmen living in France use their mother tongue in all their dealings. Is it not a pity that we carry on even some of our most important activities in English? It is my humble but firm opinion that unless we give Hindi its national status and the provincial languages their due place in life of the people, all the talk of *swaraj* is useless. It is my fervent hope and prayer to God almighty that this Sammelan may be an instrument for the solution of this great question confronting India.

(*From Hindi*)

3.10

To Students and Teachers, Surat

You must have read a summary of my speech to students in Ahmedabad. I want to talk to you about some of the things I said to them. I shall talk to your elders in the evening. Wherever I go, I like to keep alive the close contacts which I have established with students. Being myself a father of four sons, I understand the son's duty towards his parents. I was myself a son once and some persons whom I respect as elders are still living. Hence, I know very well the duty that sons owe to fathers. A son can be advised to disobey his father, if the occasion demands this. I may thus seem to be giving contradictory advice. What I am going to say to you, I have already told my sons. I have a good many sons, have had quite a few children entrusted to my care and I have brought them up. Only yesterday, a couple belonging to one of the untouchable communities expressed their desire to entrust their daughter to my care. The girl has stayed with me before now. I told her father that he could leave Lakshmi with me only if he gave up all claims on her. I did not make this condition with all parents who entrusted their children to me. Even so, I regard as my very own the children whom I have brought up. I have given my sons advice no less harsh than what I give the students these days. On the right occasion, you can rise against me, your parents and the whole world. If I did not say this, I should violate what I understand to be *dharma*. If one would prosper in *dharma*, one should, if need be, sacrifice one's parents, relations and all others in a *yajna* undertaken in real sincerity of heart as Prahlad sacrificed his father. Prahlad did not offer violent resistance to his father,

Hiranyakashiup, nor did he obey his order forbidding him to worship Vishnu —an order repugnant to his conscience—but said : "In this matter, I will obey His order who is your father, and the grand-father of your grand-father".

Your parents would say you should not leave schools and I say you should. If you understand that what I am asking you to do is your *dharma,* tell your parents respectfully that you cannot attend your schools. This is your duty if you have been sincerely moved. Why do I give such advice? What I say is not meant for students of 10 or 12 years of age. They are not free to think for themselves. They should do their parents's bidding. According to our *shastras,* a child should be lovingly reared for five years, should be disciplined for ten years—"disciplined" not with physical punishment but with instruction and persuasion,—and a son of 16 should be regarded as a friend. Why do I give such advice to young men? For many years I have co-operated with the Government, with the British Empire. Nobody could have given better co-operation than I did, for there was nothing better. My co-operation was inspired by no selfish motive. I did not want any brother or son of mine to be employed in Government service, nor did I wish to be honoured with a title. My attitude, therefore, was entirely disinterested. I gave my co-operation as a matter of *dharma,* duty. I gave obedience to this regime, not because of the punishment it can inflict, but because I thought it my duty to do so. I shall give you one illustration.

When my third son was born, I was faced with the question whether I should get him vaccinated against smallpox. I have a conscientious objection to vaccination. Yet, in 1897, I got the child vaccinated. If a child is not vaccinated within a certain number of days, one is liable to punishment. This law exists only on the statute-book. People do not respect it as they should. I felt that either I should respect it or clarify my position to the Government, which meant that I should disobey it respectfully since I do not accept as vaild the public opinion which it reflects. However, I thought it better to obey it so long as I did not get it amended and hence I got my child vaccinated. But there was an occasion afterwards to resist this same thing, vaccination. While in South Africa, we went to jail. According to the prison rules, one must be vaccinated. We non-co-operated, offered civil resistance. We told the Government that it could keep us in jail longer if it chose, but that we would not agree to vaccination. At last, the Government had to issue an order exempting people from vaccination on grounds of conscience.

How far have I not gone in co-operation? I believe it to be the highest *dharma* indeed to swallow and put up with minor harassments on the part of the Government. Even after we have won *swaraj,* fraud, robbery and Dyerism will flourish. I am not naive or hypocritical enough to say that with *swaraj* will come *Satyayuga*. After all, it will be *swaraj* in *Kaliyuga* and not in *Satyayuga*. It will be the kind of *swaraj* which the British and the Arabs enjoy. But the Dyerism of that time will be tolerable. Power will be in our hands, so that, at the most, we ourselves will have abused it, or will have allowed it to be abused. But what has happened today is not this. It has been done against our will. Had Lord Chelmsford, the Viceroy or Lord Sinha been appointed by us, it would have been a different matter. What we protest against is the way [things are done] and not the skin [of those who do them]. If my friends Dayalji and Kalyanji act unjustly, I may protest and may not even accept milk offered by them. Mr. Andrews, Mahomed Ali and Shaukat Ali are as brothers to me, but I would not accept their appointment as Viceroy since they would have been appointed by the Government. When power is in our hands, we may appoint even Lord Chelmsford as Viceroy, if we trust him, and may dismiss him when we cease to trust him. Today the whole of the country is asking Lord Chelmsford to resign, but there he is. I would give only the kind of co-operation I have explained here. Since that is not possible, I advocate non-co-operation.

I cast the accounts of the Government's rule and found that it had taken away more than it had given. I saw that the Reforms gave no reforms, but made the position worse. The Government's power is maintained not because of its machine-guns, but because of our deluded love for it. This love has taken three forms : Love for the councils, which Dwijendranath

Tagore has compared to [Sita's] infatuation for the illusory deer, love for the courts and love for education. I say nothing about titles and similar honours, for very few have them. But we are very much in the grip of the three above-mentioned infatuations. Our great leader, the learned and veteran Lala Lajpat Rai, is also their victim. Madan Mohan Malaviya, whom I have always revered, also believes that I have lost my head and that I am misleading the people. He thinks that it is *dharma* to enter councils and to attend schools. To my mind, it is a sin to enter councils and attend courts and an altogether heinous sin to attend schools.

There is a reason why I cannot succeed in convincing lawyers. I know how attached they are to things of this world. It is not easy to forsake children, to give up the arm-chair and the motor-car. But a student has no such problem. He can be led as desired. If I do not stop those who receive education for slavery and persist in attending schools and colleges, we shall not succeed in loosening the roots of the Empire. That is what I want to do. Through the students, the Empire gets the manure it needs; they are like the Niagara Falls—like the waters of the Ganga, the Yamuna and the Brahmaputra combined. This bare hint will be enough to make you see that we should have none of this education which breeds ignorance—this education for slavery. Unless I teach you the A B C of how to shake off your slavery, everything else will be unavailing. If you go on pouring milk into an unclean vessel, instead of the latter becoming clean it is the milk that will become dirty. So long as we remain like a vessel polluted by slavery, all education will be mere waste. If there are any gods above and if they see that India is like an unclean vessel, the rain of education will be to no good purpose. First, therefore, see that you are clean. If you do not learn law or medicine, India is not going to sink into the bottomless pit; with slavery, it will. It will not, then, be a country inhabited by human beings but by beasts. Not to speak out one's mind out of fear of anyone—even of a great Empire—this is to be a slave. The first lesson we have to learn is to shake off this fear. May the lesson of Jallianwala and the humiliation of Islam fill everyone with the fire which has possessed me.

The Hindus have two dangers to face. If the Muslims became slaves, through them the Hindus too would be enslaved. This is as simple as the rule of three. If we would protect Hinduism, would spend our time in devotions to Vishnu, sitting under a tree, it is our duty to help the Muslims. If the latter should behave aggressively to you in future, I would tell them to remember this time. You, too, can say that one Gandhi from among you—no matter what kind of man he was in other ways, did something on your behalf. If nothing avails, you may fight it out. I, for one, would ask you to be brave men. As between a man who is ready to lay down his life fighting and another who will do so without fighting, the latter is the braver man. How much stronger of breath must be the man who climbs the Himalayas without a stick in hand or without getting himself carried up in a *doli* than the one who climbs in this way? Having reached the top, such a man will turn to the country and greet it with a peal of happy laughter. The friend sitting by my side (Mahomed Ali) looks upon this as the weapon of the weak. Whether or no he is right, it is only in this way that one can learn even to use the sword. I told my friend Shaukat Ali that the Muslims did not have the strength to make self-sacrifices. When they have the strength to die, they will see that there is no need for a sword at all. Even so, you are welcome to draw the sword when you think it is necessary to do so. An Empire which has betrayed Islam, which made India crawl on its stomach—it is that even if one person was made to do—which forcibly remove the *purdah* off the faces of India's women this happened in the Punjab—how is it possible to co-operate with such an Empire? No matter how many metalled roads they build and what peace prevails in the country—we would rather have rivers of blood flow. Nay, even if we had to go without railways and ships and even if the administration were to break down, I would rather prefer that to the present condition. If you are fired with the same zeal that I am, even those among you who have been forbidden by their parents can leave their schools and colleges. One student's father told me that he would watch how the national school which has been started runs and then see what he should do. A man who withdrew his child from a Government school only after he had, in this manner, first satisfied himself about the working of a national school could be of no help in winning back the [freedom of the] country. One should not be exercised whether one would have education or not. Even if it were possible to teach the idea of freedom to a man who continued meanwhile in his state of slavery, one cannot teach him how to win freedom. If you feel that you have rightly understood what I am saying, give up everything. You will get all things afterwards. It is a divine law that he who lives in utter devotion to God will have all things given to him.

If all the students in Surat left their schools and colleges, how happy the result would be. The professors and teachers would then come asking you on what terms you would remain. You should tell them that, once the connection with the Government was broken off and its aid rejected, you would provide the expenses of the institutions even by begging. This was the ancient way. In those times the pupil approached the teacher with sacrificial wood in his folded hands, told him that he would fetch his fuel and look after his cattle, and prayed to be instructed. In Poona, there is one such Students' Home for orphans which the inmates maintain by begging from door to door. You should do the same rather than sacrifice your humanity by attending the present schools. Great indeed are the hopes built on you.

Here in Surat you have these two great institutions. Their students can do every fine work. Surat has lost its *surat* these days. I expect the people here to make it a point of honour to have education on their own terms or go without it altogether. If all the students showed this strength, we would have the desired result in a month's time. But even if it be that only a few stray students are convinced of this, they should leave the schools this very day. I would tell the students who did this that they had taken one step towards *swaraj,* had spoken up eloquently for the country. If you get no help from your people at home, work with your bodies. Learn, what you do not know at present, how to use your hands and feet, but do not remain in slavery. Believe it for a truth, students, that we needs must give up the love of schools, courts and councils if we want *swaraj* for the country. The first and last step towards *swaraj* is to purify ourselves. Those who have been endowed with teeth will be provided with food, not by this Government but by a Government above this Government. This is for us the first lesson, which has gone out of our minds. I for one give no credit to the Government or the rich for providing food [to the people]. Though the Government was there all the time, thousands of people died victims of the famine in Orissa. There is no dearth of rich men in the country, but even so thousands of these victims went their way to seek refuge in God. Have God's name on your lips, take courage and, without making any calculations—without balancing profit and loss—give notice to your parents and teachers that you cannot attend your schools and colleges. Do not say this, being carried away by my words. I am only trying to stimulate your heart and your reason. Unless convinced, no child has a right to disobey its parents. Only that child has such a right whose heart is on fire as mine is. In the effort to rescue parents addicted to drink from the hold of that evil habit, a son should renounce his inheritance, his home and the protection it provides. If you see that you are getting your education under the shadow of slavery, take the plunge tomorrow, even if you have to go against the wishes of your parents.

3.11

On Untouchability, Ahmedabad

Ahmedabad
April 13, 1921

I regard untouchability as the greatest blot on Hinduism. This idea was not brought home to me by my bitter experiences during the S[outh] African struggle. It is not due to the fact that I was once an agnostic. It is equally wrong to think—as some people do— that I have taken my views from my study of Christian religious literature. These views date as far back as the time when I was neither enamoured of, nor was acquainted with, the Bible or the followers of the Bible.

I was hardly yet twelve when this idea had dawned on me. A scavenger named Uka, an untouchable, used to attend our house for cleaning latrines. Often I would ask my mother why it was wrong to touch him, why I was forbidden to touch him. If I accidentally touched Uka, I was asked to perform the ablutions, and though I naturally obeyed, it was not without smilingly protesting that untouchability was not sanctioned by religion, that it was impossible that it should be so. I was a very dutiful and obedient child and so far as it was consistent with respect for parents, I often had tussles with them on this matter. I told my mother that she was entirely wrong in considering physical contact with Uka as sinful.

While at school I would often happen to touch the 'untouchables', and as I never would conceal the fact from my parents, my mother would tell me that the shortest cut to purification after the unholy touch was to cancel the touch by touching any Mussulman passing by. And simply out of reverence and regard for my mother I often did so, but never did so believing it to be a religious obligation. After some time we shifted to Porbandar, where I made my first acquaintance with Sanskrit. I was not yet put into an English school, and my brother and I were placed in charge of a Brahmin who taught us *Ramaraksha and Vishnu Puja* . The texts *"Jale Vishnuh sthale Vishnuh"* (there is the Lord present in water, there is the Lord present in earth) have never gone out of my memory. A motherly old dame used to live close by. Now it happened that I was very timid then, and would conjure up ghosts and goblins whenever the lights went out, and it was dark. The old mother, to disabuse me of fears, suggested that I should mutter the Texts whenever I was afraid, and all evil spirits would fly away. This I did and, as I thought, with good effect. I could never believe then that there was any text in the *Ramaraksha* pointing to the conduct of the 'untouchables' as a sin. I did not understand its meaning then, or understood it very imper-fectly. But I was confident that *Ramaraksha,* which could destroy all fear of ghosts, could not be countenancing any such thing as fear of contact with the 'untouchables'.

The *Ramayana* used to be regularly read in our family. A Brahmin called Ladha Maharaj used to read it. He was stricken with leprosy, and he was confident that a regular reading of the *Ramayana* would cure him of leprosy, and indeed, he was cured of it. 'How can the *Ramayana,*' I thought to myself, 'in which one who is regarded nowadays as an untouchable took Rama across the Ganges in his boat, countenance the idea of any human beings being 'untouchables' on the ground that they were polluted souls?' The fact that we addressed God as the 'purifier of the polluted' and by similar appellation, shows that it is a sin to regard anyone born in Hinduism as polluted or untouchable— that it is Satanic to do so. I have hence been never tired of repeating that it is a great sin. I do not pretend that this thing had crystallized as a conviction in me at the age of twelve, but I do say that I did then regard untouchability as a sin. I narrate this story for the information of the *Vaishnavas* and orthodox Hindus :

I have always claimed to be a *sanatani* Hindu. It is not that I am quite innocent of the scriptures. I am not a profound scholar of Sanskrit. I have read the *Vedas* and the *Upanishads* only in translations. Naturally, therefore, mine is not a scholarly study of them. My knowledge of them is in no way profound, but I have studied them as I should do as a Hindu and I claim to have grasped their true spirit. By the time I had reached the age of 21, I had studied other religions also.

There was a time when I was wavering between Hinduism and Christianity. When I recovered my balance of mind, I felt that to me salvation was possible only through the Hindu religion and my faith in Hinduism grew deeper and more enlightened.

But even then I believed that untouchability was no part of Hinduism; and, that if it was, such Hinduism was not for me.

True Hinduism does not regard untouchability as a sin. I do not want to enter into any controversy regarding the interpretation of the *shastras*. It might be difficult for me to establish my point by quoting authorities from the *Bhagavat* or *Manusmriti*. But I claim to have understood the spirit of Hinduism. Hinduism has sinned in giving sanction to untouchability. It has degraded us, made us the pariahs of the Empire. Even the Mussulmans caught the sinful contagion from us, and in S[outh] Africa, in E[ast] Africa and in Canada, the Mussulmans no less than Hindus came to be regarded as pariahs. All this evil has resulted from the sin of untouchability.

I may here recall my proposition, which is this : So long as the Hindus wilfully regard untouchability as part of their religion, so long as the mass of Hindus consider it a sin to touch a section of their brethren, *swaraj* is impossible of attainment. Yudhishthira would not enter heaven without his dog. How can, then, the descendants of that Yudhishthira expect to obtain *swaraj* without the untouchables? What crimes for which we condemn the Government as Satanic have not we been guilty of towards our untouchable brethren?

We are guilty of having suppressed our brethren; we make them crawl on their bellies; we have made them rub their noses on the ground; with eyes red with rage, we push them out of railway compartments—what more than this has British Rule done? What charge that we bring against Dyer and O'Dwyer may not others, and even our own people, lay at our door? We ought to purge ourselves of this pollution. It is idle to talk of *swaraj* so long as we do not protect the weak and the helpless, or so long as it is possible for a single *swarajist* to injure the feelings of any individual. *Swaraj* means that not a single Hindu or Muslim shall for a moment arrogantly think that he can crush with impunity meek Hindus or Muslims. Unless this condition is fulfilled we will gain *swaraj* only to lose it the next moment. We are no better than the brutes until we have purged ourselves of the sins we have committed against our weaker brethren.

(From a speech at Suppressed Classes Conference held at Ahmedabad, on April 13, 1921.)

3.12

On Conversion

[From an address to foreign missionaries]

You, the missionaries come to India thinking that you come to a land of heathens, of idolators, of men who do not know God. One of the greatest of Christian divines, Bishop Heber, wrote the two lines which have always left a sting with me : "Where every prospect pleases, and man alone is vile." I wish he had not written them. My own experience in my travels throughout India has been to the contrary. I have gone from one end of the country to the other, without any prejudice, in a relentless search after truth, and I am not able to say that here in this fair land, watered by the great Ganges, the Brahmaputra and the Yamuna, man is vile. He is not vile. He is as much a seeker after truth as you and I are, possibly more so. This reminds me of a French book translated for me by a French friend. It is an account of an imaginary expedition in search of knowledge. One party landed in India and found Truth and God personified, in a little pariah's hut. I tell you there are many such huts belonging to the untouchables where you will certainly find God. They do not reason but they persist in their belief that God is. They depend upon God for His assistance and find it too. There are many stories told throughout the length and breadth of India about these noble untouchables. Vile as some of them may be, there are noblest specimens of humanity in their midst. But does my experience exhaust itself merely with the untouchables? No. I am here to tell you that there are non-Brahmins, there are Brahmins who are as fine specimens of humanity as you will find in any place on the earth. There are Brahmins today in India who are embodiments of self-sacrifice, godliness, and humility. There are Brahmins who are devoting themselves body and soul to the service of untouchables, with no expectation of reward from the untouchables, but with execration from orthodoxy. They do not mind it, because in serving pariahs they are serving God. I can quote chapter and verse from my experience. I place these facts before you in all humility for the simple reason that you may know this land better, the land to which you have come to serve. You are here to find out the distress of the people of India and remove it. But I hope you are here also in a receptive mood and, if there is anything that India has to give, you will not stop your ears, you will not close your eyes and steel your hearts, but open up your ears, eyes and, most of all, your hearts to receive all that may be good in this land. I give you my assurance that there is a great deal of good in India. Do not flatter yourselves with the belief that a mere recital of that celebrated verse in St. John makes a man a Christian. If I have read the *Bible* correctly, I know many men who have never heard the name of Jesus Christ or have even rejected the official interpretation of Christianity will, probably, if Jesus came in our midst today in the flesh, be owned by him more than many of us. I, therefore, ask you to approach the problem before you with open-heartedness, and humility.

I cannot help recalling to you the conversation I related in Darjeeling at the Missionary Language School. Lord Salisbury was waited upon by a deputation of missionaries in connection with China and this deputation wanted protection. I cannot recall the exact words, but give you the purport of the answer Lord Salisbury gave. He said, "Gentlemen, if you want to go to China, to preach the message of Christianity, then do not ask for assistance of temporal power. Go with your lives in your hands and if the people of China want to kill you, imagine that you have been killed in the service of God". Lord Salisbury was right. Christian missionaries come to India under the shadow, or, if you like, under the protection of a temporal power, and it creates an impassable bar.

If you give me statistics that so many orphans have been reclaimed and brought to the Christian faith, I would accept them, but I do not feel convinced thereby that it is your mission. In my opinion, your mission is infinitely superior to that. You want to find men in India and if you want to do that, you will have to go to the lowly cottages not to give them something, might be to take something from them. A true friend as I claim to be of the missionaries of India and of the Europeans, I speak to you what I feel from the bottom of my heart. I miss receptiveness, humility, willingness on your part to identify yourselves with the masses of India. I have talked straight from my heart. May it find a response from hearts.

Young India, 6-8-25

3.13

The National Demand

London
September 15, 1931

(The first speech delivered at the Federal Structure Committee of the Round Table Conference)

I must confess at the outset that I am not a little embarrassed in having to state before you the position of the Indian National Congress. I would like to say that I have come to London to attend this Committee, as also the Round Table Conference when the proper time comes, absolutely in the spirit of co-operation, and to strive to my utmost to find points of agreement. I would like also to give this assurance to His Majesty's Government that at no stage is it, or will it be, my desire to embarrass authority and I would like to give the same assurance to my colleagues here, that, however much we may differ about our view-points, I shall not obstruct them in any shape or form. My position, therefore, here depends entirely upon your goodwill, as also the goodwill of His Majesty's Government. If at any time I found that I could not be of any useful service to the Conference, I would not hesitate to withdraw myself from it. I can also say to those who are responsible for the management of this Committee and the Conference that they have only to give a sign and I should have no hesitation in withdrawing.

I am obliged to make these remarks because I know that there are fundamental differences of opinion between the Government and the Congress, and it is possible that there are vital differences between my colleagues and myself. There is also a limitation under which shall be working. I am but a poor humble agent acting on behalf of the Indian National Congress. And it might be as well to remind ourselves of what the Congress stands for and what it is. You will then extend your sympathy to me, because I know that the burden that rests upon my shoulders is really very great.

THE CONGRESS is, if I am not mistaken, the oldest political organization we have in India. It has had nearly 50 years of life, during which period it has, without any interruption, held its annual session. It is what it means—national. It represents no particular community, no particular class, no particular interest. It claims to represent all Indian interests and all classes. It is a matter of the greatest pleasure to me to state that it was first conceived in an English brain : Allan Octavius Hume we knew as the father of the Congress. It was nursed by two great Parsis, Pherozeshah Mehta and Dadabhai Naoroji, whom all India delighted to recognize as its Grand Old Man. From the very commencement the Congress had Mussalmans, Christians, Anglo-Indians—I might say all the religions, sects, creeds—represented upon it more or less fully. The late Badruddin Tyabji identified himself with the Congress. We have had Mussalmans as Presidents of the Congress, and Parsis undoubtedly. I can recall at least one Indian Christian at the present moment, W.C. Bonnerji, Kalicharen Bannerji, than whom I have not had the privilege of knowing a purer Indian, was also thoroughly identified with the Congress. I miss, as I have no doubt all of you miss, the presence in our midst of Mr. K.T. Paul. Although he never officially belonged to the Congress, he was a nationalist to the full and a sympathizer of the Congress.

The Congress has, from its very commencement, taken up the cause of the so-called untouchables. There was a time when the Congress had at every annual session as its adjunct the Social Conference, to which the late Ranade dedicated his energies, among his many other activities. Headed by him you will find, in the programme of the Social Conference, reform in connection with the untouchables taking a prominent place. But in 1920, the Congress took a large step and brought in the question of the removal of untouchability as a plank on the political platform, making it an important item of the political programme. Just as the Congress considered HIndu-Muslim unity thereby meaning unity amongst all the classes to be indispensable for the attainment of *swaraj,* so also did the Congress consider the removal of the curse of untouchability as an indispensable condition for the attainment of full freedom.

The position the Congress took up in 1920 remains the same today; and so you will see the Congress has attempted from its very beginning to be what it described itself to be, namely, national in every sense of the term.

If Your Highnesses will permit me to say so, in the very early stages the Congress took up your cause also. Let me remind this Committee that it was the Grand Old Man of India who sponsored the cause of Kashmir and Mysore; and these two great Houses, I venture in all humility to submit, owe not a little to the efforts of Dadabhai Naoroji and the Congress. Even up to now the Congress has endeavoured to serve the Princes of India by refraining from any interference in their domestic and internal affairs.

I hope, therefore, that this brief introduction that I thought fit to give will serve to enable the Committee, and those who are at all interested in the claims of the Congress, to understand that it has endeavoured to deserve the claim that it has made. It has failed, I know, often to live up to the claim but I venture to submit that, if you were to examine the history of the Congress, you would find that it has more often succeeded, and progressively succeeded than failed. Above all, the Congress represents, in its essence, the dumb, semi-starved millions scattered over the length and breadth of the land in its 700,000 villages, no matter whether they come from what is called British India or what is called Indian India. Every interest which, in the opinion of the Congress, is worthy of protection, has to subserve the interests of these dumb millions; and so you do find now and again apparently a clash between several interests. But, if there is a genuine real clash, I have no hesitation in saying on behalf of the Congress that the Congress will sacrifice every interest for the sake of the interests of these dumb millions. It is, therefore, essentially a peasant organization, and it is becoming so progressively. You will even the Indian members of the Committee perhaps be astonished to find that today the Congress, through its organization, the All India Spinners' Association, is finding work for nearly 50,000 women in nearly 2,000 villages, and these women are possibly 50 per cent Mussalman women. Thousands of them belong to the so-called untouchable class. We have thus, in this constructive manner, penetrated these villages, and effort is being mde to cover every one of the 700,000 villages. It is a super human task; but if human effort can do so, you will presently find the Congress covering all of these villages and bringing to them the message of the spinning wheel.

This being the representative character of the Congress, you will not be astonished when I read to you the Congress mandate. I hope that it may not jar upon you. You may consider that the Congress is making a claim which is wholly untenable. Such as it is, I am here to put forth that claim on behalf of the Congress in the gentlest manner possible, but also in the firmest manner possible. I have come here to prosecute that claim with all the faith and energy that I can command. If you can convince me to the contrary and show that the claim is inimical to the interests of these dumb millions, I shall revise my opinion. I am open to conviction, but even so I should have to ask my principals to consent to that revision before I could usefully act as the agent of the Congress. At this stage I propose to read to you this mandate so that you can understand clearly the limitations imposed upon me.

This was a resolution passed at the Karachi session of the Indian National Congress :

> "This Congress, having considered the Provisional Settlement between the Working Committee and the Government of India, endorses it, and desires to make it clear that the Congress goal of *purna swaraj,* meaning complete independence, remains intact. In the event of a way remaining otherwise open to the Congress to be represented at any Conference with the representatives of the British Government, the Congress Delegation will work for this

> goal; and in particular, so as to give the nation control over the army, external affairs, finance, fiscal and economic policy, and to have scrutiny by an impartial tribunal of the financial transactions of the British Government in India, and to examine and assess the obligations to be undertaken by India or England and the right to either party to end the partnership at will : provided, however, that the Congress Delegation will be free to accept such adjustments as may be demonstrably necessary in the interests of India."

Then follows the appointment. I have in the light of this mandate endeavoured, as carefully as I was capable, to study the provisional conclusions arrived at by the several Sub-committees appointed by the Round Table Conference. I have also carefully studied the Prime Minister's statement giving the considered policy of His Majesty's Government. I speak as subject to correction; but, so far as I have been able to understand this document, it falls far short of what is aimed at and claimed by the Congress. True, I have the liberty to accept such adjustments as may be demonstrably necessary in the interests of India, but they have all to be consistent with the fundamentals stated in this mandate.

I remind myself at this stage of the terms of what is to me a sacred settlement the settlement arrived at Delhi between the Government of India and the Congress. In that Settlement the Congress has accepted the principle of federation, the principle that there should be responsibility at the Centre, and has accepted also the principle that there should be safeguards in so far as they may be necessary in the interests of India.

There was one phrase used yesterday. I forget by which Delegate, but it struck me very forcibly. He said, "We do not want a mere political constitution". I do not know that he gave that expression the same meaning that it immediately bore to me; but I immediately said to myself, this phrase has given me a good expression. It is true the Congress will not be and, personally speaking. I myself would never be satisfied with a mere political constitution, which to read would seem to give India all it can possibly politically desire, but in reality would give her nothing. If we are intent upon complete independence, it is not from any sense of arrogance; it is not because we want to parade before the universe that we have now severed all connection with the British people. Nothing of the kind. On the contrary, you find in this mandate itself that the Congress contemplates a partnership. The Congress contemplates a connection with the British people but that connection to be such as can exist between two absolute equals. Time was when I prided myself on being, and being called, a British subject. I have ceased for many years to call myself a British subject; I would far rather be called a rebel than a subject. But I have aspired I still aspire to be a citizen, not of the Empire, but in a Commonwealth; in a partnership if possible if God wills it, an indissoluble partnership but not a partnership superimposed upon one nation by another. Hence you find here that the Congress claims that either party should have the right to sever the connection, to dissolve the partnership. It has got to be necessarily, therefore, of mutual benefit. May I say it may be irrelevant to the consideration, but not irrelevant to me—that, as I have said elsewhere, I can quite understand the responsible British statesmen today being wholly engrossed in domestic affairs, in trying to make two ends meet. We could not expect them to do anything less; and I wondered, even as I was sailing towards London, whether we in the Committee at the present moment would not be a drag upon the British Ministers whether we would not be interlopers. And yet I said to myself : It is possible that we might not be interlopers; it is possible that the British Ministers themselves might consider the proceedings of the Round Table Conference to be of primary importance even in terms of their domestic affairs. India, yes, can be held by the sword! I do not for one moment doubt the ability of Britain to hold India under subjection through the sword. But what will conduce to the prosperity of Great Britain, the economic freedom of Great Britain an enslaved but rebellious India, or an India an esteemed partner with Britain to share her sorrows to take part side by side with Britain in her misfortunes?

Yes! If need be, but at her own will, to fight side by side with Britain not for the exploitation of a single race or a single human being on earth, but it may be conceivably for the good of the whole world ! If I want freedom for my country, believe me, if I can possibly help it, I do not want that freedom in order that I, belonging to a nation which counts one-fifth of the human race, may exploit any other race upon earth or any single individual. If I want that freedom for my country, I would not be deserving of that freedom if I did not cherish and treasure the equal right of every other race, weak or strong, to the same freedom. And so I said to myself whilst I was nearing the shores of your beautiful island, per chance it might be possible for me to convince the British Ministers that India as a valuable partner, not held by force but by the silken cord of love, an India of that character might conceivably be of real assistance to you in balancing your Budget, not for one occasion but for many years. What cannot two nations do on a handful, but brave, with a record for bravery perhaps unequalled, a nation noted for having fought slavery, a nation that has at least claimed times without number to protect the weak and another a very ancient nation, counted in millions, with a glorious and ancient past, representing at the present moment two great cultures, the Islamic and Hindu cultures; if you will, also containing not a small but a very large number of Christian population; and certainly absorbing the whole of the splendid Zoroastrian stock, in numbers almost beneath contempt, but in philanthropy and enterprise almost unequalled and certainly unsurpassed. We have got all these cultures concentrated in India. And supposing that God fires both Hindus and Mussalmans represented here with a proper spirit, so that they close ranks and come to an honourable understanding take that nation and this nation together, and I again ask myself and ask you whether, with an India free, completely independent as Great Britain is, whether an honourable partnership between these two cannot be mutually beneficial, even in terms of the domestic affairs of this great nation. And so, in that dreamy hope, I have approached the British Isles, and I shall still cherish that dream.

And when I have said this perhaps I have said all; and you will be able to dot the i's and to cross the t's, not exacting me to fill in all the details, and tell you what I mean by control over the Army, what I mean by control over external affairs, finance, fiscal and economic policy, or even the financial transactions which a friend yesterday considered to be sacrosanct. I do not take that view. If there is a stock-taking between incoming and outgoing partners, their transactions are subject to audit and adjustment; and the Congress will not be guilty of any dishonourable conduct or crime in saying that the nation should understand what it is to take over and what it should not take over. This audit, this scrutiny, is asked for not merely in the interests of India; it is asked for in the interests of both. I am positive that the British people do not want to saddle upon India a single burden which it should not legitimately bear; and I am here to declare, on behalf of the Congress, that the Congress will never think of repudiating a single claim or a burden that it should justly discharge. If we are to live as an honourable nation worthy of commanding credit from the whole world, we will pay every farthing of legitimate debt with our blood.

I do not think that I should take you any further through the clauses of this mandate and analyse for you the meaning of these clauses as Congressmen give them. If it is God's will that I should continue to take part in these deliberations, as the deliberations proceed, I shall be able to explain the implications of these clauses. As the deliberations proceed, I would have my say in connection with the safeguards also. But I think I have said quite enough in having, with some elaboration and with your generous indulgence, Lord Chancellor, taken the time of this meeting. I had not intended really to take that time, but I felt that I could not possibly do justice to the cause that I have come to expound to you, the Committee, and to the British nation of which we, the Indian Delegates, are at present the guests, if I did not give you out of the whole of my heart my cherished wish even at this time. I would love to go away from the shores of the British Isles with the conviction that there was to be an honourable and equal partnership between Great Britain and India.

I cannot do anything more than say that it will be my fervent prayer, during all the days that I live in your midst, that this consummation may be reached. I thank you, Lord Chancellor, for courtesy that you have extended to me.

3.14

On Modus Operandi

(Speech delivered at the Plenary Session of the Round Table Conference)

I do not think that anything that I can say this evening can possibly influence the decision of the Cabinet. Probably the decision has been already taken. Matters of the liberty of practically a whole continent can hardly be decided by mere argumentation, even negotiation. Negotiation has its purpose and has its play, but only under certain conditions. Without those conditions negotiations are a fruitless task. But I do not want to go into all these matters. I want as far as possible to confine myself within the four corners of the conditions that you, Prime Minister, read to this Conference at its opening meeting. I would, therefore, first of all, say a few words in connection with the Reports that have been submitted to this Conference. You will find in these Reports that generally it has been stated that so and so is the opinion of a large majority, some, however, have expressed an opinion to the contrary, and so on. Parties who have dissented have not been stated. I had heard when I was in India, and I was told when I came here, that no decision or no decisions will be taken by the ordinary rule of majority, and I do not want to mention this fact here by way of complaint that the Reports have been so framed as if the proceedings were governed by the test of majority.

But it was necessary for me to mention this fact, because to most of these Reports you will find that there is a dissenting opinion, and in most of the cases that dissent unfortunately happens to belong to me. It was not a matter of joy to have to dissent from fellow Delegates, but I felt that I could not truly represent the Congress unless I notified that dissent.

There is another thing which I want to bring to the notice of this Conference, namely : what is the meaning of the dissent of the Congress? I said at one of the preliminary meetings of the Federal Structure Committee that the Congress claimed to represent over 85 per cent of the population of India, that is to say, the dumb, toiling, semi-starved millions. But I went further : that the Congress claimed also by right of service to represent even the Princes, if they would pardon my putting forth that claim, and the landed gentry, the educated class. I wish to repeat that claim and I wish this evening to emphasize that claim.

ALL THE OTHER parties at this meeting represent sectional interests. Congress alone claims to represent the whole of India, all interests. It is no communal organization; it is a determined enemy of communalism in any shape or form. Congress knows no distinction of race, colour or creed; its platform is universal. It may not always have lived up to the creed. I do not know a single human organization that lives up to its creed. Congress has failed very often to my knowledge. It may have failed more often to the knowledge of its critics. But the worst critic will have to recognize, as it has been recognized, that the National Congress of India is a daily-growing organization, that its message penetrates the remotest village of India; that on given occasions the Congress has been able to demonstrate its influence over and among these masses who inhabit 700,000 villages.

And yet here I see that the Congress is treated as one of the Parties. I do not mind it; I do not regard it as a calamity for the Congress; but I do regard it as a calamity for the purpose of doing the work for which we have gathered together here. I wish I could convince all the British public men, the British Ministers, that the Congress is capable of delivering the goods. The Congress is the only all-India-wide national organization, bereft of any communal basis; that it does represent all the minorities which have lodged their claims here and which, or the signatories on their behalf, claim I hold unjustifiably to represent 46 per cent of the population of India. The Congress, I say, claims to represent all these minorities.

What a great difference it would be today if this claim on behalf of the Congress was recognized. I feel that I have to state this claim with some degree of emphasis on behalf of peace, for the sake of achieving the purpose which is common to all of us, to you Englishmen who sit at this table, and to us the Indian men and women who also sit at this table. I say so for this reason. Congress is a powerful organization; Congress is an organization which has been accused of running or desiring to run a parallel Government; and in a way I have endorsed the charge. If you could understand the working of the Congress, you would welcome an organization which could run a parallel Government and show that it is possible for an organization, voluntary, without any force at its command, to run the machinery of Government even under adverse circumstances.

But no. Although you have invited the Congress, you distrust the Congress. Although you have invited the Congress, you reject its claim to represent the whole of India. Of course it is possible at this end of the world to dispute that claim, and it is not possible for me to prove this claim; but, all the same, if you find me asserting that claim, I do so because a tremendous responsibility rests upon my shoulders.

THE CONGRESS represents the spirit of rebellion. I know that the word 'rebellion' must not be whispered at a Conference which has been summoned in order to arrive at an agreed solution of India's troubles through negotiation. Speaker after speaker has got up and said that India should achieve her liberty through negotiation, by argument, and that it will be the greatest glory of Great Britain if Great Britain yields to India's demands by argument. But the Congress does not hold that view, quite. The Congress has an alternative which is unpleasant to you.

I HEARD SEVERAL speakers—and let me say I have endeavoured not to miss a single sitting; I have tried to follow every speaker with the utmost attention and with all the respect that I could possibly give to these speakers—saying what a dire calamity it would be if India was fired with the spirit of lawlessness, rebellion, terrorism and so on. I do not pretend to have read histroy, but as a schoolboy I had to pass a paper in history also, and I read that the page of history is soiled red with the blood of those who have fought for freedom. I do not know an instance in which nations have attained to their own without having to go through an incredible measure of travail. The dagger of the assassin, the poison bowl, the bullet of the rifleman, the spear and all these weapons and methods of destruction have been up to now used by what I consider blind lovers of liberty and freedom, and the historian has not condemned him. I hold no brief for the terrorists. Mr. Ghuznavi brought in the terrorists and he brought in the Calcutta Corporation. I felt hurt when he mentioned an incident that took place at the Calcutta Corporation. He forgot to mention that the Mayor of that Corporation made handsome reparation for the error into which he himself was betrayed and the error into which the Calcutta Corporation was betrayed through the instrumentality of those members of the Corporation who were Congressmen.

I hold no brief for Congressmen who directly or indirectly would encourage terrorism. As soon as this incident was brought to the notice of the Congress, the Congress set about putting it in order. It immediately called upon the Mayor of the Calcutta Corporation to give an account of what was done and the Mayor, the gentleman that he is, immediately admitted his mistake and made all the reparation that it was then legally possible to make. I must not detain this Assembly over this incident for any length of time. He mentioned also a verse which the children of the forty schools conducted by the Calcutta Corporation are supposed to have recited. There were many other misstatements in that speech which I could dwell upon, but I have no desire to do so. It is only out of regard for the great Calcutta Corporation and out of regard for truth and on behalf of those who are not here tonight to put in their defence that I mention these two glaring instances. I do not for one moment believe that this was taught in the Calcutta Corporation schools with the knowledge of the Calcutta

Corporation. I do know that in those terrible days of last year, several things were done for which we have regret, for which we have made reparation.

If our boys in Calcutta were taught these verses which Mr. Ghuznavi has recited, I am here to tender an apology on their behalf, but I should want it proved that the boys were taught by the schoolmasters of these schools with the knowledge and encouragement of the Corporation. Charges of this nature have been brought against the Congress times without number, and times without number these charges have also been refuted, but I have mentioned these things at this juncture. It is again to show that for the sake of liberty people have fought, people have lost their lives, people have killed and have sought death at the hands of those whom they have sought to oust.

THE CONGRESS then comes upon the scene and devises a new method not known to history, namely, that of civil disobedience, and the Congress has been following that method up. But again I am up against a stone wall and I am told that that is a method that no Government in the world will tolerate. Well, of course, the government may not tolerate, no government has tolerated open rebellion. No government may tolerate civil disobedience, but governments have to succumb even to these forces, as the British Government has done before now, even as the great Dutch Government after eight years of trial had to yield to the logic of facts. General Smuts is a brave General, a great statesman, and a very hard taskmaster also, but he himself recoiled with horror from even the contemplation of doing to death innocent men and women who were merely fighting for the preservation of their self-respect and the things which he had vowed he would never yield in the year 1908, reinforced as he was by General Botha, he had to do in the year 1914, after having tried these civil resisters through and through. And in India Lord Chelmsford had to do the same thing; the Governor of Bombay had to do the same thing in Borsad and Bardoli. I suggest to you, Prime Minister, it is too late today to resist this, and it is this thing which weighs me down, this choice that lies before them, the parting of the ways probably. I shall hope against hope, I shall strain every nerve to achieve an honourable settlement for my country if I can do so without having to put the millions of my countrymen and countrywomen and even children through this ordeal of fire. It can be a matter of no joy and comfort to me to lead them on again to a fight of that character, but if a further ordeal of fire has to be our lot. I shall approach that with the greatest joy and with the greatest consolation that I was doing what I felt to be right, the country was doing what it felt to be right, and the country will have the additional satisfaction of knowing that it was not at least taking lives, it was giving lives; it was not making the British people directly suffer, it was suffering. Professor Gilbert Muray told me I shall never forget that I am paraphrasing his inimitable language. He said : You do not consider for one moment that the Englishmen do not suffer when thousands of your countrymen suffer, that we are so heartless? I do not think so. I do not know that you will suffer; but I want you to suffer because I want to touch your hearts; and when your hearts have been touched will come the psychological moment for negotiation. Negotiation there always will be; and if this time I have travelled all these miles in order to enter upon negotiation, I thought that your countryman, Lord Irwin, had sufficiently tried us through his ordinances, that he had sufficient evidence that thousands of men and women of India and that thousands of children had suffered; and that, ordinance or no ordinance, lathis or no lathis, nothing would avail to stem the tide that was onrushing and to stem the passions that were rising in the breasts of the men and women of India who were thirsting for liberty.

WHILST THERE is yet a little sand left in the glass, I want you to understand what this Congress stands for. My life is at your disposal. The lives of all the members of the Working Committee, the All-India Congress Committee, are at your disposal. But remember that you have at your disposal the lives of all these dumb millions. I do not want to sacrifice those lives if I can possibly help it. Therefore, please remember that I will count no sacrifice too great if by chance I can pull through an honourable settlement. You will find me always having the greatest spirit of compromise if I can but fire you with the spirit that is working in the Congress, namely, that India must have real liberty. Call it by any name you like; a rose will smell as sweet by any other name, but it must be the rose of liberty that I want and not the artificial product. If your mind and the Congress mind, the mind of this Conference and the mind of the British people, mean the same thing by the same word, then you will find the amplest room for compromise, and will find the Congress itself always in a Compromising spirit. But so long as there is not that one mind, that one definition, not one implication for the same word that you and I and we may be using, so long there is no compromise possible. How can there be any compromise so long as we each one of us has a different definition for the same words that we may be using. It is impossible, Prime Minister, I want to suggest to you in all humility that it is utterly impossible then to find a meeting ground, to find ground where you can apply the spirit of compromise. And I am very grieved to have to say that up to now I have not been able to discover a common definition for the terms that we have been exchanging during all these weary weeks.

I WAS SHOWN last week the Statute of Westminster by a sceptic, and he said : "Have you seen the definition of 'Dominion'?" I read the definition of 'Dominion', and naturally I was not at all perplexed or shocked to see that the word 'Dominion' was exhaustively defined, and it has not a general definition but a particular definition. It simply said : the word 'Dominion' shall include Australia, South Africa, Canada and so on, ending with the Irish Free State. I do not think I noticed Egypt there. Then he said : "Do you see what your Dominion means?" It did not make any impression upon me. I do not mind what my Dominion means or what Complete Independence means. In a way I was relieved.

I said I am now relieved from having to quarrel about the word 'Dominion', because I am out of it. But I want Complete Independence, and even so, so many Englishmen have said : "Yes, you can have Complete Independence, but what is the meaning of 'complete independence'?" And again we come to different definitions.

One of your great statesmen—I do not think I should give his name—was debating with me, and he said : "Honestly, I did not know that you meant this by Complete Independence." He ought to have known, but he did not know, and I shall tell you what he did not know. When I said to him, "I cannot be a partner in an Empire," he said, "Of course, that is logical." I said, "But I want to become that. It is not as if I shall be if I am compelled to, but I want to become a partner with Great Britain. I want to become a partner with the English people; but I want to enjoy precisely the same liberty that your people enjoy, and I want to seek this partnership not merely for the benefit of India, and not merely for mutual benefits; I want to seek this partnership in order that the great weight that is crushing the world to atoms may be lifted from off its shoulders."

This took place ten or twelve days ago. Strange as it may appear, I got a note from another Englishman whom also you know and whom also you respect. Among many things he writes : "I believe profoundly that the peace and happiness of mankind depend on our friendship", and as if I would not understand that, he says, "your people and mine". I must read to you what he also says, "And of all Indians you are the one that the real Englishman likes and understands." He does not waste any words on flattery, and I do not think he has intended this last expression to flatter me. It will not flatter me in the slightest degree. There are many things in this note which, if I could share them with you, would perhaps make you understand better the significance of this expression, but let me tell you that, when he writes this last sentence, he does not mean me personally. I personally signify nothing, and I know I would mean nothing to any single Englishman; but I mean something to some Englishman because I represent a cause, because I seek to represent a nation, a great organization which has made itself felt. That is the reason why he says this.

But then, if I could possibly find that working basis, Prime Minister, there is ample room for compromise. It is friendship I crave. My business is not to throw overboard the slave-holder and tyrant. My philosophy forbids me to do so, and today the Congress has accepted that philosophy not as a creed, as it is to me, but as a policy, because the Congress believes that it is the right and best thing for India, a nation of three hundred and fifty millions, to do.

A nation of 350 million people does not need the dagger of the assassin, it does not need the position bowl, it does not need the sword, the spear or the bullet. It needs simply a will of its own, an ability to say "No", and that nation is today learning to say "No".

But what is it that that nation does? Summarily, or at all, dismiss Englishmen? No. Its mission is today to convert Englishmen. I do not want to break the bond between England and India, but I do want to transform that bond. I want to transform that slavery into complete freedom for my country. Call it 'complete independence' or whatever you like, I will not quarrel about that word, and even though my countrymen may dispute with me for having taken some other word, I shall be able to bear down that opposition so long as the content of the word that you may suggest to me bears the meaning. Hence, I have times without number to urge upon your attention that the safeguards that have been suggested are completely unsatisfactory. They are not in the interests of India.

THREE EXPERTS from the Federation of Commerce and Industry have in their own manner, each in his different manner, told you out of their expert experience how utterly impossible it is for any body of responsible Ministers to tackle the problem of administration when 80 per cent of India's resources are mortgaged irretrievably. Better than I could have shown to you they have shown, out of the amplitude of their knowledge, what these financial safeguards mean for India. They mean the complete cramping of India. They have discussed at this table financial safeguards, but that includes necessarily the question of Defence and the question of the Army. Yet, while I say that the safeguards are unsatisfactory as they have been presented, I have not hesitated to say, and I do not hesitate to repeat, that the Congress is pledged to giving safeguards endorsing safeguards which may be demonstrated to be in the interests of India.

At one of the sittings of the Federal Structure Committee, I had no hesitation in amplifying the admission and saying that these safeguards must be also of benefit to Great Britain. I do not want safeguards which are merely beneficial to India and prejudicial to the real interests of Great Britain. The fancied interests of India will have to be sacrificed. The fancied interests of Great Britain will have to be sacrificed. The illegitimate interests of India will have to be sacrificed. The illegitimate interests of Great Britain will also have to be sacrificed. Therefore, again I repeat, if we have the same meaning for the same word, I will agree with Mr. Jayakar with Sir Tej Bahadur Sapru, and other distinguished speakers who have spoken at this Conference.

I will agree with them all, that we have after all, after all these labours, reached a substantial measure of agreement, but my despair, my grief, is that I do not read the same words in the same light. The implications of the safeguards of Mr. Jayakar, I very much fear, are different from my implications, and the implications of Mr. Jayakar and myself are perhaps only different from the implications that Sir Samuel Hoare, for instance, has in mind; I do not know. We have never really come to grips. We have never come to brass tacks as you put it, and I am anxious—I have been pinning to come to real grips and to brass tacks all these days and all these nights, and I have felt : 'Why are we not coming nearer and nearer together, and why are we wasting our time in eloquence, ·n oratory, in debating, and in scoring points?' Heaven knows I have no desire to hear my own voice. Heaven knows I have no desire to take part in any debating. I know that liberty is made of sterner stuff, and I now that the freedom of India is made of much sterner stuff. We have problems that would baffle any statesman. We have problems that other nations have not to tackle. But they do not baffle me; they cannot baffle those who have been brought up in the Indian climate. Those problems are there with us. Just as we have to tackle our bubonic plague, we have to tackle the problem of malaria. We have to tackle, as you have not, the problem of snakes and scorpions, monkeys, tigers and lions. We have to tackle these problems because we have been brought up under them.

They do not baffle us. Somehow or other we have survived the ravages of these venomous reptiles and various creatures. So also shall we survive our problems and find a way out of these problems. But today you and we have come together at a Round Table and we want to find a common formula which will work. Please believe me that, whilst I abate not a title of the claim that I have registered on behalf of the Congress, which I do not propose to repeat here, while I withdraw not one word of the speeches that I had to make at the Federal Structure Committee, I am here to compromise; I am here to consider every formula that British ingenuity can prepare, every formula that the ingenuity of such constitutionalists as Mr. Sastri, Sir Tej Bahadur Sapru, Mr. Jayakar, Mr. Jinnah, Sir Muhammad Shafi, and a host of other constitutionalists can weave into being.

I WILL NOT be baffled. I shall be here as long as I am required because I do not want to revive civil disobedience. I want to turn the truce that was arrived at, at Delhi, into a permanent settlement. But for heaven's sake give me, a frail man, 62 years gone, a little bit of a chance. Find a little corner for him and the organization that he represents. You distrust that organization though you may seemingly trust me. Do not for one moment differentiate me from the organization of which I am but a drop in the ocean. I am no greater than the organization to which I belong. I am infinitely smaller than that organization; and if you find me a place, if you trust me, I invite you to trust the Congress also. Your trust in me otherwise is a broken reed. I have no authority save that I derive from the Congress. If you will work the Congress for all it is worth, then you will say goodbye to terrorism; then you will not need terrorism. Today you have to fight the school of terrorists which is there with your disciplined and organized terrorism, because you will be blind to the facts or the writing on the wall. Will you not see the writing that these terrorists are writing with their blood? Will you not see that we do not want bread made of wheat, but we want bread of liberty; and without that liberty there are thousands today who are sworn not to give themselves peace or to give the country peace.

I urge you then to read that writing on the wall. I ask you not to try the patience of a people known to be proverbially patient. We speak of the mild Hindu, and the Mussalman also by contact, good or evil, with the Hindu, has himself become mild. And that mention of the Mussalman brings me to the baffling problem of minorities. Believe me, that problem exists here, and I repeat what I used to say in India I have not forgotten those words that without the problem of minorities being solved there is no *swaraj* for India, there is no freedom for India. I know that, I realize it; and yet I came here in the hope, perchance, that I might be able to pull through a solution here. But I do not despair of some day or other finding a real and living solution in connection with the minorities problem. I repeat what I have said elsewhere, that so long as the wedge in the shape of foreign rule divides community from community and class from class, there will be no real living solution, there will be no living friendship between these communities.

It will be after all and at best a paper solution. But immediately you withdraw that wedge, the domestic ties, the domestic affections, the knowledge of common birth do you suppose that all these will count for nothing?

Were Hindus and Mussalmans and Sikhs always at war with one another when there was no British rule, when there was no English face seen there? We have chapter and verse given to us by Hindu historians and by Mussalman historians to say that we were living in comparative peace even then. And Hindus and Mussalmans in the Villages are not even today quarrelling. In those days they were not known to quarrel at all. The late Maulana Muhammad Ali often used to tell me and he was himself a bit of an historian, he said, "If God"—'Allah', as he called God—"gives me life, I propose to write the history of Mussalman Rule in India; and then I will show through documents that British people have erred, that Aurangzeb was not so vile as he has been painted by the British historian; that the Mogul rule was not so bad as it has been shown to us in British history," an so on. And so have Hindu historians written. This quarrel is not old; this quarrel is coeval with this acute shame. I dare to say it is coeval with the British advent, and immediately this relationship, the unfortunate, artificial, unnatural relationship, between Great Britain and India is transformed into a natural relationship, when it becomes, if it does become, a voluntary partnership to be given up, to be dissolved at the will of either party, when it becomes that you will find that Hindus, Mussalmans, Sikhs, Europeans, Anglo-Indians, Christians, untouchables, will all live together as one man.

I do not intend to say much tonight about the Princes, but I should be wronging them, and I should be wronging the Congress if I did not register my claim, not with the Round Table Conference, but with the Princes. It is open to the Princes to give their terms on which they will join the Federation. I have appealed to them to make the path easy for those who inhabit the other parts of India, and therefore I can only make these suggestions for their favourable consideration, for their earnest consideration. I think that if they accepted, no matter what they are, but some fundamental rights as the common property of all India, and if they accepted that position and allowed those rights to be tested by the Court, which will be again of thier own creation, and if they introduced elements—only elements—of representation on behalf of their subjects, I think that they would have gone a long way to conciliate their subjects. They would have gone a long way to show to the world and to show to the whole of India that they are also fired with a democratic spirit, that they do not want to remain undiluted autocrats, but that they want to become constitutional monarchs even as King George of Great Britain is.

LET INDIA GET what she is entitled to and what she can really take, but whatever she gets, whenever she gets it, let the Frontier Province get complete autonomy today. That Frontier will then be a standing demonstration to the whole of India, and therefore, the whole vote of the Congress will be given in favour of the Frontier Province getting Provincial autonomy tomorrow. Prime Minister, if you can possibly get your Cabinet to endorse the proposition that from tomorrow the Frontier

Province becomes a full-fledged autonomous Province, I shall then have a proper footing amongst the Frontier tribes and convene them to my assistance when those over the border cast an evil eye on India.

LAST OF ALL, my last is a pleasant task for me. This is, perhaps, the last time that I shall be sitting with you at negotiations. It is not that I want that. I want to sit at the same table with you in your closets and to negotiate and to plead with you and to go down on bended knees before I take the final leap and final plunge. But whether I have the good fortune to continue to tender my co-operation or not does not depend upon me. It largely depends upon you. But it may not even depend upon you. It depends upon so many circumstances over which neither you nor we may have any control whatsoever. Then let me perform this pleasant task of giving my thanks to all—from Their Majesties down to the poorest men in the East End, where I have taken up my habitation.

In that settlement which represents the poor people of the East End of London I have become one of them. They have accepted me as a member, and as a favoured member of their family. It will be one of the richest treasures that I shall carry with me. Here, too, I have found nothing but courtesy and nothing but a genuine affection from all with whom I have come in touch. I have come in touch with so many Englishmen. It has been a priceless privilege to me. They have listened to what must have often appeared to them to be unpleasant, although it was true. Although I have often been obliged to say these things to them, they have never shown the slightest impatience or irritation. It is impossible for me to forget these things. No matter what befalls me, no matter what the fortunes may be of this Round Table Conference, one thing I shall certainly carry with me—that is, that from high to low I have found nothing but the utmost courtesy and the utmost affection. I consider that it was well worth my paying this visit to England in order to find this human affection.

It has enhanced, it has deepened my irrepressible faith in human nature that although Englishmen and Englishwomen have been fed upon lies so often that I see disfiguring your

Press, that although in Lancashire the Lancashire people had perhaps some reason for becoming irritated against me, I found no irritation, no resentment even in the operatives. The operatives, men and women, hugged me. They treated me as one of their own. I shall never forget that.

I am carrying with me thousands upon thousands of English friendships. I do not know them, but I read that affection in their eyes as early in the morning I walk through your streets. All this hospitality, all this kindness will never be effaced from my memory no matter what befalls my unhappy land. I thank you for your forbearance.

3.15

A Word to Communists

[Addressing a labour meeting in Bombay which was disturbed by some young communists Gandhiji made a Hindi speech of which the following is a condensed translation. M.D.]

I knew that there were Communists in India, but I had not met them outside the Meerut Jail, nor even heard their speeches. I made a point of interviewing the Meerut prisoners two years ago during my tour in the U.P. and thus managed to know them somewhat. I have heard one of them this evening, and I may tell them that such as they claim to win *swaraj* for the working men, I have my doubts about their ability to do so. I had made the working men's cause my own long before any of the young Communists here were born. I spent the best part of my time in South Africa working for them, I used to live with them, and shared their joys and sorrows. You must, therefore, understand why I claim to speak for labour. I expect at least courtesy from you if nothing else. I invite you to come to me and discuss things with me as frankly as you can.

You claim to be Communists, but you do not seem to live the life of communism. I may tell you that I am trying my best to live up to the ideal of communism in the best sense of the term. And communism does not, I fancy, exclude courtesy. I am amongst you today, within a few minutes I will leave you. But if you want to carry the country with you, you ought to be able to react on it by reasoning with it. You cannot do so by coercion. You may deal destruction to bring the country round to your view. But how many will you destroy? Not tens of millions. You may kill a few thousands if you had millions with you. But today you are no more than a handful. I ask you to convert the Congress if you can and to take charge of it. But you cannot do so by bidding goodbye to the elementary rules of courtesy. And there is no reason why you should be lacking in ordinary courtesy, when it is open to you to give the fullest vent to your views, when India is tolerant enough to listen patiently to anyone who can talk coherently.

The truce has done no harm to the labourers. I claim that none of my activities has ever harmed the workers, can ever harm them. If the Congress sends its representatives to the Conference, they will press for no *swaraj* other than the *swaraj* for workers and peasants. Long before the Communist Party came into existence the Congress had decided that that *swaraj* would have no meaning which was not the *swaraj* for workers and peasants. Perhaps, none of you workers here gets less than a monthly wage of Rs. 20, but, I am working for winning *swaraj* not only for you but for those toiling and unemployed millions who do not get even a square meal a day and have to scratch along with a piece of stale *roti* and a pinch of salt. But I do not want to deceive you, I must warn you that I do not bear any ill [will] to the capitalists, I can think of doing them no harm. But I want by means of suffering, to awaken them to their sense of duty, I want to melt their hearts and get them to render justice to their less fortunate brethren. They are human beings, and my appeal to them will not go in vain. The history of Japan reveals many an instance of self-sacrificing capitalists. During the last *satyagraha*, quite a number of capitalists went in for considerable sacrifice, went to jail and suffered. Do you want to estrange them? Don't you want them to work with you for the common end?

God has given you intellect and talent. Turn them to proper account. I beseech you not to lay an embargo on your reason. God help you !

Young India, 26-3-1931

3.16

At A.I.C.C. Meeting

Bombay,
August 8, 1942

I congratulate you on the resolution that you have just passed. I also congratulate the three comrades on the courage they have shown in pressing their amendments to a division, even though they knew that there was an overwhelming majority in favour of the resolution, and I congratulate the thirteen friends who voted against the resolution. In doing so, they had nothing to be ashamed of. For the last twenty years we have tried to learn not to lose courage even when we are in a hopeless minority and are laughed at. We have learned to hold on to our beliefs in the confidence that we are in the right. It behaves us to cultivate this courage of conviction, for it ennobles man and raises his moral stature. I was, therefore, glad to see that these friends had imbibed the principle which I have tried to follow for the last fifty years and more.

Having congratulated them on their courage, let me say that what they asked this Committee to accept through their amendments was not the correct representation of the situation. These friends ought to have pondered over the appeal made to them by the Maulana to withdraw their amendments; they should have carefully followed the explanations given by Jawaharlal. Had they done so, it would have been clear to them that the right which they now want the Congress to concede has already been conceded by the Congress.

(Time was when every Mussalman claimed the whole of India as his motherland. During the years that the Ali Brothers were with me, the assumption underlying all their talks and discussions was that India belonged as much to the Mussalmans as to the Hindus. I can testify to the fact that this was their innermost conviction and not a mask; I lived with them for years. I spent days and nights in their company. And I make bold to say that their utterances were the honest expression of their beliefs.) I know there are some who say that I take things too readily at their face value, that I am gullible. I do not think I am such a simpleton, nor am I so gullible as these friends take me to be. But their criticism does not hurt me. I should prefer to be considered gullible rather than deceitful.

What these Communist friends proposed through their amendments is nothing new. It has been repeated from thousands of platforms. Thousands of Mussalmans have told me that if the Hindu-Muslim question was to be solved satisfactorily, it must be done in my lifetime. I should feel flattered at this; but how can I agree to a proposal which does not appeal to my reason? Hindu-Muslim unity is not a new thing. Millions of Hindus and Mussalmans have sought after it. I consciously strove for its achievement from my boyhood. While at school, I made it a point to cultivate the friendship of Muslim and Parsi fellow students. I believed even at that tender age that the Hindus in India, if they wished to live in peace and amity with the other communities, should assiduously cultivate the virtue of [good] neighbourliness. It did not matter, I felt, if I made no special effort to cultivate the friendship with Hindus, but I must make friends with at least a few Mussalmans. It was as counsel for a Mussalman merchant that I went to South Africa. I made friends with other Mussalmans there, even with the opponents of my client, and gained a reputation for integrity and good faith. I had among my friends and co-workers Muslims as well as Parsis. I captured their hearts and when I left finally for India, I left them sad and shedding tears of grief at the separation.

In India, too, I continued my efforts and left no stone unturned to achieve that unity. It was my life-long aspiration for it that made me offer my fullest co-operation to the

Mussalmans in the Khilafat movement. (Muslims throughout the country accepted me as their true friend.)

How then is it that I have now come to be regarded as so evil and detestable? Had I any axe to grind in supporting the Khilafat movement? True, I did in my heart of hearts cherish a hope that it might enable me to save the cow. I am a worshipper of the cow. I believe the cow and myself to be the creation of the same God, and I am prepared to sacrifice my life in order to save the cow. But, whatever my philosophy of life and my ultimate hopes, I joined the movement in no spirit of bargain. I co-operated in the struggle for the Khilafat solely in order to discharge my obligation to my neighbour who, I saw, was in distress. The Ali Brothers, had they been alive today, would have testified to the truth of this assertion. And so would many others bear me out in that it was not a bargain on my part for saving the cow. The cow, like the Khilafat, stood on her own merits. As an honest man, a true neighbour and a faithful friend, it was incumbent on me to stand by the Mussalmans in the hour of their trial.

In those days I shocked the Hindus by dining with the Mussalmans, though with the passage of time they have now got used to it. Maulana Bari told me, however, that though he would insist on having me as his guest, he would not allow me to dine with him, lest some day he should be accused of a sinister motive. And so, whenever I had occasion to stay with him, he called a Brahmin cook and made special arrangements for separate cooking. Firangi Mahal, his residence, was an oldstyled structure with limited accommodation; yet he cheerfully bore all hardships and carried out his resolve from which I could not dislodge him. It was the spirit of courtesy, dignity and nobility that inspired us in those days. The members of each community vied with one another in accommodating members of sister communities. They respected one another's religious feelings, and considered it a privilege to do so. Not a trace of suspicion lurked in anybody's heart. Where has all that dignity, that nobility of spirit, disappeared now? I should ask all Mussalmans, including Qaid-e-Azam Jinnah, to recall those glorious days and to find out what has brought us to the present impasse. Qaid-e-Azam Jinnah himself was at one time a Congressman. If today the Congress has incurred his wrath; it is because the canker of suspicion has entered his heart. May God bless him with long life, but when I am gone, he will realize and admit that I had no designs on Mussalmans and that I had never betrayed their interests. Where is the escape for me if I injure their cause or betray their interests? My life is entirely at their disposal. They are free to put an end to it, whenever they wish to do so. Assaults have been made on my life in the past, but God has spared me till now, and the assailants have repented for their action. But if someone were to shoot me in the belief that he was getting rid of a rascal, he would kill not the real Gandhi, but the one that appeared to him a rascal.

To those who have been indulging in a campaign of abuse and vilification I would say, "Islam enjoins you not to revile even an enemy. The Prophet treated even enemies with kindness and tried to win them over by his fairness and generosity. Are you followers of that Islam or of any other? If you are followers of the true Islam, does it behove you to distrust the words of one who makes a public declaration of his faith? You may take it from me that one day you will regret the fact that you distrusted and killed one who was a true and devoted friend of yours." It cuts me to the quick to see that the more I appeal and the more the Maulana importunes, the more intense does the campaign of vilification grow. To me, these abuses are like bullets. They can kill me, even as a bullet can put an end to my life. You may kill me. That will not hurt me. But what of those who indulge in abusing? They bring discredit to Islam. For the fair name of Islam, I appeal to you to resist this unceasing campaign of abuse and vilification.

Maulana Saheb is being made a target for the filthiest abuse. Why? Because he refuses to exert on me the pressure of his friendship. He realizes that it is a misuse of friendship to seek to compel a friend to accept as truth what he knows is an untruth. To the Qaid-e-Azam I would say : "Whatever is true and valid in the claim for Pakistan is already in your hands. What is wrong and untenable is in nobody's gift, so that it can be made over to you. Even if someone were to succeed in imposing an untruth on others, he would not be able to enjoy for long the fruits of such coercion. God dislikes pride and keeps away from it. God would not tolerate a forcible imposition of an untruth."

The Qaid-e-Azam says that he is compelled to say bitter things but that he cannot help giving expression to his thoughts and his feelings. Similarly I would say : I consider myself a friend of the Mussalmans. Why should I then not give expression to the things nearest to my heart, even at the cost of displeasing them? How can I conceal my innermost thoughts from them? I should congratulate the Qaid-e-Azam on his frankness in giving expression to his thoughts and feelings, even if they sound bitter to his hearers. But even so why should the Mussalmans sitting here be reviled, if they do not see eye to eye with him? If millions of Mussalmans are with you, can you not afford to ignore the handful of Mussalmans who may appear to you to be misguided? Why should one with the following of several millions be afraid of a majority community, or of the minority being swamped by the majority? How did the Prophet work among the Arabs and the Mussalmans? How did he propagate Islam? Did he say he would propagate Islam only when he commanded a majority? I, therefore, appeal to you for the sake of Islam to ponder over what I say. There is neither fair play nor justice in saying that the Congress must accept a thing even if it does not believe in it and even if it goes counter to principles it holds dear.

Rajaji said : "I do not believe in Pakistan. But Mussalmans ask for it, Mr. Jinnah asks for it, and it has become an obsession with them. Why not then say 'yes' to them just now? The same Mr. Jinnah will later on realize the disadvantages of Pakistan and will forgo the demand". I said : "It is not fair to accept as true a thing which I hold to be untrue and ask others to do so in the belief that the demand will not be pressed when the time comes for settling it finally. If I hold the demand to be just, I should concede it this very day. I should not agree to it merely in order to placate Jinnah Saheb. Many friends have come and asked me to agree to it for the time being to placate

Mr. Jinnah, disarm his suspicions and to see how he reacts to it. But I cannot be party to a course of action with a false promise. At any rate, it is not my method".

The Congress has no sanction but the moral one for enforcing its decisions. It believes that true democracy can only be the outcome of non-violence. The structure of a world federation can be raised only on a foundation of non-violence, and violence will have to be totally abjured from world affairs. If this is true, the solution of the Hindu-Muslim question, too, cannot be achieved by resort to violence. If the Hindus tyrannize over the Mussalmans, with what face will they talk of a world federation? It is for the same reason that I do not believe in the possibility of establishing world peace through violence as the English and American statesmen propose to do. The Congress has agreed to submitting all the differences to an impartial international tribunal and to abide by its decisions. If even this fairest of proposals is unacceptable, the only course that remains open is that of the sword, of violence. How can I persuade myself to agree to an impossibility? To demand the vivisection of a living organism is to ask for its very life. It is a call to war. The Congress cannot be party to such a fratricidal war. Those Hindus who, like Dr. Moonje and Shri Savarkar, believe in the doctrine of the sword may seek to keep the Mussalmans under Hindu domination. I do not represent that section. I represent the Congress. You want to kill the Congress which is the goose that lays golden eggs. If you distrust the Congress, you may rest assured that there is to be a perpetual war between the Hindus and the Mussalmans, and the country will be doomed to continue warfare and bloodshed. If such warfare is to be our lot, I shall not live to witness it.

It is for that reason that I say to Jinnah Saheb, "You may take it from me that whatever in your demand for Pakistan accords with considerations of justice and equity is lying in your pocket; whatever in the demand is contrary to justice and equity you can take only by the sword and in no other manner".

There is much in my heart that I would like to pour out before this assembly. One thing which was uppermost in my heart I have already dealt with. You may take it from me that it is with me a matter of life and death. If we Hindus and Mussalmans mean to achieve a heart unity, without the slightest mental reservation on the part of either, we must first unite in the effort to be free from the shackles of this Empire. If Pakistan after all is to be a portion of India, what objection can there be for Mussalmans against joining this struggle for India's freedom? The Hindus and Mussalmans must, therefore, unite in the first instance on the issue of fighting for freedom. Jinnah Saheb thinks the war will last long. I do not agree with him. If the war goes on for six months more, how shall we be able to save China?

I, therefore, want freedom immediately, this very night, before dawn, if it can be had. Freedom cannot now wait for the realization of communal unity. If that unity is not achieved, sacrifices necessary for it will have to be much greater than would have otherwise sufficed. But the Congress must win freedom or be wiped out in the effort. And forget not that the freedom which the Congress is struggling to achieve will not be for the Congressmen alone but for all the forty crores of the Indian people. Congressmen must forever remain humble servants of the people.

The Qaid-e-Azam has said that the Muslim League is prepared to take over the rule from the Britishers if they are prepared to hand it over to the Muslim League, for the British took over the Empire from the hands of the Muslims. This, however, will be Muslim raj. The offer made by Maulana Saheb and by me does not imply establishment of Muslim raj or Muslim domination. The Congress does not believe in the domination of any group or any community. It believes in democracy which includes in its orbit Muslims, Hindus, Christians, Parsis, Jews—everyone of the communities inhabiting this vast country. If Muslim raj is inevitable, then let it be; but how can we give it the stamp of our assent? How can we agree to the domination of one community over the others?

Millions of Mussalmans in this country come from Hindu stock. How can their homeland be any other than India? My eldest son embraced Islam some years back. What would his homeland be—Porbander or the Punjab? I ask the Mussalmans : "If India is not your homeland, what other country do you belong to? In what separate homeland would you put my son who embraced Islam" ? His mother wrote him a letter after his conversion, asking him if he had on embracing Islam given up drinking which Islam forbids to its followers. To those who gloated over the conversion, she wrote to say : "I do not mind his becoming a Mussalman so much as his drinking. Will you, as pious Mussalmans, tolerate his drinking even after his conversion? He has reduced himself to the state of a rake by drinking. If you are going to make a man of him again, his conversion will have been turned to good account. You will, therefore, please see that he as a Mussalman abjures wine and women. If that change does not come about, his conversion goes in vain and our non-cooperation with him will have to continue".

India is without doubt the homeland of all the Mussalmans inhabiting this country. Every Mussalman should, therefore, cooperate in the fight for India's freedom. The Congress does not belong to any one class or community; it belongs to the whole nation. It is open to Mussalmans to take possession of the Congress. They can, if they like, swamp the Congress by their numbers, and can steer it along the course which appeals to them. The Congress is fighting not on behalf of the Hindus but on behalf of the whole nation, including the minorities. It would hurt me to hear of a single instance of a Mussalman being killed by a Congressman. In the coming revolution, Congressmen will sacrifice their lives in order to protect the Mussalman against a Hindu's attack and *vice versa*. It is a part of their creed, and is one of the essentials of non-violence. You will be expected on occasions like these not to lose your heads. Every Congressman, whether a Hindu or a Mussalman, owes this duty to the organization to which he belongs. The Mussalman who will act in this manner will render a service to Islam. Mutual trust is essential for success in the final nation-wide struggle that is to come.

I have said that much greater sacrifices will have to be made this time in the wake of our struggle because of the opposition from the Muslim League and from Englishmen. You have seen the secret circular issued by Sir Frederick Puckle. It is a suicidal course that he has taken. It contains an open incitement to organizations which crop up like mushrooms to combine to fight the Congress. We have thus to deal with an Empire whose ways are crooked. Ours is a straight path which we can tread even with our eyes closed. That is the beauty of *satyagraha*.

In *satyagraha*, there is no place for fraud or falsehood, or any kind of untruth. Fraud and untruth today are stalking the world. I cannot be a helpless witness to such a situation. I have travelled all over India as perhaps nobody in the present age has. The voiceless millions of the land saw in me their friend and representative, and I identified myself with them to an extent it was possible for a human being to do. I saw trust in their eyes, which I now want to turn to good account in fighting this Empire upheld on untruth and violence. However gigantic the preparations that the Empire has made, we must get out of its clutches. How can I remain silent at this supreme hour and hide my light under the bushel? Shall I ask the Japanese to tarry awhile? If today I sit quiet and inactive, God will take me to task for not using up the treasure. He had given me, in the midst of the conflagration that is enveloping the whole world. Had the condition been different, I should have asked you to wait yet awhile. But the situation now has become intolerable, and the Congress has no other course left for it.

Nevertheless, the actual struggle does not commence this moment. You have only placed all your powers in my hands. I will now wait upon the Viceroy and plead with him for the acceptance of the Congress demand. That process is likely to take two or three weeks. What would you do in the meanwhile? What is the programme, for the interval, in which all can participate? As you know, the spinning-wheel is the first thing that occurs to me. I made the same answer to the Maulana. He would have none of it, though he understood its import later. The fourteenfold constructive programme is, of course, there for you to carry out. What more should you do? I will tell you. Everyone of you should, from this moment onwards, consider yourself a free man or woman, and act as if you are free and are no longer under the heel of this imperialism.

It is not a make-believe that I am suggesting to you. It is the very essence of freedom. The bond of the slave is snapped the moment he considers himself to be a free being. He will plainly tell the master : "I was your bondslave till this moment, but I am a slave no longer. You may kill me if you like, but if you keep me alive, I wish to tell you that if you release me from the bondage of your own accord, I will ask for nothing more from you. You used to feed and clothe me, though I could have provided food and clothing for myself by my labour. I hitherto depended on you instead of on God, for food and raiment. God has now inspired me with an urge for freedom and I am today a free man and will no longer depend on you".

You may take it from me that I am not going to strike a bargain with the Viceroy for ministries and the like. I am not going to be satisfied with anything short of complete freedom. Maybe, he will propose the abolition of salt tax, the drink evil, etc. But I will say : "Nothing less than freedom".

Here is a *mantra,* a short one, that I give you. You may imprint it on your hearts and let every breath of yours give expression to it. The *mantra is :* 'Do or Die'. We shall either free India or die in the attempt; we shall not live to see the perpetuation of our slavery. Every true Congressman or [Congress] woman will join the struggle with an inflexible determination not to remain alive to see the country in bondage and slavery. Let that be your pledge. Keep jails out of your consideration. If the Government keep me free, I will spare you the trouble of filling the jails. I will not put on the Government the strain of maintaining a large number of prisoners at a time when it is in trouble. Let every man and woman live every moment of his or her life hereafter in the consciousness that he or she eats or lives for achieving freedom and will die, if need be, to attain that goal. Take a pledge with God and your own conscience as witness, that you will no longer rest till freedom is achieved and will be prepared to lay down your lives in the attempt to achieve it. He who loses his life will gain it; he who will seek to save it shall lose it. Freedom is not for the coward or the faint-hearted.

A word to the journalists I congratulate you on the support you have hitherto given to the national demand. I know the restrictions and handicaps under which you have to labour. But I would now ask you to snap the chains that bind you. It should be the proud privilege of the newspapers to lead and set an example in laying down one's life for freedom. You have the pen which the Government can't suppress. I know you have large properties in the form of printing presses, etc., and you would be afraid lest the Government should attach them. I do not ask you to invite an attachment of the printing press voluntarily. For myself, I would not suppress my pen, even if the press was to be attached. As you know my press was attached in the past and returned later on. But I do not ask from you that final sacrifice. I suggest a middle way. You should now wind up your Standing Committee, and you may declare that you will give up writing under the present restrictions and take up the pen only when India has won her freedom. You may tell Sir Frederick Puckle that he can't expect from you a command performance, that his Press notes are full of untruth, and that you will refuse to publish them. You will openly declare that you are whole heartedly with the Congress. If you do this, you will have changed the atmosphere before the fight actually begins.

From the Princes I ask with all respect due to them a very small thing. I am a well-wisher of the Princes. I was born in a State. My grandfather refused to salute with his right hand any Prince other than his own. But he did not say to the Prince, as I feel he ought to have said, that even his own master could not compel him, his minister, to act against his conscience. I have eaten the Princes' salt and I would not be false to it. As a faithful servant, it is my duty to warn the Princes that if they will act while I am still alive, the Princes may come to occupy an honourable place in free India. In Jawaharlal's scheme of free India, no privileges or the privileged classes have a place. Jawaharlal considers all property to be State-owned. He wants planned economy. He wants to reconstruct India according to plan. He likes to fly; I do not. I have kept a place for the Princes and the zamindars in India that I envisage. I would ask the Princes in all humility to enjoy through renunciation. The Princes may renounce ownership over their properties and become their trustees in the true sense of the term. I visualize God in the assemblage of people. The Princes may say to their people : "You are the owners and masters of the State and we are your servants". I would ask the Princes to become servants of the people and render to them an account of their own services. The Empire too bestows power on the Princes, but they should prefer to derive power from their own people; and if they want to indulge in some innocent pleasures, they may seek to do so as servants of the people. I do not want the Princes to live as paupers. But I would ask them : "Do you want to remain slaves for all time? Why should you, instead of paying homage to a foreign power, not accept the sovereignty of your own people"? You may write to the Political Department : "The people are now awake. How are we to withstand an avalanche before which even the large Empires are crumbling? We, therefore, shall belong to the people from today onwards. We shall sink or swim with them". Believe me, there is nothing unconstitutional in the course I am suggesting. There are, so far as I know, no treaties enabling the Empire to coerce the Princes. The people of the States will also declare that though they are the Princes' subjects, they are part of the Indian nation and that they will accept the leadership of the Princes, if the latter cast their lot with the People, but not otherwise. If this declaration enrages the Princes and they choose to kill the people, the latter will meet death bravely and unflinchingly, but will not go back on their word.

Nothing, however, should be done secretly. This is an open rebellion. In this struggle secrecy is a sin. A free man would not engage in a secret movement. It is likely that when you gain freedom you will have a C.I.D. of your own, in spite of my advice to the contrary. But in the present struggle, we have to work openly and to receive the bullets on our chest, without taking to heels.

I have a word to say to the Government servants also. They may not, if they like, resign their posts yet. The late Justice

Ranade did not resign his post, but he openly declared that he belonged to the Congress. He said to the Government that though he was a Judge, he was a Congressman and would openly attend the Sessions of the Congress, but that at the same time he would not let his political views warp his impartiality on the bench. He held Social Reform Conference in the very *pandal* of the Congress. I would ask all the Government servants to follow in the footsteps of Ranade and to declare their allegiance to the Congress as an answer to the secret circular issued by Sir Frederick Puckle.

This is all that I ask of you just now. I will now write to the Viceroy. You will be able to read the correspondence not just now but when I publish it with the Viceroy's consent. But you are free to aver that you support the demand to be put forth in my letter. A Judge came to me and said : "We get secret circulars from high quarters. What are we to do"? I replied, "If I were in your place, I would ignore the circulars. You may openly say to the Government : "I have received your secret circular. I am, however, with the Congress. Though I serve the Government for my livelihood, I am not going to obey these secret circulars or to employ underhand methods".

Soldiers too are covered by the present programme. I do not ask them just now to resign their posts and leave the army. Soldiers come to me, Jawaharlal and to the Maulana and say : "We are wholly with you. We are tired of the governmental tyranny". To these soldiers I would say : "You may say to the Government, 'Our hearts are with the Congress. We are not going to leave our posts. We will serve you so long as we receive your salaries. We will obey your just orders, but will refuse to fire on our own people' ".

To those who lack the courage to do this much I have nothing to say. They will go their own way. But if you can do this much, you may take it from me that the whole atmosphere will be electrified. Let the Government then shower bombs, if they like. But no power on earth will then be able to keep you in bondage any longer.

If the students want to join the struggle only to go back to their studies after a while, I would not invite them to it. For the present, however, till the time that I frame a programme for the struggle, I would ask the students to say to their professors : "We belong to the Congress. Do you belong to the Congress or to the Government? If you belong to the Congress, you need not vacate your posts. You will remain at your posts but teach us and lead us unto freedom". In all fights for freedom, the world over, the students have made very large contributions.

If in the interval that is left to us before the actual fight begins, you do even the little I have suggested to you, you will have changed the atmosphere and will have prepared the ground for the next step.

There is much I should yet like to say. But my heart is heavy. I have already taken up much of your time. I have yet to say a few words in English also. I thank you for the patience and attention with which you have listened to me even at this late hour. It is just what true soldiers would do. For the last twenty-two years, I have controlled my speech and pen and have stored up my energy. He is a true *brahmachari* who does not fritter away his energy. He will, therefore, always control his speech. That has been my conscious effort all these years. But today the occasion has come when I had to unburden my heart before you. I have done so, even though it meant putting a strain on your patience; and I do not regret having done it. I have given you my message and through you I have delivered it to the whole of India.

Mahatma, Vol. VI, pp. 154-64

3.17

The Great Trial

Ahmedabad
March 18, 1922

{Address and statement in the historical trial of Mahatma Gandhi and Shri Shankarlal Ghelabhai Banker, editor, and printer and publisher respectively of *Young India*, on charges under section 124A of the Indian Penal Code, held on Saturday, 18th March, 1922, before Mr. C.N. Broomfield, I.C.S., District and Sessions Judge, Ahmedabad}

Before reading his written statement, Mr. Gandhi spoke a few words as introductory remarks to the whole statement. He said :

Before I read this statement I would like to state that I entirely endorse the learned Advocate-General's remarks in connection with my humble self. I think that he was entirely fair to me in all the statements that he has made, because it is very true and I have no desire whatsoever to conceal from this Court the fact that to preach disaffection towards the existing system of Government has become almost a passion with me, and the learned Advocate-General is also entirely in the right when he says that my preaching of disaffection did not commence with my connection with *Young India*, but that it commenced much earlier and in the statement that I am about to read, it will be my painful duty to admit before this Court that it commenced much earlier than the period stated by the Advocate-General. It is the most painful duty with me, but I have discharged that duty knowing the responsibility that rests upon me, and I wish to endorse all the blame that the learned Advocate-General has thrown on my shoulders in connection with the Bombay, the Madras and the Chauri Chaura occurrences. Thinking over these deeply and sleeping over them night after night, it is impossible to dissociate myself from the diabolical crimes of Chauri Chaura or the mad outrages in Bombay and Madras. He is quite right when he says that, as a man of responsibility, a man having received a fair share of education, having had a fair share of experience of this world, I should know the consequences of every one of my acts. I knew that I was playing with fire. I ran the risk and, if I was set free, I would still do the same. I know that I was feeling it so everyday and I have felt it also this morning that I would have failed in my duty if I did not say what I said here just now.

"I Had to Make my Choice"

I wanted to avoid violence. I want to avoid violence. Non-violence is the first article of my faith. It is also the last article of my creed. But I had to make my choice. I had either to submit to a system which I considered had done an irreparable harm to my country, or incur the risk of the mad fury of my people bursting forth when they understood the truth from my lips. I know that my people have sometimes gone mad; I am deeply sorry for it. I am, therefore, here to submit not to a light penalty but to the highest penalty. I do not ask for mercy. I do not ask for any extenuating act of clemency. I am here to invite and cheerfully submit to the highest penalty that can be inflicted upon me for what in law is a deliberate crime and what appears to me to be the highest duty of a citizen. The only course open to you, the Judge, is as I am just going to say in my statement, either to resign your post, or inflict on me the severest penalty, if you believe that the system and the law you are assisting to administer are good for the people of this country and that my activity is, therefore, injurious to the public weal. I do not expect that kind of conversion, but by the time I have finished with my statement, you will, perhaps, have a glimpse of what is raging within my breast to run this maddest risk that a sane man can run.

Written Statement of Mahatma Gandhi

"I owe it perhaps to the Indian public and to the public in England, to placate which this prosecution is mainly taken up, that I should explain why, from a staunch loyalist and co-operator, I have become an uncompromising disaffectionist and non-co-operator, To the Court, too, I should say why I plead guilty to the charge of promoting disaffection towards the Government established by law in India.

My public life began in 1893 in South Africa in troubled weather. My first contact with British authority in that country was not of a happy character. I discovered that as a man and an Indian I had no rights. More correctly, I discovered that I had no rights as a man because I was an Indian.

But I was not baffled. I thought that this treatment of Indians was an excrescence upon a system that was intrinsically and mainly good. I gave the Government my voluntary and hearty co-operation, criticizing it freely where I felt it was faulty, but never wishing its destruction.

Consequently, when the existence of the Empire was threatened in 1899 by the Boer challenge, I offered my services to it raised a volunteer ambulance corps and served at several actions that took place for the relief of Ladysmith. Similarly in 1906, at the time of the Zulu revolt, I raised a stretcher-bearer party and served till the end of the rebellion. On both these occasions I received medals and was even mentioned in despatches. For my work in South Africa I was given by Lord Hardinge a Kaiser-i-Hind Gold Medal. When the war broke out in 1914 between England and Germany, I raised a volunteer ambulance corps in London consisting of the then resident Indians in London, chiefly students. Its work was acknowledged by the authorities to be valuable. Lastly, in India, when a special appeal was made at the War Conference in Delhi in 1918 by Lord Chelmsford for recruits, I struggled at the cost of my health to raise a corps in Kheda and the response was being made when the hostilities ceased and orders were received that no more recruits were wanted. In all these efforts at service, I was actuated by the belief that it was possible by such services to gain a status of full equality in the Empire for my countrymen.

The first shock came in the shape of the Rowlatt Act, a law designed to rob the people of all real freedom. I felt called upon to lead an intensive agitation against it. Then followed the Punjab horrors beginning with the massacre at Jallianwala Bagh and culminating in crawling orders, public floggings and other indescribable humiliations. I discovered, too, that the plighted word of the Prime Minister to the Mussalmans of India regarding the integrity of Turkey and the holy places of Islam was not likely to be fulfilled. But, in spite of the forebodings and the grave warnings of friends, at the Amritsar Congress in 1919, I fought for co-operation and working the Montagu-Chelmsford reforms, hoping that the Prime Minister would redeem his promise to the Indian Mussalmans, that the Punjab wound would be healed and that the reforms, inadequate and unsatisfactory though they were, marked a new era of hope in the life of India. But all that hope was shattered. The Khilafat promise was not to be redeemed. The Punjab crime was whitewashed and most culprits went not only unpunished, but remained in service and some continued to draw pensions from the Indian revenue, and in some cases were even rewarded. I saw, too, that not only did the reforms not mark a change of heart, but they were only a method of further draining India of her wealth and of prolonging her servitude.

"Administration of Law Prostituted"

I came reluctantly to the conclusion that the British connection had made India more helpless than she ever was before, politically and economically. A disarmed India has no power of resistance against any aggressor if she wanted to engage in an armed conflict with him. So much is this the case that some of our best men consider that India must take generations before she can achieve the Dominion status. She has become so poor that she has little power of resisting famines. Before the British advent, India spun and wove in her millions of cottages just the supplement she needed for adding to her meagre agricultural resources. This cottage industry, so vital for India's existence, has been ruined by incredibly heartless and inhuman processes as described by English witnesses. Little do town-dwellers know how the semi-starved masses of India are slowly sinking to lifelessness. Little do they know that their miserable comfort represents the brokerage they get for the work they do for the foreign exploiter, that the profits and the brokerage are sucked from the masses. Little do they realize that the Government established by law in British India is carried on for this exploitation of the masses. No sophistry, no jugglery in figures can explain away the evidence that the skeletons in many villages present to the naked eye. I have no doubt whatsoever that both England and the town-dwellers of India will have to answer, if there is a God above, for this crime against humanity which is perhaps unequalled in history. The law itself in this country has been used to serve the foreign exploiter. My unbiased examination of the Punjab Martial Law cases has led me to believe that at least ninety-five per cent of convictions were wholly bad. My experience of political cases in India leads one to the conclusion that in nine out of every ten cases the condemned men were totally innocent. Their crime consisted in the love of their country. In ninety-nine cases out of hundred, justice has been denied to Indians as against Europeans in the Courts of India. This is not an exaggerated picture. It is the experience of almost every Indian who has had anything to do with such cases. In my opinion, the administration of the law is thus prostituted consciously or unconsciously for the benefit of the exploiter.

The greatest misfortune is that Englishmen and their Indian associates in the administration of the country do not know that they are engaged in the crime I have attempted to describe. I am satisfied that many English and Indian officials honestly believe that they are administering one of the best systems devised in the world and that India is making steady though slow progress. They do not know that a subtle but effective system of terrorism and an organized display of force on the one hand, and the deprivation of all powers of retaliation or self-defence on the other, have emasculated the people and induced in them the habit of simulation. This awful habit has added to the ignorance and the self-deception of the administrators. Section 124-A under which I am happily charged is perhaps the prince among the political sections of the Indian Penal Code designed to suppress the liberty of the citizen. Affection cannot be manufactured or regulated by law. If one has no affection for a person or system, one should be free to give the fullest expression to his disaffection, so long as he does not contemplate, promote or incite to violence. But the section under which Mr. Banker and I are charged is one under which mere promotion of disaffection is a crime. I have studied some of the cases tried under it, and I know that some of the most loved of India's patriots have been convicted under it. I consider it a privilege, therefore, to be charged under it. I have endeavoured to give in their briefest outline the reasons for my disaffection. I have no personal ill will against any single administrator, much less can I have any disaffection towards the King's person. But I hold it to be a virtue to be disaffected towards a Government which in its totality has done more harm to India than any previous system. India is less manly under the British rule than she ever was before. Holding such a belief, I consider it to be a sin to have affection for the system. And it has been a precious privilege for me to be able to write what I have in the various articles tendered in evidence against me.

"Non-co-operation with Evil—A Duty"

In fact, I believe that I have rendered a service to India and England by showing in non-co-operation the way out of the unnatural state in which both are living. In my humble opinion, non-co-operation with evil is as much a duty as is co-operation with good. But, in the past, non-co-operation has been deliberately expressed in violence to the evil-doer. I am endeavouring to show to my countrymen that violent non-co-operation only multiplies evil and that, as evil can only be sustained by violence, withdrawal of support of evil requires complete abstention from violence. Non-violence implies voluntary submission to the penalty for non-co-operation with evil. I am here, therefore, to invite and submit cheerfully to the highest penalty that can be inflicted upon me for what in law is a deliberate crime and what appears to me to be the highest duty of a citizen. The only course open to you, the Judge, is either to resign your post and thus dissociate yourself from evil, if you feel that the law you are called upon to administer is an evil and that in reality I am innocent; or to inflict on me the severest penalty if you believe that the system and the law you are assisting to administer are good for the people of this country and that my activity is, therefore, injurious to the public weal.

Judgement

The Judge, Mr. Broomfield, then delivered the following judgement :

"Mr. Gandhi, you have made my task easy in one way by pleading guilty to the charge. Nevertheless what remains, namely, the determination of a just sentence, is perhaps as difficult a proposition as a Judge in this country could have to face. The law is no respecter of persons. Nevertheless, it will be impossible to ignore the fact that you are in a different category from any person I have ever tried or am likely to have to try. It would be impossible to ignore the fact that, in the eyes of millions of your countrymen, you are a great patriot and a great leader. Even those who differ from you in politics look upon you as a man of high ideals and of noble and of even saintly life. I have to deal with you in one character only. It is not my duty and I do not presume to judge or criticize you in any other character. It is my duty to judge you as a man subject to the law, who has by his own admission broken the law and committed what to an ordinary man must appear to be grave offences against the State. I do not forget that you have constantly preached against violence and that you have on many occasions, as I am willing to believe, done much to prevent violence, but having regard to the nature of your political teaching and the nature of many of those to whom it is addressed, how you could have continued to believe that violence would not be the inevitable consequence it passes my capacity to understand.

"There are probably few people in India who do not sincerely regret that you should have made it impossible for any Government to leave you at liberty. But it is so. I am trying to balance what is due to you against what appears to me to be necessary in the interests of the public, and I propose, in passing sentence, to follow the precedent of a case, in many respects similar to this case, that was decided some 12 years ago, I mean the case against Mr. Bal Gangadhar Tilak under this same section. The sentence that was passed upon him as it finally stood was a sentence of simple imprisonment for six years. You will not consider it unreasonable, I think, that you should be classed with Mr. Tilak, and that is the sentence, two years' simple imprisonment on each count of the charge, i.e., six years in all, which I feel it my duty to pass upon you and I should like to say in doing so that, if the course of events in India should make it possible for the Government to reduce the period and release you, no one will be better pleased than I."

Turning to Mr. Banker, the Judge said : "I assume you have been to a large extent under the influence of your chief. The sentence that I proposed to pass upon you is simple imprisonment for six months on each of the first two counts, that is to say, simple imprisonment for one year and a fine of a thousand rupees on the third count, which six months' simple imprisonment in default".

"Association with Tilak's Name—An Honour"

Mr. Gandhi, addressing the Judge, then said : "I would only say one word. Since you have done me the honour of recalling the trial of the late Lokmanya Bal Gangadhar Tilak, I just want to say that I consider it to be the proudest privilege and honour to be associated with his name. So far as the sentences itself is concerned, I certainly consider that it is as light as any Judge would inflict on so and me far as the whole proceedings are concerned, I must say that I could not have expected greater courtesy".

Index